Radio by the Book

ALSO BY TIM DEFOREST

Storytelling in the Pulps, Comics, and Radio: How Technology Changed Popular Fiction in America (2004)

Radio by the Book

*Adaptations of Literature and
Fiction on the Airwaves*

TIM DEFOREST

McFarland & Company, Inc., Publishers
Jefferson, North Carolina, and London

LIBRARY OF CONGRESS CATALOGUING-IN-PUBLICATION DATA

DeForest, Tim, 1960–
 Radio by the book : adaptations of literature and fiction on the airwaves / Tim DeForest.
     p.   cm.
 Includes bibliographical references and index.

 ISBN 978-0-7864-3972-0
 softcover : 50# alkaline paper ∞

 1. Radio plays, American — History and criticism.
 2. Radio adaptations — History and criticism.   I. Title.
 PS336.R33D44   2008
 809.2'22 — dc22   2008022968

British Library cataloguing data are available

©2008 Tim DeForest. All rights reserved

No part of this book may be reproduced or transmitted in any form or by any means, electronic or mechanical, including photocopying or recording, or by any information storage and retrieval system, without permission in writing from the publisher.

Cover image © 2008 Shutterstock

Manufactured in the United States of America

McFarland & Company, Inc., Publishers
 Box 611, Jefferson, North Carolina 28640
  www.mcfarlandpub.com

To all my fellow old-time radio enthusiasts:
yes, we are smarter than everyone else
and it is okay to acknowledge it.

Table of Contents

Preface 1
Introduction 3

PART I: MYSTERY
The Saint   7 • Flashgun Casey   13 • The Falcon   19
Boston Blackie   23 • The Lone Wolf   28 • Frank Merriwell   33
Bulldog Drummond   36 • Charlie Chan   41 • Mr. Moto   46
Perry Mason   52 • Nick Carter   58 • Philo Vance   63
Ellery Queen   69 • Hercule Poirot   74 • Nero Wolfe   79
Sherlock Holmes   85 • Mr. and Mrs. North   91
The Thin Man   97 • The Fat Man   101 • Sam Spade   105
Philip Marlowe   113 • Michael Shayne   119 • The Shadow   124
The Avenger   132 • The Green Lama   136
Fu Manchu   141 • *Molle Mystery Theater*   146

PART II: ADVENTURE
Tarzan   153 • *Escape*   159

PART III: WESTERNS
Hopalong Cassidy   167 • The Cisco Kid   172

PART IV: SCIENCE FICTION
Buck Rogers   179 • *Dimension X* and *X Minus One*   185
Exploring Tomorrow   190

PART V: GENERAL ANTHOLOGIES
The Damon Runyon Theater 195 • *Favorite Story* 199
The Mercury Theatre on the Air and *The Campbell Playhouse* 203
The World's Great Novels and *NBC University Theater* 211
Mystery in the Air 215 • *The Weird Circle* 218
NBC Presents: Short Story 221 • Miscellaneous Adaptations 225

Bibliography 229
Index 231

Preface

When I was about thirteen years old, the *CBS Radio Mystery Theater* would come on at just about my bedtime. I would often have it playing on the radio while I lay in bed.

I have a lot of fun memories of that show, but the best memory comes from listening to an adaptation of "The Fall of the House of Usher." When it came to the climax — the part where Madeline has clawed herself out of her premature grave and is stalking her brother Roderick through the decaying mansion — I had to turn the radio off. It was literally too scary for me to handle.

Within a few years, I had opportunity to learn more about the joys of radio drama. A local station played reruns of *The Lone Ranger* on weekday evenings. About the same time, I saw a long-playing record containing two Shadow episodes in a music store. I'm not sure now if this was before or after I had begun reading paperback reprints of the original Shadow novels, but I do remember I badly wanted that record. If memory serves, I whined to my mother until she agreed to buy it. Never mind that I was several years too old to be whining about anything — it worked.

It wasn't until I was an adult, though, that I began to make a conscious point of collecting episodes. Back in the olden days, when we hunted antelope with sharp rocks and used cassette tapes for recording sounds, this was a time and space consuming activity, but it was well worth the effort. Slowly but surely, I become reasonably knowledgeable about old-time radio in general.

When I started having some minor success as a writer, I wanted to write about old-time radio. The trouble was a number of excellent works on the subject, especially those by John Dunning and Jim Harmon, had already been done. I needed to find an original approach, or at least think of some aspect of old-time radio that hadn't been thoroughly covered already.

Finally, I hit upon the idea of a book that exclusively examines old-time radio shows based on prose fiction. The examination of how these two different forms of storytelling were brought together would be, I hoped, interesting and informative. Besides, it was the sort of thing for which the research would usually be a lot of fun. I'd be reading books and stories that I would have been reading for enjoyment anyway. Same with the radio shows — it would almost always be something I'd listen to just for fun even if I weren't writing a book. I did have to fight my way through a few of the novels I didn't care for (curse you, Philo Vance), but these were relatively rare exceptions.

Additional background information was available through many of the best existing works on the old-time radio. John Dunning's *On the Air: The Encyclopedia of Old-Time Radio* is the Ur-book on the subject, covering nearly every show from radio's Golden Age. Jim Harmon's *The Great Radio Heroes* doesn't cover quite as much ground, but discusses a number of key shows and characters with wit and enthusiasm.

Over three quarters of the shows I would be writing about were from the mystery and detective genres, so William DeAndrea's *Encyclopedia Mysteriosa: A Comprehensive Guide to the Art of Detection in Print, Film, Radio, and Television* and Otto Penzler's incredibly fun *The Private Lives of Private Eyes, Spies, Crime Fighters, and Other Good Guys* were enormous helps. These entertaining and exhaustive works are invaluable to anyone interested in the mystery genre.

The end result of all this research is a book that examines individual characters who jumped from prose to radio. I also take a look at a number of anthology shows that specialized in dramatizing short stories or novels. We'll start with the mystery and detective shows, then move on to adventure, westerns, and science fiction before ending with the general anthologies. Following the discussion of each character or show is a list of the air date range and broadcast network, along with the voice actor or actors portraying the primary character (or the host, in the case of anthology programs). In the case of shows based upon characters, the character's first appearance in print is also included. We will explore how the writers and producers approached the source material for each show. We'll look at what they changed, what they kept and what they left behind. The results of their efforts were almost always highly entertaining radio — examples of a form of storytelling much more engaging and satisfying than most of what has since replaced it in popular culture.

Introduction

The various outlets for popular fiction have always cross-pollinated one another. Mary Shelley's novel *Frankenstein*, for instance, was being adapted into various stage plays almost immediately after its publication in 1818. *The Searchers*, to use a slightly more modern example, was first a novel by Alan Lemay, then adapted into a 1956 movie by John Ford and John Wayne. The Dell Publishing Company then produced a comic book adaptation of the movie.

The Lone Ranger began his career on radio, then expanded into both prose and comic books before leaving radio behind for television (eventually in both live-action and animated form). He appeared in a 1938 movie serial and, during the 1950s, several feature films.

Superman was created to be a newspaper comic strip, but first appeared instead in a comic book. He soon got his daily strip as well, then jumped to radio, a 1942 novel, cartoons, two movie serials and eventually television and feature films.

You can't keep a good fictional character down. During the first half of the 20th century, when radio still ruled over the living rooms of America, the hunger for engaging stories and characters could not be sated. Three national networks plus a good number of independent stations took up an awful lot of air time. Comedy, adventure, mystery, drama, music—all these bases had to covered and then covered again the very next night. George Burns, coming to radio from vaudeville, once noted that fifteen minutes of good material would last for months when you were on stage, playing to a different audience each night. Fifteen minutes of good material on radio, though, lasted just fifteen minutes, after which you had to have something new.

So it's not surprising that radio's producers and writers (like theatrical and film producers before and after) looked to outside sources for inspiration. But you can't just take, say, *Treasure Island*, assign the dialogue as is to the actors, and have them read it into a microphone. Radio is different from prose — what works dramatically on the page doesn't necessarily work the same way on the airwaves. Besides, it all had to fit to the second into the proper time slot. Stories had to be abridged — scenes had to be shifted around — dialogue had to be altered or condensed. And all this had to be done without losing the entertainment value of the work being adapted.

And, of course, sometimes you were taking just a character from a prose source and dropping him into original stories on radio. This gave you a hero (or heroine) and probably an overall thematic feel, but you still had to come up with a new plot each week.

It was a tricky job, but radio proved to be up to it. It was a medium that did not really allow for mediocrity. Without visuals, the Theater of the Mind had no choice but to tell its stories well. When it failed, there were no pretty girls, graphic violence, or visual editing tricks available to keep the audience from spinning the dial to another channel. Bad radio faded away quickly. Good radio endured. Above all else, this book is a celebration of some of the best that came out of that medium's Golden Age.

Part I

Mystery

The Saint

Simon Templer's nickname was meant to convey irony and it certainly succeeded in this regard. The Saint—"The Robin Hood of Modern Crime"—started out as a pretty violent guy. Created by Leslie Charteris in 1928, Simon Templer did not hesitate to off someone — often in cold blood — in order to get his job done.

His saving grace, of course, was that the people he killed were invariably criminals and murderers of the worst sort. Simon made his living (and a rather good one at that) stealing from crooks. But he's also the champion of the innocent. Come to him for help and he will help you. If you're a gorgeous babe, he'll help that much more quickly.

Mostly, though, Simon did what he did for the sheer love of adventure, finding it regularly both in his native England and across the globe. In the short story "The Angel's Eye," we are told "For just as a musician would be electrified by a cadence of divine harmonies, so could the Saint respond to the tones of new and fabulous adventure." Simon loved life-threatening danger more than anything else.

Charteris built the Saint from the basic "suave gentleman adventurer" mold that had long existed in popular culture, but gave him both enough charm and enough of an edge to make him stand out from the crowd. For a half-century, Charteris produced countless Saint short stories, novellas and novels to enormous commercial success.

The best of these stories hold up completely for the modern reader. Charteris wrote third-person narration with a wit that mirrored the Saint's ironic humor and carried the plots along smoothly. His best prose is simply fun to read. He wisely varied the types of adventure the Saint would have, never letting the character grow stale. One tale might emphasize Simon's skill as a burglar or con artist. Another would be a traditional whodunit. Some stories were character studies; others were adventure yarns.

Considering the sheer volume of his work, it's not surprising that Charteris occasionally dropped the ball. He had a tendency to overwrite — he once stretched a description of Simon tackling an armed adversary to six paragraphs, making *absolutely* sure we knew just how skilled and inherently cool the Saint was in a dangerous situation.

But Charteris was too good a writer to do this too often. Most of the time, his prose was smooth and his plots would twist and turn nicely. He obviously liked his creation, once saying "To me he is tremendously personal, and yet in a way he is as impersonal as any character can be, because more than anything else, he is only an attitude of mind."*

Simon Templer represents the desire to live life completely on one's own terms, unfettered by the rules of society. This freedom is balanced by a sense of honor and a slightly skewed but still viable moral sense, making Simon work as both hero and rebel.

One of the best Saint stories is the novel *The Saint in New York*, first published in 1934. Simon has been hired by a wealthy man named William Valcross, whose son was murdered by New York mobsters. Valcross offers the Saint a cool one million dollars to clean up the city.

Simon takes on the seemingly impossible job. He publicly announces his intention to kill a mobster who is on trial for murdering a cop. The trial is fixed and it's pretty much open knowledge that the mobster will either be found not guilty or simply be pardoned.

Disguised as a nun, Simon carries out the assassination on the courthouse steps in full view of police and reporters, then handily makes his getaway. A few hours later, he's in the home of a corrupt judge, relieving that man of $20,000 in bribe money.

The action continues at breakneck speed. Simon forms an uneasy alliance with a cop and learns that the New York mobs are run by someone known only as "the Big Fellow." He rescues a kidnapped girl, whacking another mob lieutenant along the way. He begins to get secret help from a woman named Faye Edwards, who seems to be a part of the mob but apparently has her own agenda. Toward the story's climax, there's an excellent and very suspenseful sequence in which Simon is captured and taken for a ride by a pair of coldly professional hit men.

Two factors, aside from good plot construction, make the novel really work. First, the Saint is not infallible and is subject to reasonable human limits. Sometimes, Simon's wit, bravery and physical skill threaten to spill him over into a level of super-heroism that would have made the story

Barer, 3–4.

dull. But Charteris never quite lets that happen — just when it seems Simon could do not do wrong, he'll make a mistake that would threaten his life.

At one point, he misjudges the motive of a mobster who offers to rat out his compatriots and thus loses an opportunity to gain vital information. A moment of carelessness soon afterwards gets him captured and nearly killed. Later in the story, exhausted and wounded, we are told that "the vast weariness which had enveloped him had dragged him down to the point where he could do little more than wait with outward stubbornness for whatever Fate had in store. If he must go down, he would go down as he had lived, with a jest and a smile — but the fight was sapped out of him." By balancing Simon's endless supply of witticisms with moments of fallibility and vulnerability, Charteris kept the level of suspense in the novel high.

Another strength of the novel comes from the expression of a sincere righteous anger towards corrupt officials. Dishonest politicians, judges and district attorneys — those who betray the people they have sworn to serve — are treated with outright contempt.

Simon starts out as a mercenary, "hired by Valcross to do an outlaw's work; but ... whether he acknowledged it or not, whether they believed it or not, he was the champion of seven million [New Yorkers]...." It was an acknowledgement that there is such a thing as good and evil and that each of us must choose sides. Despite their illegality, the choices Simon makes give *The Saint in New York* a strong moral backbone.

So the Saint slogs on, doing an outlaw's work in the interests of justice. When he turns down a large bribe to let a mobster go free, the mobster babbles "'If it isn't money, what do you want? Damn, it, what is your racket?'

"'Death,' said the Saint in a voice of terrible softness. 'Death is my racket.'"

In later years, the Saint mellowed a little, depending more often on his wits and less often on his gun or the throwing knife he kept concealed up his sleeve. No longer an open outlaw, he more often worked with the police or government officials, though his casual attitude toward breaking the law often resurfaced.

Charteris took advantage of the Saint's lasting popularity, selling rights to the character to movies, comic books, radio and television, proving that crime (if committed by proxy through a literary creation) can pay quite well.

The Saint first came to radio in 1938 in England. He jumped across the Atlantic in 1945, with Edgar Barrier and Brian Aherne both playing the title role on NBC and CBS respectively. Vincent Price took over the role in 1947, on a series that jumped between three networks in a more-or-less continual run that lasted until 1951. (Barry Sullivan filled in for Price in several episodes in 1950, while Tom Conway played a more English Simon for the last few episodes of the series.) The earlier runs do not survive, but fortunately many of the Vincent Price episodes are still available.

The writers on *The Saint* were tasked with adapting stories about a character who regularly broke the law to a medium whose standards would not allow its protagonists to be criminals. Thus, only the basic outline of the original Saint remains. He's still the suave gentleman and ladies man. He still has a penchant for one-liners. But, despite being described as the "Robin Hood of Modern Crime" in the opening narration of every episode, he does not work outside the law. The radio's Saint never executes a mobster on the courthouse steps. Heck, he doesn't even usually carry a gun.

Nor is he British. Price's Saint is based in New York. He doesn't work for a living and, since he gives the rewards he occasionally earns to charity, he is apparently independently wealthy. Can we theorize he's living on the proceeds of his outlaw past? We're never told. We are told that he is well-known to the public as the Saint and that when someone knocks on his door looking for help, he always has plenty of time on his hands.

But despite the changes, *The Saint* was a delightful series. Writers Louis Vittes, Dick Powell and others constructed clever well-plotted mysteries. But perhaps more importantly, they gave Vincent Price an unending supply of wonderful one-liners. And Price was the perfect radio Saint — the listener had no trouble accepting him as a charming, witty man who faced danger with imperturbable calm.

To provide Simon with someone with whom he could trade one-liners (and with whom he could also trade expository dialogue), he is given a semi-regular sidekick. Louie the cabdriver (played by radio stalwart Lawrence Dobkin) had a New Yorker common man demeanor that played off quite nicely against Simon's upper class sensibility. At first, Louie and Simon were mildly antagonistic towards each other — every time Simon flagged a cab, it just happened to be Louie's. But this changed into a friendlier relationship before the conceit grew stale and Louie became Simon's driver-of-choice.

It's interesting to compare Louie to the Shadow's cabbie/comic relief Shrevvy, whom we'll meet in a later chapter. Whereas Shrevvy was often awkwardly inserted into a plot (and never really that funny), Louie fit just fine into *The Saint* and did indeed provide laughs. Credit for this goes as much to Dobkin's skillful performance as to the writers.

The opening scene of an episode from Christmas Eve, 1950, showcased Price's skill with clever dialogue and his rapport with Dobkin. Simon, dressed to play Santa Claus at a charity event, is confronted at his apartment door by a lady with a gun. It's a case of mistaken identity that leads to a confused and hilarious exchange of dialogue, simultaneously generating laughter and setting up a mystery involving jewels stolen by someone else in a Santa suit:

> GIRL: Reach!
> SAINT: For what?
> GIRL (uncertain): The chandelier.
> SAINT: We can't.
> GIRL: Why not?
> SAINT: No chandelier.
> GIRL: Oh, a wise guy, huh?
> ...
> GIRL: How would you like to be plugged in the ... the ...
> SAINT (in helpful tone): Bread-basket?
> GIRL: Where?
> SAINT: Let's pass lightly over that. I wouldn't want to get plugged anywhere.
> ...
> GIRL: Look, Fats, are you going to stop stalling and hand over the stuff, or am I going to have to shoot?
> SAINT: Well, since I'm not Fats Boylen and I have no stuff to hand over, you'll just have to shoot.
> LOUIE: Mr. Templer, that could be fatal!
> ...

Price and Dobkin's seemingly effortless readings of their parts made the bizarre and silly situation completely acceptable.

The plots of most episodes were reasonably clever and always progressed logically, giving the show the necessary backbone to work as both a mystery and a comedy. An episode from July 16, 1950, for instance, begins when a beautiful woman knocks on Simon's door. She's desperately frightened — a couple of odd-looking thugs are lurking on the street outside, looking for her. He escorts her to Grand Central Station, where she abruptly leaves him without explaining what is going on. Arriving back at his apartment, he's greeted by a man with a European accent and a Lugar. The man tells him he shouldn't have decided to work for "them" instead of "us."

Simon has no idea what's going on — both the girl and the gunman have assumed he was already involved in whatever it is. The inexplicable delivery of a whiskey glass to his apartment only adds to the confusion.

Simon gets the drop on the gunman and starts to gradually put the puzzle together. He's captured by the odd-looking thugs, but manages to think and talk his way out of trouble.

The girl shows up again and fills in the blanks. She's part of an organization that hunts Nazi war criminals. The whiskey glass contains the fingerprints of a Nazi who was assumed to be dead. The girl needs it to prove to the authorities that he is still alive.

The episode climaxes when Simon (this time along with the girl) is re-captured by the thugs. Simon jumps them, capturing the Nazi also. A nice twist involving the Nazi's true identity brings the episode to an end.

Taken as a plain mystery, it would have been a good episode. Combined with Price's fine portrayal as the Saint and the humor he brought to the role, it was excellent. It would have been nice to listen to a more faithful version of Leslie Charteris's outlaw hero on the radio, but the Saint we were given was himself a superbly entertaining addition to popular culture. Both Charteris's witty prose and Vincent Price's witty performance brought us their own individual types of fun.

The Saint on radio:
NBC: 1/6/45–3/31/45
The Saint: Edgar Barrier
CBS: 6/20/45–9/12/45
The Saint: Brian Aherne
CBS: 7/9/47–6/30/48
Mutual: 7/10/49–5/28/50
NBC: 6/11/50–10/14/51
The Saint: Vincent Price, Barry Sullivan, Tom Conway
First prose appearance: *Meet the Tiger* (1928), by Leslie Charteris

Flashgun Casey

The hard-boiled school of detective fiction was born in the pages of *Black Mask* magazine in 1923 with the publication of stories by Carroll John Daly and Dashiell Hammett. It was a new kind of detective fiction, completely different from the Conan Doyle–inspired works that had dominated the genre for a generation. It was gritty and cynical, set in a violent world that was rife with corruption and betrayal. The heroes themselves walked very close to an ethical line in the sand, often more determined to uphold a personal code of honor than the law. The writing style of the hard-boiled school was sparse. No words were wasted and stories with often complex plots were clearly told in the space of relatively few pages.

It was, at first, a purely American genre and it quickly began to influence American film. The Warner Brothers gangster movies of the 1930s were infused with hard-boiled elements. Film Noir, a genre which produced some of the finest films ever, is generally considered to have begun with the 1941 adaptation of Hammett's *The Maltese Falcon*.

Radio, though, was a little late in jumping aboard the hard-boiled bandwagon. It wasn't until the late 1940s that shows such as *Sam Spade*, *Philip Marlowe*, *The Voyage of the Scarlett Queen*, *Pat Novak for Hire*, and a number of other quality efforts demonstrated that the genre could be faithfully and entertainingly adapted to the airwaves. Why radio waited a couple of decades before doing this would make for an interesting debate in and of itself. Perhaps the genre did not seem adaptable to radio, though the flood of successful adaptations that eventually came along make that seem unlikely. Perhaps radio executives were initially nervous about broadcasting such cynical and violent material into the living rooms of America.

For our purposes here, this meant that poor Jack Casey, the tough, hard-drinking, Boston-based news photographer who was the protagonist in an excellent series of stories in *Black Mask* magazine, came to radio a few years too early. When Casey was brought to the airwaves in 1943, he was plopped into a more traditional whodunit, without the cynical edge or rapid-fire pacing that makes the hard-boiled genre so appealing. His show still makes for good radio, but anyone familiar with the original stories can't help be think about just how much better it could have been.

"Flashgun" Casey was created by George Harmon Coxe. The first story, "Return Engagement," appeared in the March 1934 issue of *Black Mask*. Casey, "a big, thick-chested fellow with curly brown hair and a profane manner," is almost a supporting character in this initial effort, as he helps a new photographer named Wade infiltrate a mobster's hideout to get a front page photo. But the story still serves as a good introduction to the character—we know Casey is loyal to his friends and profession and that he's tough as nails in a dangerous situation.

Later stories in the series expanded on the character a little. We discover that Casey has both a sense of decency and an empathetic nature. When he deals with someone dishonest or sleazy, he feels depressed. When he's able to help a good person in need, he feels exhilarated.

He'll hold back potentially newsworthy photographs from his editor (and information from the police) to protect someone innocent from being hurt or publicly embarrassed. At the same time, he's loyal to his newspaper and his profession—he loves his job and takes pride in doing it well.

It's these qualities in Casey that make him an effective hard-boiled hero. The best stories from the genre combines its cynical world-view with the knowledge that there actually is a difference between right and wrong. The protagonist, by upholding his code of honor, would give the stories a moral backbone that raised them to a level they would not have otherwise reached. The code was often a very personal thing, centering around keeping one's word and remaining deeply loyal to one's friends or profession. It reminded us that, though we might be up to our hips in corruption, we were each still individually responsible to hang on to our own moral worth.

In "Once Around the Clock," from May 1941, Casey runs across a drunken ex-con named Lew Bronson and helps him back to his apartment. When the cops show up a few minutes later to arrest Bronson for murder, Casey (almost by instinct) gives him a chance to slip away.

Subsequent events result in Bronson and Casey both being held at gunpoint by the real killer. But when the killer also threatens the life of a girl Bronson loves, the ex-con shows some backbone. Until this point,

Casey (along with everyone else) had considered Bronson to be a weak-willed loser. But now "courage was in [Bronson] ... Casey found it in his eyes, and written across the thin white face as he took another slow step in the face of the gun. Seeing all these things so clearly now, Casey was ashamed and knew that somehow, Bronson should not be left to fight alone."

Coxe had a talent for such characterizations — taking the drunks and losers that Casey ran across and believably infusing them with a degree of nobility. It was people like this that largely motivated Casey throughout the series.

Several multi-part Casey stories were serialized in *Black Mask*, then later reprinted as novels. "Killers are Camera Shy," from 1941, was published as a novel titled *Silent are the Dead* the following year. It's a great yarn, just a noche below the best of the hard-boiled genre.

As the novel opens, a former D.A. named Endicott has been busted by the cops, caught red-handed in a scheme to sell stolen bonds back to the company that had insured them. When Endicott is released on bail, Casey and another "camera" named Perry Austin go to his office to take his picture. They find him murdered. Casey snaps a shot of a fleeing car, but he's unsure if he got a clear image of either the driver or the license plate. He gives Austin the film-holder containing the negative and sends him off. While he's waiting for the police, a woman arrives at Endicott's office. Casey gets a shot of her before she flees.

It's here that Casey's sense of empathy starts to complicate his life — he assumes the girl was not the killer and so refrains from telling the police about her. This decision ends up bringing him a fair amount of trouble before the novel ends.

On top of this, Austin and the film negative both vanish. A couple of thugs try to take Casey for a ride and he narrowly escapes with his life. He eventually finds Austin's dead body — along with evidence that Austin was a blackmailer. Yet *another* young lady is present at *that* crime scene.

Casey by now has a number of motives driving him. He's not a detective and is perfectly willing to let the police figure out who the killer or killers are. But he has a responsibility to his newspaper to get good pictures; a responsibility to his conscience to protect the privacy of those he perceives as innocent; and a responsibility to his profession to find and destroy Austin's blackmail information while preventing knowledge of how Austin had shamed that profession from becoming public.

One aspect of the novel is a bit contrived — two beautiful women showing up at two different murder scenes to be conveniently photographed by Casey was too much of a stretch. But otherwise the plot is very well-constructed and because of this the contrivance isn't overly bothersome. Casey and his police contact Lt. Logan, sometimes working together and sometimes not, methodically uncover clues that eventually tie everything together. There's one moment of Sherlock Holmes–type deduction on Casey's part at the denouement, but for the most part the investigation follows a logical progression in the style of a police procedural.

Along the way, we get several occasions in which Casey demonstrates he's as good with his fists as he is with his camera. In fact, all the action scenes, including a tense sequence near the finale when Casey sets himself up as bait to flush out a killer, are done very well.

Little things not directly relating to the plot nonetheless add to Casey's character. He climbs to a second floor window to get an interesting angle for photographing a crime scene, reminding us he's a skilled professional. At another time, he's stuck at a fine arts show, trying to fake his way through conversations by mentioning painters at random and feeling so uncomfortably out-of-place he might as well have been on another planet.

The supporting characters are also well-drawn. The cops, the crooks and all those in between are given real personalities. A twist at the end involving one particular character is genuinely touching.

It all hangs together with Casey acting as the anchor. One passage in particular gives us a clear snapshot of the protagonist:

> There was a great loyalty in Casey.... He had been a photographer a long time and for all his crabbing and profanity, his clashes with [his editor], his grumbling over the injustices he suffered, he would not change his job with the President....
> ...That's how it was. Day after day. Picturing the contemporary drama of life but never thinking of it that way; thinking of it only as a job he liked and always knowing one thing: if you got a picture, no one could ever deny it. Stories could be faked but to get a picture you had to be there.

As stated earlier, a somewhat softer version of Casey appeared on the CBS radio network. He was played briefly by Matt Crowley and then Jim Backus from July to September 1943, then by Staats Cotsworth through 1950 and again during a 1954–55 run.

Only a few Crowley episodes and none of the Backus episodes survive, so it's Cotsworth's portrayal that defines the radio Casey. He played the photographer as a quick-witted and determined professional with a knack for deductive reasoning. Homicide detective Lt. (later Captain)

Logan was also brought along from the original stories, giving Casey a convenient point of contact with the police. Casey and Logan often worked together, with Casey freely jumping in with questions of his own when suspects or witnesses were being questioned.

All this helped turn the photographer from a distinctive hard-boiled personality into yet another in a long line of amateur detectives. Several new characters were created for the radio series to further facilitate this change. Ann Williams was a young female reporter who became Casey's regular partner, giving him someone with whom to verbally share information — thus passing the same information on to the audience. A 1945 episode implied a romantic relationship between Casey and Ann, but this was never followed up.

Ethelbert, the bartender at the Blue Note Café, was the second new-to-radio character. The episodes were usually structured so that at some point, Casey and Ann would be stuck for a lead in their current case. They'd stop by the Blue Note, where Ethelbert would act both as a sounding board and as minor comic relief. We'd also get to hear some pretty good jazz piano playing in the background until Casey abruptly made the deductive leap that would solve the crime.

A 1946 episode, "The Red Raincoat," begins with a woman getting shot down in the street. A witness at first identifies the body as Nora Gelhorn, the owner of the coat the victim is wearing. But a closer look reveals the victim to be Nora's co-worker, Emma Randall. At first, it looks like the murder was a case of mistaken identity and evidence points to Nora's husband as being the killer. Casey, though, thinks the husband's been framed. A picture he took of the Randall bedroom reveals a clue that points to someone else as the real killer. Casey and Ann confront the suspect, arranging events in such a way as to use a nosey neighbor as a witness to a confession.

It's all good stuff, providing the listener with the comfortable familiarity of a well-written whodunit. As was usual for radio of that era, an excellent pool of character actors provided voices for the various crooks, cops, witnesses and victims, giving the show added verisimilitude.

The main characters are likable if not particularly memorable and anyone who hadn't read Coxe's original stories would have no real objections to the show. But those of us who know the empathetic tough guy who lived between the covers of *Black Mask*, dealing with both the human tragedy and the human triumph that infused the best hard-boiled stories, can't help but wish *that* was the Casey who made it to radio. He could have easily held his own alongside Marlowe, Spade and Pat Novak. *Casey,*

Crime Photographer was at the same time an entertaining mystery show and a lost opportunity.

Flashgun Casey on radio:
CBS: 7/7/43–11/16/50; 1/13/54–4/13/55
Casey: Matt Crowley, Jim Backus, Staats Cotsworth
First prose appearance: "Return Engagement" (1934), by George Harmon Coxe

The Falcon

The Falcon began life in a 1940 short story by Michael Arlen. Titled "The Gay Falcon" and published in *Town and Country Magazine*, it was that character's only literary appearance.

The story's protagonist, who is actually (and, from a modern perspective, rather unfortunately) *named* Gay Falcon, is the sort-of suave gentleman adventurer that had already become a pop culture stereotype. The story breaks no new ground, but Leslie Charteris' best "Saint" stories prove that it is possible for a good writer to wrap entertaining plots and characterizations around exactly this sort of stereotype. Arlen's tale, involving jewel thievery and murder, is well-constructed and there's a nice double-twist at the denouement.

The Falcon doesn't have the same level of charisma exhibited by Simon Templer — both his one-liners and his antagonistic encounter with a plodding police detective have a little bit of a "been-there, done-that" quality to them. But he manages to carry the story along quickly all the same and the reader comes away satisfied.

It was in other media that the Falcon really took flight. George Sanders, fresh from playing the Saint in five films, brought the character to movie screens four times in 1941 and 1942. Tom Conway (playing the original Falcon's brother after Sanders' character was killed by Nazi spies) took over for nine more films. Conway, of course, would get his chance to play the Saint on radio a few years later.

Our main concern, of course, is the radio show. *The Falcon* premiered on the NBC Blue network in April 1943. That run ended six months later. In 1945, it popped up again on Mutual and ran more or less steadily on that network or on NBC until November 1954.

On radio, Falcon became a nickname — the character's real name was now Michael Waring. With virtually no background provided from the original Arlen story (other than the concept of the charming and witty detective), the show's creative staff was basically starting from scratch.

They choose New York for the setting and made Waring a freelance detective who was "always ready with a hand for oppressed men and an eye for repressed women." Berry Kroeger played him in the initial run, with James Meighan taking over in 1945. These two played Waring with a suave upper class flavor. Later actors who cycled through the role — Les Tremayne, Les Damon & George Petrie — gave Waring more of a hard-boiled edge.

We are never provided with any detailed background information for Waring. He only rarely seems to charge a fee for his detective work — there's an impression that he's independently wealthy, but this is never spelled out. He has no regular girlfriend or sidekick and no particular cop to act as either friend or nemesis. Even his nickname is never explained. We're told all we need to know about him in the first few seconds of each episode.

The show always began with a phone call — usually a woman calling to confirm a date with Waring for that night. But he inevitably has to beg off— there's a murder to be solved and he's the only one who can solve it. "There's a party around," he'll explain, "that's been shown how to parley a two-bit pocket knife into a killing; so naturally he's going to make a stab at it."

Many times, these opening puns were (like this one) a bit much; often they didn't actually relate to that episode's plot. But they helped to quickly establish the narrow character template upon which Michael Waring was built. He's a ladies man with a penchant for one-liners and a talent for solving crimes. He also did a bit of espionage from time to time, helping out the Military Intelligence boys during World War II and in later years getting drafted into occasionally doing a bit of Cold War spying.

So far, like the original Arlen story, there's nothing really original happening. But despite this, *The Falcon* was quite good — over half-a-century later, it's still fun to give it a listen.

The basic appeal of a well-constructed mystery is one reason for this. The Falcon as a character is, after all, something of a cipher. Certainly he doesn't have the same level of appeal as, say, Sherlock Holmes or Nero Wolfe. But he was set down amidst good, solid mysteries — in which the plot advanced logically and the clues made sense.

"The Case of the Curious Cop," from May 1951, began with a dishonest detective named Kraven trying to shake down a gambler for a pay off. The cop ends up getting shot and his equally dirty partner, named Walsh, is killed soon afterwards.

Walsh's wife is suspected of killing him, so she goes to the Falcon for help. During Waring's investigation, the gambler turns up dead. Kravan then unexpectedly turns up alive, making *him* the most likely suspect. But Waring manages to put several small clues together and unveil the identity of the real killer. It's an enjoyable mystery, perfectly satisfying to any fan of the genre.

Another advantage *The Falcon* had — shared by just about any radio show produced in New York during the late 1940s and 1950s — was the pool of actors available to play the various guest parts each week. Radio drama was at its absolute best at this time and there was no shortage of actors who could step into a variety of roles and play them with conviction.

A 1952 episode, "The Case of the Dirty Dollar," highlights this nicely. The characters involved in this one include a weak-willed small-time gambler, a wife who loves him despite his faults, a mobster attracted to her, and the mobster's intensely loyal bodyguard. The plot itself was fine, providing some nice twists, but extra tension was generated throughout the episode by the emotions motivating these characters. Both the writers *and* the actors created a real sense of humanity, steadily building upon our sympathies and making the actions of the characters believable.

"The Case of the Vanishing Visa," another 1952 episode, has the Falcon being recruited by Army Intelligence to travel to Vienna and help a female agent named Trudi escape from the country. But before Waring enters the story, there's an interesting prologue; Trudi meets her contact, a drunken expatriate American, in a Vienna hotel to pass information to him. The American is burned out, convinced he's a danger and that he'd talk if captured.

When the Secret Police show up at the door, the American gives Trudi time to get away and then shoots himself to avoid any chance of betraying her — thus proving himself much braver than he had credited himself. The entire scene runs maybe three minutes, but in that short time, well-written dialogue and good acting give it real emotional impact. The rest of the episode, involving the Falcon's battle of wits with the head of the Secret Police, is very good, but that first few minutes are absolutely wonderful.

In the end, *The Falcon* does not rate among the best of old-time radio, but it was still worthwhile. It's sort of like stopping at a hot dog stand for lunch rather than a swanky restaurant. You know the food's not going to be the same quality, but if you're in the mood for a hot dog, it still tastes awfully good.

The Falcon on radio:
NBC Blue: 4/10/43–12/29/43

Mutual: 7/3/45–4/30/45

NBC: 7/7/50–9/14/52

Mutual: 1/5/53–11/27/55

The Falcon: Berry Kroeger, James Meighan, Les Tremayne, Les Damon, George Petrie
First prose appearance: "The Gay Falcon" (1940), by Michael Arlen

Boston Blackie

Boston Blackie, like the Falcon, found fame in other media after a relatively brief literary career. An active thief in the original stories, Blackie reformed from overt villainy when he came to radio, using his wits to catch crooks rather than commit crimes.

The Blackie stories were written by Jack Boyle, a former newspaper reporter who turned to crime to support his opium habit. Boyle was in prison in 1914, doing a stretch for armed robbery, when a magazine called *The American* published the first Boston Blackie story. (Boyle initially used the byline "No. 6606"—his prisoner number—but soon started using his own name.)

This first story is very contrived in terms of plot, but it does an effective job of delineating Blackie's character. He's a thief and completely unrepentant about it. But when breaking into a wealthy couple's mansion one night, he finds a young boy home alone, left there by an irresponsible nanny. He quickly befriends the boy. When the boy's mother comes home with another man, Blackie overhears enough conversation to realize that her marriage is on the rocks. Well, this won't do—the boy is *not* growing up in a broken home. Blackie quickly improvises a plan that breaks up the mother's illicit romance and gets her on the road to reconciliation with her husband. Then he steals her jewelry anyway, figuring he's done more than enough to earn it.

That's Blackie—a thief with a sense of honor and an intense loyalty to his friends. We also soon learn that the bulk of his loyalty is given to his loving wife, Mary.

To populate the world around Blackie, Boyle created a criminal society that never really existed—where all but a few despised snitches live under a strict code of honor that involves helping one another and, of course, never ratting on each other.

Realistic or not, this view of an honorable underworld is a perfectly acceptable conceit for a work of fiction, providing it is done well. But throughout the Boston Blackie stories, Boyle never really succeeds in making the idea completely believable — stretching himself too thin when he tries to make nearly all his criminal characters the "good guys." He expects us to sympathize not just with the sort-of noble Blackie, but also with guys we have no reason not to want to see in prison.

Had Blackie alone been living by his own individual but strict code of honor, or if Boyle spent more time establishing the police as brutal or government officials as corrupt or oppressive, then the stories might have generated a reasonably satisfying Robin Hood feel. But the crooks aren't giving their stolen money to the poor or railing against a corrupt society. Blackie might pause from his latest burglary to tuck a small boy back into bed and save a marriage, but everyone else is just robbing us blind. Perhaps most importantly, though Blackie himself doesn't kill, he casually helps those who do commit murder avoid capture.

Still, Blackie's and Mary's intensely loyal relationship is appealing and the later stories do improve. Blackie's clever schemes to pull off a job or break someone out of prison make for entertaining reading.

The final story in the series — "Boston Blackie's Mary" — is the best of the lot and includes mystery writers James M. Cain and Rex Stout among its admirers. Blackie has finally been caught and sent to prison — though to get him there the cops had to frame him for a crime he didn't commit. When brutal Deputy Warden Martin Sherwood bans Mary from writing or visiting her husband, Blackie engineers an escape. He and Mary reunite and plan to flee the country.

Sherwood's a great character. He's brutal and vindictive, but also smart and fearless. He comes up with an ingenious plan to track down Blackie and Mary, eventually confronting them in an out-of-the-way rooming house.

Blackie gets the drop on him, though, and realizes he has to kill the brutal warden in order to ensure his escape. But he can't bring himself to pull the trigger. He offers Sherwood a chance to shoot it out with even odds. Sherwood refuses, calling Blackie's bluff.

Out of morally acceptable options, Blackie surrenders. Then Sherwood, impressed by the love and loyalty that Blackie and Mary have expressed towards each other, decides to let them go. The couple escapes together to South America. It's an undeniably corny ending, but good characterizations and good prose make it believable and effective.

Boston Blackie appeared in many films, both silent and sound, in the years between the two world wars. Chester Morris, who played the likable thief in fourteen films for Columbia Pictures, brought him to radio in 1944 in a summer replacement series for NBC.

As with the Saint, there was no way the networks could get away with making an active criminal the hero of a series broadcast on the public airwaves. But this had been true in the movies as well, so the revised premise used there was simply transferred to radio. Besides, the movies had been popular and there was no reason to tinker with proven success. So, by the time he came to radio, Blackie had given up crime and now spent his spare time (and he had a lot of spare time) catching murderers.

Like the Falcon and the Saint, Blackie did not work for a living and seemed to be independently wealthy. Presumably, he's living off the ill-gotten gains of his former career. But whatever the source of his income, he can now afford to enjoy life, at least until a friend — or just someone in trouble — comes to him for help. He is, we are told in the opening narration of each episode, the "enemy to those who make him an enemy — friend to those who have no friends." Often, the friend in need is falsely accused of murder or some other crime, obligating Blackie to track down the real criminal. He's now almost the polar opposite of Boyle's original creation, who spent *his* spare time helping criminals get away.

The series got off to an awkward start with its premier episode. Broadcast on June 23, 1944, it began with a young lady named Lee Moray accusing Blackie of having robbed her grandfather. Blackie is arrested by police inspector Faraday, an old enemy of the former thief who wants nothing more than to see him back behind bars. (Faraday had been Blackie's nemesis in the Columbia B-movies, brought to radio along with the idea that Blackie had reformed.)

Miss Moray visits Blackie in his cell and admits to making up the story about the robbery — the false accusation was simply the only way she could think of to contact him. She really wants his help in recovering a diamond stolen from her apartment. The diamond belonged to her fiancé and she's going to be in big trouble if it's not recovered.

Blackie agrees to help her and then quickly and easily escapes from his cell. This is the sort of plot hole that plagued early episodes of the series — why didn't the girl just drop the charge against him?

Blackie finds the diamond at the fiancé's apartment. Soon, he uncovers a plot by the rotten cad to use the diamond to pay off gambling debts while blaming his girlfriend for its disappearance. Blackie is recaptured by Faraday before figuring everything out, but then the Inspector inexplicably lets him go to help recover the diamond and round up anyone who had actually done something illegal.

Illogical plot development always stands out like a sore thumb in radio drama — there are no visual tricks available to hide them. The writers seemed to be trying too hard to establish the ambiance and characters — so determined to show us how clever Blackie is that they sacrificed basic story construction along the way.

Things were soon looking up, though. Future plots were better constructed and when the show returned as a syndicated series in 1945 (with Richard Kollmar now playing Blackie), it was consistently well-written. Kollmar was charming in the lead role. Mary, his wife in the original stories, was absent from the 1944 summer series, but returned in 1945 as Blackie's girl friend. Played by Lesley Woods, she established a nice rapport with Kollmar.

The one mistake the show made and never corrected was the character of Inspector Faraday. Played at first by Richard Lane and later by Maurice Tarplin, the poor policeman bumbled around annoyingly in every single episode, doing little to either advance the plot or entertain the audience.

It was a pity. Lane had played Faraday opposite Morris' Blackie in the B-movie series. In that medium, Faraday was competent and reasonably intelligent. This helped emphasize just how clever Blackie was — it took at least a little bit of effort to outsmart the cop. The two men were somewhat friendly adversaries and the relationship was dramatically viable. But once on radio, poor Faraday was reduced to a mere dunce.

In nearly every episode, he storms up to Blackie and threatens to arrest him for a recent murder — whether or not he had any reason to actually do so. Just as often, he'd end up having to accept Blackie's help to catch the real killer. It was contrived, predictable and unnecessary.

Many fictional detectives have their police nemeses. Nero Wolfe, for instance, had Inspector Cramer. But Cramer was a good cop and his conflicts with Wolfe were always a logical outgrowth of the plot. Sherlock Holmes encountered slow-witted policemen, but not in every story and Holmes occasionally worked with a competent detective. Faraday, on the other hand, lacked believability and was a dramatically awkward character.

Still, good plots with fair clues more or less balanced this out. An episode from April, 1947 begins with the murder of a jewel thief by a gangster named Rudy Carter. Carter then forces Jimmy Saunders, who owes him $50,000 in gambling debts, to introduce a girl to Jimmy's baseball star brother Sammy. When Jimmy comes to Blackie for help, the ex-thief assumes Carter wants Sammy to throw games. Sammy keeps hitting homers, though, disproving this theory.

Faraday enters the case when he accuses Blackie of killing the jewel thief, as per the show's rigid formula. Blackie is warned to stay away from the case. He, of course, ignores the warning and continues to investigate.

It turns out that Sammy is being used to unwittingly smuggle jewels (stolen by the thief Carter murdered) from city to city as he travels with his team. Faraday must once more swallow his pride in order to back up Blackie when Carter is confronted with evidence of his crimes.

It's a solid mystery and the supporting characters — most notably Carter and Sammy Saunders — are nicely personalized. It's too bad Faraday always remained such a stereotypical dunce; *Boston Blackie* could have been much better than it was.

Boston Blackie on radio:
NBC: 6/24/44–9/15/44
Blackie: Chester Morris
Syndicated: 4/11/45–10/25/50
Blackie: Richard Kollmar

First prose appearance: "The Price of Principle" (1914), by Jack Boyle (writing as "no. 6606")

The Lone Wolf

Michael Lanyard, aka the Lone Wolf, might very well have been separated at birth from Boston Blackie. Both men were thieves. Both men were "born" when their premier stories were published in 1914. Both men eventually reformed, turning from committing crimes to solving them.

The Lone Wolf, though, reformed much quicker; where Blackie didn't turn away from crime until he jumped from prose into the B-movies, Lanyard did so partway through his first adventure.

Louis Joseph Vance's novel *The Lone Wolf* starts off with a succinct one-chapter biography of Lanyard, quickly letting us know who he is and how he became a skilled thief. He'd been abandoned as a young child at an out-of-the-way hotel in Paris called Troyon's. Put to work there by the uncaring proprietors, he took to snitching money from the guest rooms. He also took to reading, teaching himself both French and English letters and "thereby took his first blind step toward salvation."

When he's eleven years old, he makes the mistake of trying to steal from an Irishman named Bourke, who catches him red-handed. Michael is unconcerned, though. He has already deduced that Bourke is himself a thief and is convinced the Irishman will not turn him in.

Impressed, Bourke sort of adopts Michael and teaches him the tricks of the high-class criminal trade — everything from cracking a safe to proper table manners. Most importantly, he teaches him to always work alone. A truly successful criminal must have no ties. "To make a friend of a man you must lower your guard," Bourke tells him. "As for Woman, remember this, m'lad: to let love into your life you must open a door no mortal hand can close. And God only knows what'll follow in."

The story then jumps ahead some years. Bourke is dead and Lanyard, known by reputation as the Lone Wolf, comes to Paris from London after successfully relieving a wealthy dowager of her jewelry. The child petty thief has grown up into a sophisticated and charming gentleman and connoisseur of the arts. He's still a thief, of course, but now he's really, really good at it.

But he soon discovers that his identity has finally been compromised. A gang of criminals identifying themselves as "The Pack" have learned that Lanyard and the Lone Wolf are one and the same. They leave him a message, demanding that he join their organization and share his plunder with them. He meets with the leaders of the gang, but contemptuously refuses to throw in with them, responding neither to blackmail nor threats of violence.

Soon, he finds himself in a war of sorts. He tries to fence the jewels, but his usual contact abruptly refuses to do business with him anymore. Next, a Scotland Yard detective in the hotel room next to his own is brutally murdered. Lanyard foils an attempt by the Pack to frame him for the murder, but now he's on the run for his life. He's also broke, having unwisely blown his emergency cash at a roulette table.

Lanyard might have still managed to take care of the Pack and regained control over his life if it wasn't for one thing—he'd fallen in love. By this point in the story, he has met Lucy Shannon, a young woman who had been forced against her will to do the bidding of the Pack's leader. She was on the run along with him and, as they hid out for the night in an unoccupied apartment, he had something of an epiphany. He was no longer alone and he suddenly discovered that he "was concerned less for himself, even now when he should be gravely so, than for another."

So he vows to go straight. That leaves him with two problems—returning the stolen jewels (which he accomplishes by a sort of reverse burglary at the Paris home of his victim) and getting out of Paris alive. This second problem seems insoluble, especially after Lucy abandons him under circumstances that seem to indicate she was playing him for a fool.

Disillusioned, he considers returning to crime, but finds he's already developed too much of a conscience to allow this. He's nearly captured by the police and takes to hiding in plain sight as a taxi driver. This leads to a wild car chase through Paris when the Pack finally identifies him again.

He reconnects with Lucy and discovers she left him because she feared she was endangering him. Finally, the two arrange to leave Paris by airplane. The Pack sends a second plane after them, leading to a midair exchange of pistol shots in what must be one of the earliest dogfights to appear in fiction.

At the end, Lanyard and Lucy do make it to England safely. By this time, the various members of the Pack are dead or in prison and Lanyard has befriended a member of the British Secret Service. He and Lucy seem to be safe.

But, of course, they're not. Vance's novel was successful enough to warrant sequels and you can't be named the Lone Wolf if you're hauling a wife along with you. When the first sequel, *The False Faces*, was published in 1918, we discover that poor Lucy and her young son have been murdered. Lanyard is out for revenge, taking time to do some spying for the Allies at the same time.

Future adventures always included a lovely damsel in distress (another reason, probably, for doing away with Lucy) and often involved an old enemy seeking revenge. There were six more novels altogether, the last one in 1934. All were melodramatic in terms of both the plot and the style of the prose, but it's skillfully written melodrama that generates an appropriate level of suspense as it carries the story along. Lanyard's tendency toward introspection and moral consideration is both a virtue and a flaw. On occasion, his introspective moments slowed the action down a little too much. But those moments also gave him more depth than Boston Blackie, while his concern for justice and his sense of personal honor make him a godfather for future gentleman adventurers such as the Saint.

The Lone Wolf's first appearance on radio was on the popular CBS anthology show *Suspense*, in an episode broadcast in July 1943. At the time, actor Warren Williams had been starring as Lanyard in a series of B-movies produced by Columbia Pictures. Eric Blore co-starred as Jameson, a comic relief butler who had been created for the movie series. Both men simply transferred the roles they were playing on screen to radio.

In the movies — and on the *Suspense* episode — Lanyard is publicly known as a former thief who is now a "gentleman of leisure." But, as he explains at the beginning of the radio show, "there are still times when I am obliged — or should I say forced — to ... resort to the somewhat questionable talents of the Lone Wolf." In other words, he constantly finds himself involved in murder investigations, forced to find the real killer to clear himself of suspicion. This format is identical to the Boston Blackie films also being produced by Columbia Pictures in the 1940s.

Williams, experienced in the role by now, handles himself well on radio. The story finds him finds both he and Jameson at a party, where they inevitably discover a body. Lanyard, naturally, is suspected of the crime, but after avoiding a death trap, finding a second body and using his old skills to crack a safe in order to get evidence, he manages to identify the real killer. It's a pretty good mystery, though Lanyard's banter with Jameson is a bit forced at times.

The Lone Wolf finally made it to his own series in 1948. He wasn't a big success on radio, running for only about six months on the Mutual network. Played initially by Gerald Mohr (who had also portrayed Lanyard in three B-movies produced about the same time) and later by Walter Coy, the radio Lone Wolf has set up shop as a gentleman detective with a reputation that often sends distressed damsels running to him for help.

It's particularly interesting that the original Lone Wolf novels were an influence on Leslie Charteris' stories of the Saint. By 1948, both characters were settled in on radio and, in most respects, were now indistinguishable from one another. In fact, the one surviving episode of *The Lone Wolf* was written by Louis Vittes, who also wrote for *The Saint*.

But in that one episode, Walter Coy fails to exude the same level of charm that Vincent Price gave to Simon Templer. He's not bad at all— he's just not as good.

The story itself is fine. One evening as Christmas approaches, a young woman named Peggy approaches Lanyard and asks him to help find a small solid-gold figurine of Santa Claus that she's lost. She's visited several nightclubs that evening, so she and Lanyard back track her route. But the waiters at every nightclub they visit claim not to have seen Peggy that night.

Peggy began the evening having dinner with some friends, so the pair stops to see them next. One of the friends, a sleazy guy named Joe, claims to know where the Santa is. But the lights go out and Joe is gunned down before he can say anything else.

Lanyard discovers that Peggy has eyes for the rich husband of her former best friend. A trip to the husband's home finds *him* dead and the missing Santa at his feet. By now, though, Lanyard has the clues he needs to identify the killer. He gathers the suspects together and explains his deductions, then escorts the guilty party to headquarters.

It was a plot that could have been used on *The Saint* virtually without change. And that's the problem. Michael Lanyard is not given his own distinctive personality—he's simply copying what Simon Templar had been doing at CBS for nearly a year prior to the premier of *The Lone Wolf*.

But with only the one episode from which to judge the show, it would be hasty to condemn it outright. It's possible that other scripts presented Coy better opportunity to give Lanyard his own individuality. Perhaps Gerald Mohr—a skilled radio veteran—did the character more justice when he assayed the role.

Jameson, the comic relief butler, was a regular character on the series, played by Jay Novello, but does not appear in "The Golden Santa." We can't now know how well Lanyard and Jameson played off each other or to what degree their banter might have added any element of uniqueness to the show. If Jameson's personal history was carried over from the movies intact — he was a former pickpocket who missed being a criminal, but stayed honest at Lanyard's insistence — then there was a lot of room to have fun with the character.

So how good a show was *The Lone Wolf*? It's a mystery that would drive us to see Michael Lanyard himself if he were still in business.

The Lone Wolf on radio:
Mutual: 6/29/48–1/1/49

The Lone Wolf: Gerald Mohr, Walter Coy
First prose appearance: *The Lone Wolf* (1914),
by Louis Joseph Vance

Frank Merriwell

Frank Merriwell was one heck of a guy. He was an honors student *and* a star athlete, first at prep school and later at Yale. He played just about every sport, but still found time between classes and games to catch an occasional crook, help a lady in distress, or see a bully get his comeuppance.

Frank was created by dime novel writer William Gilbert Patton (using the pen name Bert L. Standish) in 1896. The character was an immediate hit with younger readers. Appearing weekly in the dime novel *Tip Top Weekly*, Frank helped boost circulation to 200,000 copies. Eventually, around one thousand Merriwell stories saw print, with the hard-working Patton writing nine-tenths of these. The term "dime novels" at that time was a misnomer. Most, including *Tip Top*, were thirty-two page pamphlets that cost a nickel. But even taking into account the short length of each individual story, it still adds up to a lot of Merriwell.

Frank was undeniably a stereotype. Even his name was meant to highlight his virtues. Frank=frankness; Merry=happy disposition; Well=health and vitality. When we meet him in his premier adventure, "Frank Merriwell, or the First Days at Fardale," he's standing up to a bully. In later stories, he'd continue to show himself to be honest, brave, stalwart, resourceful, and prone to getting kidnapped a lot.

Usually he was kidnapped by gamblers just before the big game. He'd always escape, of course, arriving at the field just in time to kick a field goal or hit a home run. Frank stumbled onto all sorts of other adventures as well, both at school and during his fairly regular travels abroad. He foiled the evil plots of many a thief and saboteur, showed many a wayward youth the error of his ways, and was such an all-around fine fellow you'd often find yourself guiltily wishing he'd just once lose his temper and cuss someone out.

In "Frank Merriwell's Nobility, or the Tragedy of the Ocean Tramp," from 1899, Frank and some of his fellow students are sailing to Europe for the summer. Also on board, though, is a crooked gambler named Harris who had clashed with Frank in an earlier story. Harris tries to kill Frank, but he's caught and clapped in irons.

Soon after, Frank exposes yet another crooked gambler who's cheating at poker. (Frank is not gambling himself, of course — only observing.) Then the ship catches fire and Frank risks his life to save Harris from his prison in the hold. He gives Harris his spot on an overcrowded life boat, fights a sword duel with the other gambler, and uses a life preserver to escape from the doomed ship in the nick of time. All this happens in the space of just thirty-two pages.

It's full of stilted dialogue and contrived situations, but Patton was a good enough writer to weave a modicum of real emotion into the tale. Frank's compassion towards his enemies comes across as a little bit touching despite the contrivances. It's not hard to understand Frank's popular appeal. It wasn't just that he's so good at everything — he is also a really nice guy.

Frank's adventures, with occasional stories about his brother Dick and eventually Frank Merriwell, Jr., continued on in dime novels until 1912. Comic books and Little Big Books followed with continued commercial success.

Frank first came to radio in a short-lived 1934 serial on NBC that does not survive. A more successful run on the same network debuted in 1946 and ran for three years, with Lawson Zerbe playing Frank.

There was no attempt to modernize Frank or change him in any way. The stories were set at the turn of the century and went for nostalgia right from the start. With the sound of clopping hooves on cobblestone streets in the background, announcer Mel Brant would exclaim "There it is — an echo of the past — an exciting past — a romantic past. The era of the horse-and-carriage, gas lit streets and free-for-all football games."

Frank was still encountering crooks and bullies between classes. The same sort of plots that fit nicely in a 32-page dime novel fit just as well in a 30-minute time slot.

In one episode, Frank and his best friend Bart escape from a cave in which they'd been trapped to foil the machinations of a spy. In another, Frank kicks the winning extra point in a game against Rutgers. When the game ball is stolen, both Rutgers and Yale fans threaten to riot. Frank tracks the ball down and recovers it, thus averting violence. In yet another adventure, Frank and Bart are spending their summer vacation working as life guards at Atlantic City, where they have a run-in with gun smugglers. The bad guys capture them and plan to shanghai them onto a South American freighter, but the boys soon gain the upper hand. In each case, Frank's ingenuity and determination see him and his friends through.

Actually, the radio show was better written than the dime novels. Dialogue flowed more naturally and the plots unfolded without as much contrivance. But themes and basic plot structures remained unchanged. Frank Merriwell wasn't broken, so no one tried to fix him.

Despite a half-century of enormous popularity, poor Frank has been largely forgotten today. He was one of many characters from his era who represented the best we could be. Some of these — such as the Lone Ranger and Dick Tracy — are still recognizable to many people today. But others, like Frank, have faded away. Perhaps in his case it's simply because Yale in 1900 doesn't have the same level of mythic appeal as the Old West or Prohibition-era Chicago. In fact, on radio at least, the nostalgic setting for *The Adventures of Frank Merriwell* never really mattered. Many episodes could have been given what would have then been a contemporary setting without any major changes.

All the same, Frank did all right for himself. In all those years, he never did lose his temper and cuss someone out. And that's exactly as it should be.

Frank Merriwell on radio:
NBC: 3/26/34–6/22/34 (serial)
Frank: Donald Briggs

NBC: 10/5/46–6/4/49
Frank: Lawson Zerbe

First prose appearance: "Frank Merriwell,
or the First Days at Fardale" (1896),
by William Gilbert Patton (writing as Bert L. Standish)

Bulldog Drummond

"Demobilized officer finding peace incredibly tedious, would welcome relief."

When Captain Hugh Drummond, D.S.O., MC, grew bored in the years following the Great War, he ran the above advertisement in the newspaper. A response to the ad was quick in coming — soon he was up to his neck in an adventure involving murder, kidnapping, torture, a damsel in distress, a hand-to-hand fight with a gorilla, stolen pearls and a plot to overthrow the British government.

All this took place in *Bulldog Drummond*, a novel written in 1920 by Colonel H.C. McNeile. McNeile, a twelve-year veteran of the military, initially wrote under the pen name "Sapper"— the slang term for a military engineer.

Bulldog Drummond, yet another protagonist who doesn't have to work for a living, is the bane of many vicious criminals, but has been known to get on the nerves of some of his readers as well. He balances precariously on an odd line between being enjoyable and being really, really annoying. The courage and resourcefulness he displays while foiling villainous plots make him fun to read about, but his speech mannerisms and casual bigotries can eventually start your left eye twitching in barely-suppressed aggravation.

Drummond, along with nearly everyone he meets *and* the novel's third-person narrator, all talk with the sort of "assumed flippancy" and understated humor that is stereotypical of the British public school class. (Mystery writer William DeAndrea referred to it as "the 'old bean' school of writing and speech so skillfully skewered by P.G. Wodehouse."*)

It's unrelenting throughout McNeile's prose. If Drummond is cap-

---

*DeAndrea, 315.

tured and threatened with torture, he casually remarks that he's in for "a cheery night." When he comes up with a plan of action, he comments that he's "got a perfect cerebral hurricane raging."

If it were just Drummond, then it would have been acceptable — his remarks are fairly witty and it is, after all, the same template that would later be used successfully by the Saint and the Falcon. But during the course of his premier adventure, he rounds up several old army buddies to aid him and, so help me God, they all talk exactly the same way. It gets so that you want to just slap one of them to make him stop.

McNeile's plot construction leaves something to be desired as well. Drummond does a lot of listening outside windows — he always seems to be in just the right place at the right time to overhear the bad guys discuss their plans in detail. He gets captured a lot, but his captors never kill him outright even if they have no reason not to do so. And any henchman left guarding Drummond is bound to be as dumb as a post, making his eventual escape possible.

But despite his flaws as a writer, McNeile found a large audience for his Bulldog Drummond novels and short stories, producing them regularly until his death in 1937. Another writer, Gerald Fairlie, took over the character and wrote seven more Drummond novels, with the last published in 1954. The inevitable series of B-movies featuring Drummond were produced in the 1930s and '40s.

McNeile was successful — and still readable today — because his virtues just barely manage to outweigh his vices. His plots might be awkward, but he moves them along briskly and crams in a lot of cool stuff before the denouement.

In Drummond's first adventure, his advertisement is quickly answered by the beautiful Phyllis Benton, who has fallen afoul of master criminal Carl Peterson. Drummond looks into the matter and discovers that Peterson has kidnapped American millionaire Hiram C. Potts. Drummond and Peterson (the two are destined to be archenemies) spend some time successively rescuing or recapturing poor Mr. Potts. Drummond himself is captured a couple of time, once after being forced to kill Peterson's pet gorilla in hand-to-hand combat, but always manages an appropriately narrow escape.

Gradually, Drummond uncovers Peterson's insidious plot to help the Bolsheviks take over England — with Peterson planning on betraying his partners and skipping the country with a fortune in loot. After dodging an assassination attempt by a pygmy with a blowgun, Drummond and his band of ex-army buddies crush the conspiracy. Drummond and Phyllis get engaged. Peterson's sadistic partner comes to a deservedly horrible end, but the master criminal himself escapes and plots his revenge.

It's all presented in a prose enthusiastic enough to hurdle over its flaws. There are a number of truly exciting set pieces — both Drummond's fight with the gorilla and his encounter with the pygmy in a pitch dark room are excellent. In a quite wonderful scene, Drummond is trapped on a rooftop, surrounded by Peterson's men. He starts singing loudly, attracting the attention of a dozen or so bystanders. This allows him to simply climb down and walk away, with the thugs helpless to stop him in front of so many witnesses.

Peterson, brilliant and coldly calculating, is a great villain and Drummond — almost despite himself — is a fun hero. We may vainly wish the adventurer would just *once* speak in a straightforward declarative sentence, but we'll have a fair amount of fun tagging along with him as he dodges death traps and foils evil to make it all worthwhile (with wet cloth still pressed to forehead to help that twitching eye).

Bulldog Drummond came to radio on the Mutual Network in 1941 for a very respectable eight-year run (with a brief revival in 1954). The radio show simplified Drummond's life quite a bit, leaving out his wife and his gaggle of ex-army comrades. The only character who follows him from his prose adventures is his butler Denny.

This was an understandable change on two levels. First, that many characters would not fit comfortably into a half-hour's worth of story. Second, the change highlights one of radio's few storytelling limitations: without visual cues, a large cast would make it difficult for the listeners to keep track of who was who. Voice differences alone were not always adequate. The Tarzan radio serials we'll be examining in a later chapter were able to juggle multiple characters because many of them had distinctive national accents, but a large all-British cast would have been inherently confusing.

Initially, the series was set in Drummond's native England. But after a few months, he and Denny emigrated to the United States. Here, the pair encountered killers, smugglers and kidnappers on a weekly basis.

Drummond's motivation remained the same. At the beginning of one episode, he describes the lure of adventure as "the element of surprise which turns seemingly dull situations into gripping experiences and prosaic places into areas of excitement." He certainly found his excitement on that particular occasion — he soon witnesses a murder, with the victim quoting Shakespeare before expiring and thus providing a clue that allowed Drummond to uncover two overlapping murder plots.

One might wonder why poor Denny puts up with all this, but he does. He may, in fact, be the single most loyal manservant in the history of the world, with duties that extend far beyond making tea or picking up the dry cleaning. No matter what sort of trouble Drummond gets into, Denny is there at his side. Apparently, the otherwise staid butler considers following a suspect or confronting an armed killer to be a normal part of his established responsibilities. He's the sort of butler no gentleman-adventurer should be without.

The radio Drummond had a talent for deductive reasoning that his prose counterpart only occasionally exhibited. Any one episode balanced out his straight detective work with a few attempts on his life. Quite often both he and Denny were dropped into a death trap of some sort near the climax. In general, the stories were less bizarre but better plotted than in the original stories.

Drummond's "old bean" dialogue was toned down quite a bit. It's tempting to say this was a relief (and to a degree it was) but, ironically, this left him with less personality. During the show's initial run, Drummond was played by George Coulouris, Santos Ortega and Ned Wever. Cedric Hardwicke took the role during the '54 revival. All were fine actors, but Drummond, like the Falcon, was never more than a template upon which to build a mystery story.

A 1942 episode starts with the owner of an amusement park found dead on his own roller coaster. His daughter Isabel thinks he was forced onto the ride with the intention of causing his weak heart to give out. She goes to Drummond for help.

Drummond collects information and soon deduces that the girl's father was indeed murdered. He and Denny dodge a few bullets before they uncover the motive. An oyster bar near the amusement park is the center of a dope-smuggling ring, using a rather clever trick to sneak the drugs in and out. The park owner had seen something incriminating and had to be silenced.

Drummond, Denny and Isabel are captured and taken aboard a yacht. The two men are locked up in the anchor chain room, where they'll be crushed when the anchor is raised. They, of course, manage to escape and confront the chief smuggler. Isabel avenges her father by personally knocking the villain unconscious.

It was a good story, well-constructed and nicely atmospheric. Still, it could have been better, as could the show as a whole. The idea of an independently wealthy man bouncing around the country with his faithful butler, investigating crimes just for the fun of it, is inherently entertaining. But Drummond on the radio was a little too staid — a trait that was a much better fit on Denny than on the good captain. Had Drummond been given more personality — had a little more of McNeile's enthusiasm made the leap to radio while still leaving his flaws behind — *Bulldog Drummond* might have been one of the true classics of radio's Golden Age.

Bulldog Drummond on radio:
Mutual: 12/13/41–1/12/49
Drummond: George Coulouris, Santos Ortega, Ned Wever

Mutual: 1/3/54–3/28/54
Drummond: Cedric Hardwicke

First prose appearance: *Bulldog Drummond* (1920), by Colonel H.C. McNeile (writing as Sapper)

Charlie Chan

Charlie Chan is always both the smartest *and* the most likeable guy in the room. When Chan was created by Earl Derr Biggers in the 1925 novel *The House Without a Key*, it was these two attributes that best defined the character, carrying him through six well-written mystery novels, seemingly countless B-movies and several radio series. All the novels, by the way, were initially serialized in the *Saturday Evening Post* before being republished in book form. Chan was a success in every medium in which he appeared.

In the premier novel, we first see Chan through the eyes of a character named John Quincy Winterslip, a Bostonian who comes to Hawaii on family business and becomes caught up in the investigation of the murder of a relative. Winterslip himself is a nicely realized character — full of a sense of New England propriety and engaged to the right sort of girl back home, he's drawn to the sense of freedom he finds in the tropics and is soon falling in love with a girl in a lower social circle. Though a bit stuffy at first, he eventually acquits himself well both in confronting killers and in affairs of the heart.

But it's Charlie Chan, the short, fat, Chinese American police sergeant running the investigation, who most commands the reader's attention. We know he's smarter than we are from nearly the moment we meet him. And, as we get to know him, we can't help but like him.

First, he's an excellent cop with a talent for deductive reasoning and a firm grasp of human nature. In this first adventure, he finds a set of clues at the crime scene (a cigarette butt of a certain brand, a calendar book with a page torn out, etc.) that all seem potentially valuable. One by one, the clues lead to dead ends, but the information he collects while following up on them allows him to zero in on the killer, arriving just in time to save Winterslip's life.

Through the years, Chan has been accused of being a stereotypical character, in part because of his sometimes stilted use of English as typified by dialogue such as "Humbly begging pardon to be so abrupt ... the moment of our appointment is eminent." It's true he never completely gets the hang of English, occasionally leaving out a noun or preposition or using words like "unsignificant." But Biggers' skill at characterization is perhaps most apparent in that Chan's problems with English never lessen our opinion of his intelligence. There is no lack of either brains or dignity inherent in his speech patterns.

He's also a devoted family man. In most of the novels, we are given a glimpse of his large family and it's clear that he loves them all dearly. The contrast between he and his children is notable — he's still very Chinese in his speech and attitudes, while they are thoroughly Americanized. But he's proud of their American citizenship, even if he deplores their incessant use of slang. "Vast English language is spread out before you," he once tells his one of his sons, "and you select for your use the lowliest words. I am discouraged." But his discouragement is always momentary, trumped by love and devotion.

Finally, Chan is a thoroughly decent human being. He's a policeman because he wants to see justice done, but he's polite and considerate toward everyone he meets — rich, poor, honest or criminal.

In *The Black Camel* (1926), Chan is confronted with a murder involving confusing, contradictory clues. Someone is also planting false clues and various suspects are lying to him for various reasons. But though he can be tough if he had to be and expresses mild annoyance with an inept assistant, he never loses his temper or treats anyone with disrespect or discourtesy, even when it seems likely that that person has stabbed a woman to death.

It's not surprising that a character as appealing as Charlie Chan would be snatched up for use in other media. He was first brought to radio in 1932–33 in a series of direct adaptations of several of the novels, with Walter Connolly playing the lead. Unfortunately, no recordings of these survive.

In the meantime, Chan began appearing in motion pictures produced by Twentieth-Century Fox, the first of which was released in 1929. In 1931, Swedish actor Warner Oland took over the role of Chan and the studio soon had a hit series on its hands. As with Boston Blackie, the films would have a direct influence on later radio adaptations, so we must detour into that medium for a few moments.

The Chan movies receive the greatest amount of criticism regarding stereotyping, in large part because the lead was never actually played by a Chinese actor. By itself, this is a fair and important criticism, highlighting the racism that was an accepted part of Western society at the time. It's unlikely that the filmmakers ever gave thought to actually casting a Chinese actor to play the great detective.

But there's no denying that Oland was very appealing in the role. The same reasons we like Chan so much in the book — his intelligence and his common decency — are just as apparent in Oland's portrayal of the detective. Once again, Chan is both the smartest and the most likeable guy in the room.

The movies also played up Chan's love of his family. But the movie Chan did not stay put in Hawaii — instead, the detective is traveling the world to consult with other police departments. This gave limited opportunity to show Chan with his wife and children. So, in the 1935 film *Charlie Chan in Shanghai*, we meet Chan's "Number One Son" Lee, played with charm and enthusiasm by Keye Luke.

Lee becomes a regular character in the films, often traveling with his father and always insisting he be allowed to help out with the current case. His love for and pride in his pop are apparent in his every action. Often he is a help. Other times, his excess enthusiasm leads him into trouble. But the younger Chan never comes across as dumb even when he goofs up badly. This is largely due to Luke's excellent job as an actor, giving charm and dignity to a role that could have degenerated into stereotypical comic relief. And, though he can get on his father's nerves from time to time, it's clear that Charlie returns his love.

As for the plots, they were never as clever as in the original novels, but they were always serviceable. Besides, we watch and enjoy the Charlie Chan films mostly because we just enjoy hanging out with the man. The mysteries he solves were sufficient to that end.

Another slight modification from the books was building on Chan's habit of spouting aphorisms. Chan did this in the original novels from time to time, some of which were pretty good: *Moment comes when gold and pearls can not buy back the raven locks of youth.* But the movie Chan had an endless supply of wise sayings covering nearly every subject known to man. *Admitting failure like drinking bitter tea; All forgotten, like last year's bird's nest; Hope is sunshine which illuminate darkest path; Bad alibi like dead fish — cannot stand test of time.*

Warner Oland's chronic alcoholism lead to a tragic early death and Sidney Toler took over the role in 1938, followed by Roland Winters in 1947. If neither actor was quite as good as Oland, both still brought the same appealing qualities to the role. The Chan series continued until 1949, making it one of the most successful in the history of cinema.

Charlie Chan returned to radio in 1936 as a fifteen-minute daily serial on the Mutual network. This ended in 1938. A weekly half-hour show began on NBC in 1944, then jumped back to a daily serial format for a time. A 1947–48 half-hour show back on Mutual finished his radio career. During this time, he was played by first by Ed Begley and later by Santos Ortega. Leon Jamey most often played "Number One Son."

All these versions looked to the movies rather than the original books for their inspiration. Lee Chan becomes a regular character, now taking an active part in criminal investigations with the approval of his father, who hopes he will also one day join the police department. As in the movies, Charlie's speech is stilted and formal, while Lee is total Americanized. And, of course, Charlie spouts aphorisms at the drop of a hat, the best one regarding a criminal who had been murdered by his compatriots: "Nemesis is exceedingly accurate bookkeeper — wages of sin must be paid to the last penny."

Not enough of the daily serials survive to give us more than fragments of a few storylines. What does survive, though, hints at well-constructed mysteries — which, of course, makes the fact that so many episodes are missing that much more aggravating.

The surviving half-hour mysteries are adequate, but far from the best of which radio is capable. Each episode opens with the reminder that Charlie Chan "combines the wisdom of the East with the Science of the West," then uses a third-person narrator to set up the situation and introduce the characters. In "The Curious Ride of the Sea Witch," two escaped convicts steal a boat and ride out to a yacht in hopes of hijacking it. Aboard the yacht, the wealthy woman owner is forbidding her daughter to marry the man she loves. Soon after, the woman is murdered. The convicts have been caught by the crew and everyone assumes they are guilty. But Chan, with Lee tagging along, investigates and quickly deduces that someone else is guilty. It's an okay plot, but flawed in that the convicts were too obviously red herrings and the solution could be predicted almost from the moment the murder occurred.

The main problem, though, was with the actors. Both Begley and Ortega were excellent character actors and both were good as Chan. Leon Jamey, though, never seemed authentic as Lee and his relationship with his father always comes across as a little forced.

Is this a case in which we must grit our teeth and admit that a medium other than radio did a better job of storytelling? On this occasion, yes — the movies were consistently better than the radio shows. But not, we must hasten to add, because of any inherent problems with radio's storytelling potential. In this case, it's simply because the movies found the perfect actors for the job in Warner Oland and Keye Luke. The chemistry between those two actors was something that radio shows were never fortunate enough to match.

Charlie Chan on radio:
NBC Blue: 12/2/32–5/26/33 (serial)
Chan: Walter Connolly
Mutual: 9/17/36–4/22/38
NBC: 7/6/44–9/28/44
NBC Blue: 10/5/44–4/5/44
ABC: 6/18/45–11/30/45 (serial)
Chan: Ed Begley
Mutual: 8/11/47–6/21/48
Chan: Ed Begley, Santos Ortega

First prose appearance: *The House Without a Key* (1925), by Earl Derr Biggers

Mr. Moto

Mr. I.A. Moto is a small, obsequiously polite Japanese man who once explained that he had worked as a valet while attending an American University. He can also tend bar, perform carpentry, navigate boats, speak a number of languages and — when it seems necessary to do so in service to his Emperor — slit your throat from ear to ear. He will afterwards offer regretful apologies for the necessity, though.

Mr. Moto was created to fill the gap left by the death of Earl Derr Biggers, the author of the Charlie Chan novels. He came about when the *Saturday Evening Post*, looking for a new and (hopefully) equally popular Oriental detective character, sent John P. Marquand to China to dig up ideas.

Marquand was just the right man for the job. A great writer, he would eventually win the Pulitzer Prize for his 1937 novel *The Late George Apley*, a satire about upper-class New England manners. The Moto novels, he later said, were a "literary disgrace. I wrote about [Moto] to get shoes for the baby."*

The Moto novels may not have anything to do with New England or the foibles of the upper class, but they are all well-crafted, exciting spy stories and there is nothing disgraceful about them. Marquand, benefiting from his trip to the East, used a smooth, clear prose to both tell the story and provide a vivid sense of atmosphere. Five of the six Moto novels were written in the 1930s or early '40s — at a time when neither Japanese nor Chinese culture had been much influenced by the West. To most Americans, the Far East was close to being an alien world and pretty much beyond their understanding. This was the setting for most of the Moto novels and Marquand often emphasized the differences in Eastern and

*DeAndrea, 234.

Western cultures to introduce elements of suspense into the stories. But he did so without resorting to stereotypes. The characters in the novels are very different from one another — sometimes completely baffled by the actions or attitudes of each other — but all of them are believable, three-dimensional people. The world they inhabit may be different from anything the American readers were familiar with, but it still seemed very real. For instance, this passage from *Thank You, Mr. Moto* (1936) shows how Marquand could quickly give us the feel of a strange city:

> *There is no place in the world as strange as Peking at night, when the darkness covers the city like a veil, and when incongruous and startling sights and sounds come to one out of that black. The gilded carved facades of shops, the swinging candle lanterns, the figures by the tables in the smoky yellow light of teahouses, the sound of song, the twanging of stringed instruments, the warm strange smell of soybean oil, all come out of nowhere to touch one elusively and are gone.*

The really interesting thing about the Moto novels is that Mr. Moto is never actually the main character. In the premier novel, serialized in 1935 as "Mr. Moto Takes a Hand" and later published as *No Hero*, the protagonist is an alcoholic American named Casey Lee.

Lee is a former Navy pilot who flew in combat and later made a name for himself by completing transatlantic and transcontinental solo flights. We meet him when he's in Tokyo, preparing to make a trans–Pacific flight to both earn money and to salvage a fading reputation. But he's drinking too much and when he receives a telegram telling him his sponsors have pulled their support for the flight, he loses his temper. He publicly bashes the United States, tearing up his passport and declaring, "There are plenty of other countries."

Mr. Moto is nearby and helps the drunken Lee to his room. The next day, a Russian woman named Sonya Karaloff takes Lee to an out-of-the-way restaurant to meet Moto again. Moto suggests that the Japanese government would be willing to sponsor Lee's flight. First, though, Lee needs to sail to Shanghai and mingle with American government and military officials there, reporting whatever interesting tidbits he might overhear.

Still bitter, Lee agrees, finding a way to rationalize in his own mind his decision to spy against his country. But this doesn't last. On the ship to Shanghai, he is contacted by a desperate Chinese man who wants him to sneak a written message to an American Intelligence officer. The Chinese never gets to give him the message, though, before he turns up in Lee's cabin with a knife in his back.

The situation has made Moto suspicious of Lee — and with good reason. To his own astonishment, Lee finds that he is unwilling to work against the United States. "Men die for their faith who have never been inside a church," he explains, "and men die for their country, although they may have spent their lives criticizing all its works. The amazing thing is that they are probably surprised by their irrational willingness to die."

The Russian woman, Sonya, is also on board the ship and has by now revealed herself to have an agenda of her own. She and Lee are forced to work together, finding themselves attracted to each other without knowing if they can trust one another. With Sonya's help, Lee manages to get away from the ship as it approaches Shanghai and swim ashore. Here he ends up in the hands of a Chinese crime lord named Wu Lai-fu, who has his own motivations for being involved.

Eventually, Lee figures out where the message he was meant to deliver is hidden. But so does Moto. The message tells the location of a formula for a new method of fuel production that could change the balance of military power in the region.

Lee, with Sonya's help, dodges an attempt to kill him. One step ahead of Moto, the two get hold of a plane and fly to a remote Chinese village to retrieve the formula. But Lee wants it for the U.S., while Sonya wants it for a band of White Russian exiles who plot to overthrow the Soviet government. And Mr. Moto, who wants it for Japan, hasn't given up yet....

It's a fast-moving story, building up suspense throughout until it comes to its nicely complex but believable finale. Mr. Moto is technically the villain, but he's really the coolest guy in the story. He is willing to act ruthlessly, but we understand throughout that he does what he does in service to *his* country. We may root against him, but we still respect him. Extremely intelligent and capable, it takes a lot of work to stay ahead of him, making him a great adversary.

There were four more Moto novels written before America entered the Second World War in 1941. They all follow a similar pattern — an American, emotionally burnt-out or otherwise given up on life, becomes involved in something dangerous and finds an opportunity to redeem himself. This was formulaic to a degree, but because of Marquand's skill at characterization, it was never corny or stilted.

Sometimes Mr. Moto was an adversary, but he could also be an ally. In *Thank You, Mr. Moto*, the protagonist is Tom Nelson, a former lawyer who had grown sick of the American rat race and moved to Peking. Now he just drifted through life, his favorite observation being "It doesn't really matter, does it?"

But it does turn out to matter. Nelson becomes a target for assassination when it is believed that he has learned about the plans of a Chinese bandit named Wu Lo Feng to seize control of the city. Feng is being backed by a militaristic faction of the Japanese government. Mr. Moto shows up to fight against Feng — he himself defends Japanese imperialism, but belongs to a political faction that wants the expansion to be slower and less violent.

Nelson, Moto, and several other characters are eventually captured by the bandits. Nelson, by now, has found his backbone and takes the lead in an escape attempt — though his unfamiliarity with firearms nearly gets them all killed at one point. With Moto politely pointing out the wisest course of action, though, they do manage to get away. Moto is then able to stop the Feng's uprising before it can begin, giving us one last reminder that the small Japanese man can be extremely ruthless when the situation demands it.

Twentieth-Century Fox produced eight Mr. Moto movies between 1937 and 1939, with Hungarian-born actor Peter Lorre doing wonderful work in the lead role. In the movies, Mr. Moto is initially a successful importer who works as a detective both as a hobby and to look out for his own business interests. Eventually, he became an active agent for the "International Police," often (and ironically, considering his role in the books) looking after the interests of the Western political powers. Though the plots and situations are very different from the books, Lorre captures that same combination of politeness, intelligence and violence that makes the character so interesting. The Moto movies are among the best in the genre.

Pearl Harbor put an end to both the books and the movies — it had abruptly become impossible to have a Japanese hero (or even a likable adversary) in American popular culture. Marquand would return to the character one more time in the 1957 novel *Stopover Tokyo*, with an aging Moto playing a small role in foiling a Communist plot to overthrow the Japanese government. After that, Mr. Moto appears to have retired.

Had Moto come to radio in the 1930s, he probably would have been based more on the B-movies than the books — this being the usual procedure with such characters at that time. But World War II got in the way and the character didn't get to radio until 1951, after the bitterness of the war had some time to fade. By this time, the Moto films were long gone from the public eye and the radio series looked back to the original books for its inspiration.

All the same, when *Mr. Moto* aired on NBC from May to October 1951, there were some drastic changes. Obviously, Mr. Moto couldn't work for a government that no longer existed. Nor would it be appropriate in a weekly series for the title character to play a supporting role.

So Moto was moved from Japan to the United States. In fact, he had apparently changed into a native-born U.S. citizen, mentioning in one episode that he grew up in San Francisco. The unswerving loyalty the original Moto felt towards the Emperor was shifted over to America. The radio Moto is an agent for an unnamed U.S. Intelligence service, working behind the scenes to serve his country.

The opening narration for each episode varies a little each week. In one, Moto is described at an "international agent extraordinaire — the inscrutable, crafty and courageous Oriental." In another, we're told "Across the world, from Japan to Jersey, from Cape Horn to Murmansk, Mr. Moto is fighting the evils of Communism quietly, ruthlessly, courageously." In yet another, he is described as "the world's most brilliant espionage agent."

Whatever the exact wording, the point is the same. Moto is still a highly trained and skilled agent, quite able to either outthink or outfight his adversaries. He's just working for a different side now.

The radio series also retained the basics of the original Moto's personality: his unfailing politeness counter-pointed by his willingness to act violently when he is forced to do so. Good scripts and the performance of James Monks as Moto brought these apparently contradictory traits across in a believable manner, giving the short-lived show its own unique feel.

An episode titled "Smoke Screen" begins with Moto telling us:

> The boy, unbelievably young, writhed on the floor of my New York apartment. His legs convulsed in the ropes that tied them together. His thin, adolescent wrists strained hopelessly at the handcuffs. It is impossible not to feel sympathy for a human being possessed by such a devil. He had bitten his forefinger almost through. He screamed about a white, crippled cat that clawed at him.

The boy is going through cold-turkey drug withdrawal and Moto is refusing him any help at all until he comes across with the location of a large cache of smuggled opium. But it's made clear that Moto will also do anything he can to help the boy kick the habit and get back on his feet. "You are young," Moto tells him. "You can be strong again."

It's a very effective scene, skillfully structured and acted, bringing out Mr. Moto's complex personality while still moving the story along briskly.

The opium was being smuggled in by a Chinese Communist submarine; other episodes are also steeped in Cold War villainy. "Project 77" found him in Japan, searching for a kidnapped Naval officer who has vital information about an experimental jet-powered torpedo. He eventually learns that a man posing as a local missionary is actually a Russian agent.

But this takes time, giving the enemy spy opportunity to break the kidnapped officer through torture and get the information he needs. The officer is disposed of and the agent begins to make arrangements to smuggle the information to Russia.

Moto gets unexpected help from the fake missionary's Japanese wife. She had married him knowing he was a spy, hoping for an opportunity to one day foil his plans. With her help, the spy is caught and killed before the information can be passed on to the Soviets. It was yet another well-written story, with several nice bits of characterization from among the supporting characters adding spice to the story.

This ability to give substance to the supporting roles and play them effectively off Mr. Moto was perhaps the show's greatest strength. This was one of the key qualities of the original novels; writer-director Harry W. Duncan was wise to imitate it.

In one case, Duncan also copied one of Marquand's original plots. "The Karaloff Papers" uses the plot from *No Hero*, but shifts Moto into Casey Lee's role. Moto's original part as the villain is now played by Wu Lai-fu, the Chinese crime lord who was a supporting character in the novel. Mr. Moto really can seem to do anything — whether it be switching nationalities or switching parts within a story.

About a dozen episodes of *Mr. Moto* survive, which probably represents the bulk of those produced. Today, the character is remembered mostly through the Peter Lorre films. They're really fun movies and this is fine by itself, but it's worthwhile to remember that Mr. Moto also acquits himself well in other media. Always polite and occasionally deadly, he's worth getting to know in all his incarnations.

Mr. Moto on radio:
NBC: 5/20/51–10/20/51
Mr. Moto: James Monks

First prose appearance: *No Hero* (1935), by John P. Marquand

Perry Mason

During the 1920s and 1930s — the heyday of the pulp magazines — a former lawyer named Erle Stanley Gardner discovered he had a talent for writing entertaining stories. He had a knack for creating fun characters, each of whom could star in his own series of mystery or adventure tales. The best of them might have been Lester Leith, a con man who came up with complex plans to rob criminals of their ill-gotten gains. Then there was the short and lightweight private eye Donald Lam, who worked for an agency run by 250-pound tough-gal Bertha Cool. Other Gardner creations included characters with names like Sydney Zoom, the Human Fly, and Hard Rock Hogan.

But Gardner really hit literary gold with the creation of Perry Mason in the 1933 novel *The Case of the Velvet Claws*. By the time Gardner passed away in 1970, he had produced eighty Perry Mason novels, selling over two hundred million total copies. It was the single best-selling mystery series in the history of American literature.

Today, due to the popularity of the books and the 1957–66 television series starring Raymond Burr, most people think of Mason as the brilliant lawyer who uses his sharp, quick intelligence and awesome legal skills to help clear his inevitably innocent clients and expose the real killer. He didn't start out that way, though. When we first meet Mr. Mason, he totes a pistol, urges witnesses to lie, beats up a reporter, bribes a cop to trace a phone number and is in general pretty casual about breaking the law if that's the best way to help his client. He does use his expertise as a lawyer on occasion, but for the most part he is indistinguishable from a hard-boiled private eye. In fact, at one point he brags about how his cases rarely reach the courtroom — he'll have wrapped them up one way or another long before they reach even the preliminary hearing stage.

He is, above all else, loyal to his clients. "There's only one rule in this game," he once said, "and that is that when you do take [a client], you've got to give them all you got."

This rule holds even when the client is actually pretty rotten. In *The Case of the Velvet Claws*, Mason is approached by a woman who gives her name as Eva Griffin and needs help dealing with a blackmailer. Mason knows almost right away that she's giving a phony last name and address, but he agrees to help her out regardless. The case quickly grows complicated: Eva is being blackmailed over an extra-marital affair by the editor at a newspaper specializing in scandals and gossip. The secret owner of the paper — the man thus heading the blackmail ring — turns out to be Eva's husband, who has no idea his own wife was one of his marks.

When the husband turns up dead, it looks as if Eva is guilty. To make sure Mason will continue to help her, she lies about hearing him in the house speaking to her husband just before the murder. Her assumption is that Mason *has* to help her or risk being framed for the crime himself.

But this crude extortion attempt is unnecessary. Mason sees sticking by his client as his one overriding duty. With the help of his private secretary Della Street and private detective Paul Drake, Mason follows up clues and gradually puts enough facts and deductions together to name the real killer. He then collects his fee from Eva without really bothering to hide his disdain for her. She had been innocent of murder, though, and he had come through for her.

It's a well-plotted mystery with several good twists at the end. As was usual for Gardner, his prose carries the story along using dialogue and short descriptions of action, making *Velvet Claws* a fast, fun read.

Characterizations are pretty basic in the Mason novels, but we get to know Perry, Della, and Paul Drake pretty well over the course of the series. Della is especially interesting. She comes from an upper class family, but insists on earning her own way through life. It's soon obvious that she and Perry are in love. In fact, he proposes to her at least five times during the course of the series. But she refuses every time, once telling him "You're not the marrying kind, but I know damn well you need a secretary who's willing to go to jail occasionally to back your play."

She does land in the pokey from time to time, as well as putting in long and unusual hours, doing undercover work and always acting with competence and intelligence. Like Bulldog Drummond's butler Denny, she goes above and beyond the call of duty on a regular basis. And it's clear she wouldn't want to have it any other way.

Mason also depends on the Paul Drake Detective Agency for help, calling Drake at a moment's notice and often in the wee hours of the night, asking him to put his men on the job tailing a suspect or looking for a stolen item. Drake, in fact, acts as a sort of built-in deus ex machina, providing Mason with a plausible means of finding clues quickly in the midst of the fast-paced stories.

Mason continued his hard-boiled ways for several years, often clashing with a brutish, dishonest police Sergeant named Holcombe. But in the 1940s, Gardner began to serialize some of the new Mason novels in the respectable *Saturday Evening Post*. Writing to a new audience, Gardner toned down Mason's more violent activities and began to take him into the courtroom on a regular basis. His adversary Sergeant Holcombe was reduced to just occasional appearances, while the more intelligent and honest Lieutenant Tragg became a series regular. Perpetually aggravated D.A. Hamilton Burger came to play a larger role, as he and Mason verbally clashed with each other in the always entertaining courtroom scenes.

Gardner kept his dialogue-heavy prose style, though, and his plots remained strong. The new formula fit Mason perfectly and the novels from the late 1940s on are without fail solid, pleasurable mysteries.

A client would come to Mason for legal advice on some important matter. Inevitably, someone would soon end up dead and the client would be charged with the crime. Mason, Della and Drake would investigate. Then, usually at the preliminary hearing (the cases rarely made it to a jury trial), Mason would employ his considerable skills as both a lawyer and a detective to prove his client's innocence and expose the true murderer. It never grew tiresome, carried along with renewed freshness each time by Gardner's fast-moving prose, well-constructed plots and likeable protagonists. The courtroom sequences alone are quite riveting.

The Case of the Sun Bather's Diary (1955) begins with Mason receiving a phone call from Arlene Duvall. Arlene has literally been robbed of everything—her car and trailer home were stolen while she was sun bathing. She's calling *au naturel* from a remote phone booth.

Della takes her some clothes and brings her to meet Mason. Arlene wants Mason to find the trailer, but doesn't want to involve the police. It turns out that her father is in jail for stealing nearly $400,000 dollars from the bank that had employed him. The money was never recovered. Arlene claims she has been trying to find evidence to clear her father's name. But she won't say where the money she's living on comes from. Mason agrees to help her, but tells her up front that if she's using the stolen money, he'll turn her over to the police and collect the reward.

To the surprise of absolutely no one reading the novel, someone is soon killed. Mason is very personally involved this time — he'd been in the victim's house, talking to him, just moments before the man was killed.

Burger thinks Mason is lying about something to shield his client and subpoenas him to appear before a grand jury. Mason is truthful under oath, but withholds information that would be harmful to his client when Burger's line of questioning leaves him with a loophole for doing so. Burger is convinced Mason has perjured himself and vows to bring charges as soon as Arlene Duvall is prosecuted for murder.

But Mason stays on top in the end. At Arlene's hearing, he picks apart the Burger's case. When he himself is called to the stand as a hostile witness for the prosecution, he nearly drives Burger to apoplexy when he's able to present a piece of surprise evidence. Then he succinctly explains how both Arlene and her father must be innocent, names the guilty parties, and solves both the murder and the bank theft at the same time.

And so it went time and time again. There are several conceits to the novels that the reader must accept. One wonders, for instance, how poor Hamilton Burger kept his job as D.A. after trying to prosecute so many innocent people; or why apparently all of Mason's clients end up pretty much falling over corpses so regularly after hiring him. But each individual novel is done so well that these conceits actually become strengths rather than weaknesses.

The format for a Perry Mason novel probably could have been brought to radio with reasonable faithfulness. Perhaps the plots would have had to be simplified a little to cut down on the number of suspects and witnesses (remember that radio drama's one inherent weakness is keeping track of a large number of characters without visual cues), but the basic formula and most especially the courtroom scenes would have translated quite well.

But Perry Mason came to radio as a fifteen-minute per weekday soap opera in 1943, running on CBS in that format for twelve years. Bartlett Robinson, Donald Briggs and Santos Ortega each cycled through the role of Mason, with John Larkin taking over in 1947 for the last eight years of the run. Della Street was successively played by Gertrude Warner, Jan Miner and Joan Alexander. Gardner himself tried writing scripts at first, but soon admitted he had no talent for that form of storytelling.

Gardner looked upon the show as a source of additional royalties and as an advertisement for his books, but he was still unhappy with the initial quality of the stories. In 1946, Irving Vendig joined the show as a writer and managed to inject stronger plots and characterizations into the proceedings.

And, in fact, it wasn't a bad effort. The main problem for a modern listener is the dearth of surviving episodes. Of the approximately 3,200 episodes produced during the show's run, only about one out of ten survive. To this author's knowledge, no complete storylines exist. We are forced to jump into the middle of a plot and try to figure out what's going on without all the information we need. More annoyingly, it's not unusual for the episodes that conclude a storyline to be missing.

Also, it *was* a soap opera and didn't hesitate to occasionally step away from the current mystery to deal with the romances or family troubles of various supporting characters. This would have been fine if the show had simply been a traditional soap opera, but anything that doesn't deal directly with a corpse or a clue doesn't really belong in a Perry Mason story.

When the plot did stick to the crime at hand, it was pretty good. Most of the surviving episodes feature John Larkin as Mason, who endowed the lawyer with a strong personality. Though there are a few episodes taking place in a courtroom, the radio Mason returned to the more active roots of early novels. In one partially surviving sequence, he himself is on the run from the cops, with Della and Paul Drake accompanying him, as he plots to trap those who have framed his client. On other occasions, he would accompany Lt. Tragg and pretty much act as a partner to the cop, helping question witnesses and even subdue suspects.

But both the flaws and the strengths of the show are trumped by the simple fact of too many missing episodes. It makes it difficult to critically examine the show with any real fairness. The show certainly found an audience when it first aired and it was done with enough skill and expertise to make this understandable. But it never really did the classic Mason novels justice.

In 1955, there were discussions to bring the show to television in the soap opera format. Gardner, though, refused to allow any storylines in which Mason and Della become romantically involved. So Mason and his co-protagonists were simply dropped. The show came to TV as the soap *The Edge of Night*.

Two years later, Perry Mason finally did come to television in the classic black-and-white series starring Raymond Burr and Barbara Hale. With plots often based directly on the original novels, it is one of the rare examples of television that is actually intelligent and entertaining. Earlier, we were forced to admit that Charlie Chan was better represented in the movies than on radio. Now, in an act that will cause a burst of intense pain to shoot through the liver of any old-time radio aficionado, we must acknowledge that Perry Mason did better in the vast wasteland of television than he did on dramatic radio. It just goes to show that anything, no matter how unlikely, can happen at least once.

Perry Mason on radio:
CBS: 10/18/43–12/30/55 (serial)
Mason: Bartlett Robinson, Santos Ortega,
Donald Briggs, John Larkin

First prose appearance: *The Case of the Velvet Claws* (1933),
by Erle Stanley Gardner

Nick Carter

It was lucky for Nick Carter that as a child he didn't harbor any secret desires to play baseball or dance ballet — otherwise he might have grown into a very unhappy and maladjusted adult.

Nick Carter's father trained him almost from birth to be an expert detective. He was developed physically into an immensely strong and expert fighter (with both fists and guns) and was taught everything from science to art to languages to acting and disguise tricks. Though small in stature, his physical strength earned him the nickname Little Giant and he was said to be able to "fell an ox with one blow of his small, compact fist." He was good at just about everything and eventually put his many talents to work bringing criminals to justice. He usually operated out of New York City, but he traveled around often enough to foil evil plots the world over. He seemed happy enough, though one can't help but wonder if he didn't occasionally look out at a sandlot ball game and let out a soft sigh of regret.

Nick's first appearance was in "The Old Detective's Pupil, or the Mysterious Crime of Madison Square," published in the September 18, 1886 issue of the *New York Weekly*. The *Weekly* was one of hundreds of dime novels that ruled over popular literature during the latter half of the 19th century. As mentioned earlier, "dime novel" was something of a misnomer. The phrase was coined in 1858, when the publishing firm Beadle and Adams began to issue a series of novel-length books that cost a dime apiece. Within a few years, "dime novel" was the generic expression for any regularly published source of popular fiction — most were pamphlet-sized booklets that cost a nickel.

At first, the most popular dime novels were frontier stories or westerns, but after the Civil War, with industrialization drawing more and more of the population into the cities, a more urban hero was needed. The first detective character to regularly appear in a dime novel series was named Old Sleuth, who solved his first case in 1872. He was soon joined by hundreds of other detectives, with the genre eventually outselling the westerns.

When Nick Carter joined the crowd in 1886, he was in many ways no different from the rest. He, like nearly all his peers, was an expert in disguise who solved his cases by following the bad guys around, listening in on their conversations, avoiding a death trap or two, then making his arrests. The same sort of contrived plots and stilted dialogue that cursed the rest of the dime novel universe infested Nick's tales as well.

But Nick managed to stand out from the rest. He appeared in over one thousand dime novels, most of them written by Frederic Merrill van Rensselaer Dey, whose contribution to the Nick Carter mythos eventually totaled about 20,000,000 words. Nick was still around when the last of the dime novels faded away in 1915 — the detective promptly jumped over to the pulp magazines. Original stories were still being regularly written about Nick for *Detective Story Magazine* through 1927, with reprints and a few smatterings of new material still popping up in various places through the 1940s. There were, of course, a few B-movies and a number of comic book appearances.

What kept Nick going when most other dime novel cops faded away? For one thing, Nick's origin was fairly original and some of his individual tricks of the trade (such as keeping a revolver in a spring-loaded holster up each of his sleeves) were kind of neat. The villains he encountered stood out from the crowd as well. His eventual arch-enemy, mad scientist and serial killer Dr. Jack Quartz, was the perhaps the most memorable, but Nick also went up against more than his share of ruthless females: Zanoni the Woman Wizard and Zelma the Female Fiend being just two examples.

In an effort to give younger readers someone with whom to directly identify, Nick eventually acquired help from a number of youthful assistants. Chick Valentine was a "homeless waif" rescued by Nick and eventually adopted by him. Patrick "Patsy" Walker was a newsboy/shoe shine boy who also joined Nick's growing crew of young crimebusters. Ten Ichi was a son of the Emperor of Japan, sent to Nick to learn detective skills for reasons never really explained. Other assistants, both male and female, came and went.

For a two-year period from 1895 to 1897, Nick retired from active investigations to run a detective school for boys. Dime novel readers were treated to the adventures of these intrepid students, with Nick acting as advisor and mentor. Then Nick abruptly returned to duty and his poor students were never mentioned again.

None of this would ever help qualify a Nick Carter dime novel as great literature, but all of it was potentially useful fodder for entertaining melodrama. Sadly, few if any of Nick's stories stand the test of time. Popular fiction of this sort can make for wonderful escapism — characters from a few decades later such as Zorro or the Shadow are examples of this. But such stories require good, solid plots that make sense in the context of the fictional world in which they are set. Most importantly, the hero must fight or think his way out of trouble on his own merits. Too many of Nick's stories depend on plain dumb luck to allow them to be truly satisfying.

In "Nick Carter, Detective: The Solution of a Remarkable Case," from 1891, Nick investigates the mysterious death of popular dancer Eugenie La Verde, who had been strangled in her bed ("...the murderer had left not a single clew, however slight, by which he could be traced").

Donning a disguise for no other reason than he always dons a disguise, Nick searches the crime scene. He finds nothing useful there, but when stopping for lunch at a nearby restaurant, he happens to overhear two thugs discussing the murder. So his big break in the case comes — as it all too often did — through plain dumb luck. Why his dad put all that time and effort into actual detective training is beyond analysis.

What follows is not all bad. Nick is captured by the villains, but escapes. It turns out one of the bad guys is a snake charmer — Eugenie was strangled by a python and Nick must dodge a cobra attack. At the climax, the snake charmer is crushed by one of his own pets.

It's frustratingly close to being fun, but the dependence on dumb luck and the fact that the crooks *always* happen to be talking about important matters when Nick is hiding nearby pretty much spoils it.

In "Scylla, the Sea Robber; or, Nick Carter and the Queen of the Sirens," from 1905, Nick goes up against the lady pirate Scylla and her crew of thirteen lovely distaff cutthroats. He's captured and taken to their underwater base, accessible through a secret entrance in a government buoy marker. Nick is tossed into the ocean with one hundred pounds of iron tied to his legs — only to be rescued through the most unforeseen and poorly explained deus ex machina in the history of fiction. Once again, the reader desperately wants to enjoy the story, but his desire for escapism is crushed under the weight of too many awkward contrivances.

It was on radio that Nick Carter finally comes through for us. *The*

Return of Nick Carter premiered on the Mutual network in 1943. Soon retitled *Nick Carter, Master Detective*, it ran for twelve years, with Lon Clark playing Nick for the entire run. For most of its existence, it was a standard half-hour show, but it did try out a fifteen-minute serialized format for a short time in 1944.

For radio, most of Nick's young assistants were dropped. In a sort of literary sex-change, "Patsy" Walker, shoe-shine boy, became Patsy Bowen, lovely girl secretary, played first by Helen Choate and later by Charlotte Manson. Nick's adopted son Chick also popped up in the spin-off series *Chick Carter, Boy Detective*, which ran on Mutual from 1945–47.

Nick was still a private detective, though like many other radio detectives he rarely seems to accept a fee for his work. (In a 1946 episode, he does mention that at least one insurance company keeps him on retainer.) Occasionally, he stumbled across a murder, but it's more usual for the police or another interested party to come to him for help. The show had a fun opening — someone would be knocking persistently on a door. Patsy would open the door and ask "What is it?"

"Another case!" was the inevitable answer.

Played with steady intelligence by Clark, Nick became a worthy addition to the traditional detective genre. The stories were interesting and the clues were fairly presented as Nick depended on actual deductive reasoning to solve cases. He was still quite capable in a fight and still an expert with disguises, though this last trait was no longer so badly overused. But mostly he depended on his brains.

In "Double Disguise; or, Nick Carter and the Mystery of the Kidnapped Heiress," (the show kept the dime novel tradition of using double titles), Nick runs across an attempt to frame an innocent man named Chester Brown for murder. The motive is to steal a fortune that Brown's wife was about to inherit. Nick deduces the identity of the real killer as an old enemy named Bartow and attempts to infiltrate the crook's hideout while in disguise. But it's a trap — Bartow set things up to lure Nick there and quickly sees through the disguise. Nick and Brown, who has also been captured, are hanged from the ceiling and left rapidly strangling to death. Bartow and his men flee as the police enter the building.

It seems as if Nick is doomed. But he uses a clever and reasonably believable trick to save both himself and Brown. He and the police then tail Bartow to yet another hideout, where they get the drop on him.

The dime novel conceits of captures and death traps were still there, but they were elements that fit naturally within a well-plotted story, with Nick's deductive skills being nicely emphasized throughout. Other episodes didn't worry as much about getting Nick into a death trap, but were content with allowing him to show off his cerebral skills. A 1945 episode titled "The Make-Believe Murder," for instance, begins with an invitation for Nick to join the exclusive Alphabet Club. For his initiation, he must solve a make-believe murder staged by club members for his benefit. But one of the members is really murdered during the fake investigation, shot dead when the lights go out. The only gun in the room, though, was a toy cap pistol. Later, another club member was murdered with a toy sword.

Nick figures it all out by the end, of course, identifying both murderer and motive and deducing how the seemingly impossible crime was committed. It was, once again, well-written and completely fair to the audience in the presentation of the clues. This quality was maintained throughout the run of the show. Finally, here was a Nick Carter whose adventures we can enjoy with a clear conscience.

Nick Carter on radio:
Mutual: 4/11/43–9/25/55 (briefly a serial in 1944)
Nick: Lon Clark

First prose appearance: "The Old Detective's Pupil,
or the Mysterious Crime of Madison Square" (1886),
by Frederick Van Rensselaer Dey

Philo Vance

In "The Simple Art of Murder," Raymond Chandler's important essay about detective fiction, Chandler refers to Philo Vance as "the most asinine character in detective fiction."

Chandler was right. Philo Vance *is* an asinine jerk—a rude, Nietzschean snob who holds most of the people he meets and the things he sees in utter disdain. He's an insufferable smarty-pants, always convinced he's right and that everyone else is wrong. Of course, he *is* always right, but that doesn't make him any less of a jerk.

Philo Vance was created in the 1926 novel *The Benson Murder Case*, written by Willard Huntington Wright under the pen name S.S. Van Dine. The book was enormously successful and Van Dine produced eleven more, with the last one being published in 1939. Though their popularity fell off towards the end, sales of the Philo Vance novels during their heyday were credited with keeping the publishing company Scribners afloat during the worst of the Depression.

Why Philo Vance was so popular is something of a mystery today. It might have been that—in terms of plot, at least—the mildly clever plots were better than most of what was available to mystery fans at the time. Agatha Christie's vastly superior books were only just appearing in the American marketplace and most of her best was yet to come. The hardboiled style of fiction was still young and, good as it was, there would still be those readers who preferred a more traditional take on their murder investigations.

Also, Vance did have a unique personality. A completely unappealing personality, perhaps, but certainly different from anything else you might find at the newsstand in 1926.

Some of the most iconic characters in mystery fiction are insufferable smarty-pants. Sherlock Holmes and Nero Wolfe are the best examples of this—they nearly always outsmart everyone else and they are not above displaying their egos on their sleeves from time to time. But we still *like* Holmes and Wolfe. We'd jump at an opportunity to have dinner with either of them and there's no doubt we would enjoy their company.

This is because they are balanced characters. They have their faults—which both their creators and their fans recognize *as* faults—making it easier to identify with them. Their stories include strong supporting characters with definable personalities of their own, which helps give readers a more balanced perspective. And, though both Holmes and Wolfe are not above arrogance, they also each have a sense of justice and the ability to treat others (regardless of social status) with respect.

But Philo Vance has no balance to his character at all. In the eyes of S.S. Van Dine, he doesn't have any faults. His arrogance and condescending attitude are justified by his genius. He acts like he's better than everyone else because it is the author's intent to show us that he is indeed our superior.

And Vance is determined to show us over and over again just how smart he is, inserting non-sequitur mini-lectures into his conversations. While waiting a few minutes for a witness to be brought into a room for questioning, he abruptly launches into a lesson on the virtue of patience, quoting Shakespeare, Longfellow, Milton, Cervantes, Rousseau, Virgil and Horace in the space of one relatively short paragraph. (The last two in the original Latin, of course.) This is supposed to remind us that Vance is a polymath and a genius. What it really reminds us of is that Vance is pompous without really being interesting.

The characters surrounding Vance have no real personalities of their own, allowing Vance's traits to completely dominate the novels. Van Dine inserts a version of himself into the novels to act as the Watson, but he never says a single word or does anything other than tag along with Vance. Most of the time, we literally forget he's there. Other characters are sometimes annoyed with Vance in the early novels, but later tend to simply worship at his feet in appreciation of his brilliant mind. The cumulative effect of all this grates severely on the nerves of the readers. Even the little things, like Vance's faux British accent which Van Dine insists on spelling out phonetically, seem purposely designed to aggravate us. We just don't like Philo Vance at all and we'll gladly stop for a badly cooked Big Mac rather than have to spend an evening dining with him.

When we first meet Philo Vance in the *Benson Murder Case*, Van Dine wastes no time in telling us where we stand with the snooty protagonist: "An aristocrat by birth and instinct, [Vance] held himself severely aloof from the common world of men. In his manner there was an indefinable contempt for inferiority of all kinds."

Vance has plenty of time to be contemptuous. He's independently wealthy after a rich aunt left him her fortune and he passes his time collecting art. Educated at Harvard and Oxford, he is an expert in the art of many cultures and time periods.

It's this interest in art that convinces him he can also solve crimes. "Every crime is witnessed by outsiders," he explains, "just as is every work of art. The fact that no one sees the criminal, or the artist, actu'lly at work, is wholly incons'quential." In other words, just as an art expert can tell Rubens painted a particular portrait by studying its style and theme, a skilled detective should be able to identify a murderer by studying the scene of the crime. It's all a matter of applied psychology. Material clues, things like cigarette butts found near the body, are meaningless. In fact, such clues inevitably lead one to wrong conclusions.

From a strictly realistic point of view, this is complete nonsense. But, if handled with consistency and cleverness, it can be made to work in the confines of a mystery novel. The overwhelming majority of stories in the genre take place in a world just a little bit removed from real life; a world where amateur detectives abound and subtle deductive reasoning is more important than the dull routine of real police work. If psychology in Philo Vance's world is a more exact science than in reality, allowing him to deduce the identity of criminals by studying the styles and themes of the crime, then that's just fine.

In fact, the novel does handle this with reasonable consistency. Vance doesn't ignore material clues the way he initially expounds everyone should. Instead, he reinterprets them in terms of what he knows about the apparent psychology of the killer. When District Attorney Markham and the police jump to a wrong conclusion based on those cigarette butts, Vance is soon able to prove them wrong. When a suspect eventually confesses, Markham is satisfied the case is closed. But then Vance questions the suspect and demonstrates the confession to be false.

It's not for some time that Vance reveals that he knew who the killer was five minutes after arriving at the crime scene. But he also realized that no one would believe him until he proved his theories about crime solving were correct. He then presents "proof," based on evidence found at the scene, that one particular suspect is guilty.

Markham is convinced. Then Vance announces that that suspect is *not* guilty. "I had an irresistible longing," explains Vance, "to demonstrate to you how utterly silly your circumst'ntial and material evidence is.... Its theory is not unlike that of our present-day democracy. The democratic theory is that if you accumulate enough ignorance at the polls, you produce intelligence; and the theory of circumst'ntial evidence is that if you accumulate a sufficient number of weak links, you produce a strong chain."

Markham is annoyed, but he's pacified somewhat when Vance then explains how yet another suspect must be guilty. Of course, then Vance reveals this isn't true either — he was just emphasizing his point.

By now, no jury in the world would have convicted Markham if he'd pushed Vance out a window. But Vance finally gets around to explaining who the real killer is and where to find the evidence to prove it. Markham is amazed and grateful, failing utterly to give Vance a good strong shove at the right moment.

It's a pretty good story and it's held up by its own internal logic, but, by golly, putting up with Vance makes it a chore to read.

This author would like to point out that he's not just being individually cranky. Contemporaries of Van Dine recognized Vance's faults as well. Aside from Chandler, poet Ogden Nash gave us the following couplet:

> *Philo Vance*
> *Needs a kick in the pance.*

Modern critics also have a hard time with him. William DeAndrea wrote "Vance is the kind of person you'd cross a street to avoid."*

Vance never really got any better. If anything, in later novels, he got worse. Eventually, his Nietzschean attitude leads him to knocking off murders on his own without having to bother with a justice system he considered to be "an elaborate invention of imbeciles."

The closest he ever comes to acting human was in *The Garden Murder Case* (1935). He meets and falls in love with a young lady named Zalia Graem. But, in rare burst of sincere humanity, he realizes he'd make a lousy husband and he gives her up. Afterwards, he goes back to being an insufferable smarty-pants.

The next to last Vance novel is *The Gracie Allen Murder Case* (1938). This bizarre book was written to accompany a movie starring Warren Williams as Vance and comedienne Gracie Allen as, well, Gracie Allen.

---

*DeAndrea, 362.

Following along in the novel as Vance acts as a surrogate George Burns, trading quips with Gracie, is a truly surreal experience.

The last novel, *The Winter Murder Case*, was published in 1939 just after Van Dine's death. Philo Vance's career continued through the 1940s in an occasional B-movie. He finally came to radio in 1945.

Philo Vance first radio appearance was a brief run on NBC in 1945. Jose Ferrer played Vance. No episodes of this run, or of a short-lived 1946 ABC series with an unknown cast, survive.

Vance's radio career today is remembered through a syndicated series produced from 1948 to 1950, with Jackson Beck playing Vance. A good number of these episodes are still around, allowing us to pass fair judgment on them.

Fortunately, the creative staff of the show realized that Philo Vance would never work on radio if he were lifted as is from the books and he was toned down considerably. Vance was now a private detective, complete with the requisite lovely secretary. The secretary, Ellen Deering, was played by Joan Alexander. District Attorney Markham was played by George Petrie. Beck played Vance with a cultured, upper class accent, but the arrogance and snobbishness of the book Vance is gone. He's simply a really smart guy who is good at figuring out whodunit.

Most episodes involved Markham (or Detective Sergeant Heath — another character brought over from the books) going to Vance for help. Though it's never spelled out, Vance is apparently still independently wealthy and thus able to help out the cops as needed. In one episode, a suspect offers him a lot of money to prove his innocence. Vance tells him if he's guilty, the detective won't be bought off. But if he's innocent, he won't need to pay any money.

In the "Tick Tock Murder Case," from 1949, Markham asks Vance to help investigate the murder of a man named "Tick-Tock" Maxwell, a former watchmaker turned racketeer. While Vance follows up on this, Markham and Heath investigate a safe-cracking case.

Vance thinks Maxwell's partner, Frank Carter, is guilty. But Carter has a perfect alibi — he was robbing the safe at the time. Carter's fingerprints were found on the safe. Carter is arrested for the safe job and released on bail. But a girl friend of Maxwell's, Maisie Evans, meets Vance to pass on information about Carter's involvement in the murder. Carter later kidnaps Evans, planning to murder her.

When Vance confronts Carter about the girl, a henchman knocks the detective out. Vance and Evans are tied up and locked in a closet together. They manage to untie each other. Vance then tricks the henchman into opening the closet door and knocks *him* out. The detective is then able to use a peculiar aspect of Carter's fingerprints on the safe to break his alibi, proving that the crook was *not* robbing the safe at the time of the murder.

It was a good mystery, with a perfectly fair clue and a rare chance to see Vance handling himself well in a dangerous situation. Beck, an excellent character actor, gave a solid performance in the lead role. If Vance no longer had much of a personality beyond his skills as a detective, Beck still endowed him with intelligence and sincerity.

Philo Vance is not one of radio's best shows, but it is still a good, solid example of its genre. The episodes were very much dialogue-driven, with little dependence on sound effects — and, incidentally, perhaps a bit too much dependence on stereotypically dramatic organ music to establish mood and act as a bridge between scenes.

The emphasis on dialogue allowed the scripts to cover a lot of ground in terms of collecting clues and interviewing suspects. The conceit from the book — that Vance could treat crime like a work of art open to psychological interpretation — was gone completely. In its place was old fashioned deductive reasoning often using the sort of clues that the book Vance had despised. Thematically, it was not original at all, but it was a professionally produced and entertaining show.

Most importantly, of course, was the fact that on radio, Philo Vance was no longer annoying. He is now someone with whom we might be willing to have dinner. Poor rejected Zalia Graem might have been happy being married to this version of Vance. Today, S.S. Van Dine's novels are dated and barely readable. But the radio show is still worth listening to.

Philo Vance on radio:
NBC: 7/5/45–9/27/45
Vance: Jose Ferrer

ABC West: 1946
Vance: unknown

Syndicated: 1948–1950
Vance: Jackson Beck

First prose appearance: *The Benson Murder Case* (1926), by Willard Huntington Wright (writing as S.S. Van Dine)

Ellery Queen

When we first meet Ellery Queen in the 1929 novel *The Roman Hat Mystery*, we can't help but think that he's a little bit of a snot. Obviously influenced by the commercial success of Philo Vance, Ellery's creators initially endow him with some of Vance's less admirable traits. Arrogant and rude, with annoying physical and speech mannerisms (the third or fourth time he calls his father "pater" you really want to smack him one), he's a little difficult to like. He's not nearly as bad as Vance, though, and he's much more than just a clone of that character. Ellery is a mystery writer with a knack for deducing the identities of real-life killers. "I've handled crime facts so long in fiction," he explains in a later novel, "that I've-uh-acquired a certain dexterity in handling them in real life."

Ellery was dreamed up by writers Frederic Dannay and Manfred B. Lee, cousins from Brooklyn whose decades-long collaboration resulted in some of the finest mystery stories ever written. They actually wrote the Ellery Queen mysteries under the pen name "Ellery Queen." The conceit was that we were reading fictionalized accounts of cases handled by the "real life" Ellery. Told in the third person almost entirely from Ellery's point-of-view, the short stories and novels are written in intelligent and occasionally verbose prose that mirrors Ellery's own speech patterns.

Ellery is a bachelor, sharing a New York apartment with his father, police Inspector Richard Queen. The two have a healthy, friendly relationship — one of the factors that make up for Ellery's more annoying attributes. Also, of course, having a cop for a father gives Ellery a believable entry point into murder investigations.

The elder Queen is presented as a good cop, smart and capable. But he recognizes and appreciates his son's genius, calling on his help without resentment or jealously for particularly difficult cases.

And there are quite a few difficult cases. Dannay and Lee were experts at creating complex mysteries that nonetheless had fair solutions to them. We're presented with the same clues as Ellery, giving us a fair chance to ourselves identifying the killer. We hardly ever do, though, because the clues are just a bit too subtle for most of us to recognize their true significance. When Ellery beats us to it and explains how he knew, we often want to kick ourselves because the solution was right there in *front* of us! Few mystery writers created problems in deduction as consistently fair and ultimately satisfying as we find in the Queen canon.

But good mysteries — even great mysteries — still need a likable protagonist to support them on a long term basis. As Dannay and Lee developed a better grasp on Ellery's character, the more exasperating mannerisms faded away. He took to simply calling his father "Dad," stopped wearing a pince-nez, and ceased to make a major production out of lighting a cigarette. Throughout the 1930s, he grew from barely tolerable to downright affable, developing a sense of compassion and social justice that added depth to his character.

The 1942 novel *Calamity Town* represented a sort of turning point in the series. Ellery travels to the small town of Wrightsville to soak up the atmosphere while writing his latest novel. He befriends Patricia Wright, a member of the town's most prestigious family. But soon, the two stumble across an apparent plot to murder Pat's sister Nora.

Someone is eventually murdered — apparently by accident in an attempt to poison Nora. Nora's husband Jim is arrested and the evidence against him seems incontestable.

But Ellery and Pat work to clear him. At this point, Ellery has no logical reason to doubt Jim's guilt — but by now he's become attached to the Wright family as a good friend. For the first time in his career, he's not an outside observer, but an active participant. It's not a comfortable position for him to be in and the novel consequently has a degree of angst weaving through it that we hadn't seen in previous stories.

Adding to this angst is an examination of the mob mentality that's also a part of the story. Driven by pettiness and jealously, the townspeople convict Jim in their own minds even before he's arrested. Ellery helps save Jim from a mob at one point. The Wright family becomes social pariahs. Ellery does eventually run across the clue that allows him to finger the real killer, but not before the Wrights suffer irrevocable tragedy.

All this is balanced out by the generosity and nobility of individual characters we meet along the way. One character sacrifices himself for another — the Wrights and a few of their steadfast friends stick together as a family. Aside from being a solidly written mystery, *Calamity Town* presents a balanced view of the human race as a whole — showing us both the worst and the best we can be.

After *Calamity Town*, the Ellery Queen canon can be very roughly divided into two categories. The many short stories remain clever mysteries — puzzles that challenge the reader to just *once* beat Ellery to the guilty party. One common conceit was the use of a "dying clue," in which the victim, unable for some reason to simply write down the name of his killer, leaves some sort of subtle clue before expiring. This could be anything from a beard painted on a lady's portrait to initials scrawled in the dirt. In one case, the "dying clue" was actually left by the killer to frame someone else. But whatever the source of the clue that would lead Ellery to the truth, it was always there for us to see as well.

The novels, though, were more in-depth in terms of characterization and often contained a level of angst equal to that found in *Calamity Town*. In *Ten Days' Wonder* (1948), Ellery makes one of several return trips to Wrightsville, where he again becomes involved in a murder case. (Wrightsville is, in fact, a lousy vacation spot considering its per capita murder rate.) This time, he makes a wrong deduction, which arguably leads to a man's death.

Ellery swears off criminal investigations after that, but in the 1949 novel *Cat of Many Tales* a serial killer known as the Cat has New York City on the verge of panic. Ellery is drawn into the case and soon appointed Special Investigator by the mayor. The killings seem to be random, but Ellery picks up on a pattern. Soon, he and his father have identified the Cat (or have they?) and set a trap. In the meantime, Dannay and Lee again examine the tragic effects of mob mentality — this time being driven by fear rather than pettiness.

Cat of Many Tales builds up an incredible level of suspense as Ellery and Inspector Queen try to trap the Cat, and there's an absolutely shocking twist at the end. It is arguably the best of the Ellery Queen novels, working both as an excellent mystery and a sharp character study.

Dannay and Lee continued to produce Ellery Queen stories into the 1960s, with other writers also helping out on a few of the later works. The quality never dropped and Ellery remains one of the mystery genre's greatest characters.

Ellery came to radio on CBS in 1939, with Hugh Marlowe playing Ellery and the ever-present Santos Ortega playing his father. The show jumped back and forth between the major networks during the 1940s, eventually ending its run on ABC in 1948. Carleton Young, Sydney Smith, Lawrence Dobkin, and Howard Culver all took their turns in the lead role, while Bill Smith and Herb Butterfield would each eventually step in as Inspector Queen. A new character, secretary Nikki Porter, was also a regular character and eventually jumped over to the prose stories to join Ellery there as well.

The show ran in the standard thirty-minute format and wisely chose to follow the straight mystery format found in the short stories rather than the more complicated character-driven plots used in the novels. It's a decision that can leave us wondering what a serial adaptation of, for instance, *Cat of Many Tails* might have sounded like. But the show did such a nice job presenting us with fair mystery puzzles that there's really no room to complain.

The show's main strength was that Dannay and Lee were still at the helm — producing solid scripts each week. When Dannay left the show in 1944, mystery writer Anthony Boucher helped Lee maintain the same level of quality.

The Adventures of Ellery Queen really embraced the "armchair detective" idea. Each week, one or two "experts" were introduced and given a chance near the end of the story to identify the guilty culprit. The experts included a wide variety of celebrities such as voice-over master Mel Blanc, band leader Guy Lombardo, photographer Margaret Bourke-White, writer Norman Corwin, and actor John Wayne. We'd hear the story, then the action would pause just before the denouement. Ellery and Inspector Queen — still in character — would give the "expert" a chance to solve the crime. (Usually, this was fairly straightforward, but in a 1947 episode, Inspector Queen spent several minutes drooling over stripper Gypsy Rose Lee before allowing her to admit she had no idea who the killer was.)

The experts were rarely correct, but the clues were always there. If the mysteries weren't quite as clever in general as they were in the prose stories, they were pretty close. We end up kicking ourselves for not getting it before Ellery's explanation just as often after a radio episode as we do after a short story. In fact, a few of the radio plots were later adapted by Dannay and Lee into prose.

Even the actors on the show were often fooled. None of the cast was shown the last scenes of a script until the final dress rehearsal, "so that the one playing the murderer wouldn't blow the show by trying too hard to sound innocent." The regular cast got into the habit of holding a pool as they tried to guess the killer's identity. Ted de Corsica, who played the supporting role of the usually clueless Police Sergeant Velie, was the most frequent winner.*

For a time, the "experts" were drawn from the studio audience and, late in the run, a panel of mystery writers were able to zero in on the killer with a higher success rate. But regardless of the precise format, the armchair detective idea was an entertaining part of a well-written show.

Occasionally the experts were invited on the show because they had some connection to elements of the plot. In the "Adventure of the Circus Train," from 1943, the experts included a member of a railroad police force and a publicity director from the Ringling Brothers circus. Ellery, his dad and Nikki are traveling home from Chicago to New York. When their train reservations are canceled they book passage on a circus train. Their traveling companions include an eight-foot giant, a midget, and a fortune teller. The circus' owner announces that he's closing up the circus and flashes quite a bit of cash around. Soon after, he's found murdered in his compartment — his head dashed in with one of the giant's oversized shoes. The cash is missing.

Several other pairs of shoes have been mixed together. The poor "experts" are stumped, but Ellery deduces a pattern to the way the crime was committed that tells him where the missing cash is hidden and identifies the killer. Once again, he gets there way before we do. But what can we do? Dannay and Lee, working through the mind of Ellery Queen, are just plain smarter than we are.

Ellery Queen on radio:
CBS: 6/18/39–9/22/40
Ellery: Hugh Marlowe
NBC: 1/10/42–12/30/44
Ellery: Carleton Young, Sydney Smith
CBS: 1/24/45–4/16/47
Ellery: Sydney Smith
NBC: 6/1/47–9/21/47
Ellery: Lawrence Dobkin
ABC: 11/27/47–5/27/48
Ellery: Lawrence Dobkin, Howard Culver

First prose appearance: *The Roman Hat Murder* (1929), by Frederic Dannay and Manfred B. Lee (writing as Ellery Queen)

---

*Nevins, 28.

Hercule Poirot

"I don't think I shall ever forget my first sight of Hercule Poirot," recalled the narrator of *Murder in Mesopotamia*. "...I don't know what I imagined — something rather like Sherlock Holmes — long and lean with a keen, clever face.... When you saw him you just wanted to laugh! ... To begin with, he wasn't above five feet five, I should think — an odd, plump little man, quite old, with an enormous moustache, and a head like an egg. He looked like a hairdresser in a comic play!"

Comical as his appearance is, Hercule Poirot is a brilliant detective, able to gather up confusing and contradictory clues and put them in the proper order necessary to identify the murderer. A native of Belgium, he is a monumental egotist, but he has the chops to back up his high opinion of himself. In a career that stretched from 1920 to 1975, he investigated and solved some of the most cleverly constructed mysteries that have ever graced the pages of a novel.

Poirot is, along with Miss Jane Marple, one of the two most famous creations of Agatha Christie, arguably the finest writer in the history of the genre. She wrote the first Poirot novel, *The Mysterious Affair at Styles*, in 1916, though it wasn't published until 1920. She hit the bestseller list in 1926 with the Poirot novel *The Murder of Roger Ackroyd*, a whodunit with an absolutely shocking but still satisfying and fair ending.

Poirot, when we first meet him, is already a veteran detective, having recently fled his native country after it was occupied by the Germans during the Great War. No longer official, he often works as a private investigator, with his reputation bringing clients to him for help. It is just as common, though, for him to simply happen to be nearby when someone gets murdered.

Christie used Poirot in numerous novels and short stories, with the best of these seeing publication in the 1920s and 1930s. What made the vain little detective so popular is the same thing that keeps Christie's books in print today (with total sales across the decades that are exceeded only by the Bible and Shakespeare): the plots are absolutely brilliant, with subtle clues scattered throughout that are always fair but nearly impossible for most readers to spot. Christie was a master at having a "least likely suspect"—the one person who couldn't *possibly* have done it—turn out to be guilty. In fact, Christie was so good at this that even if we simply assume the least likely suspect is guilty because he or she always is, we'll still be wrong. It will turn out to be someone so much more unlikely that we didn't even consider him a suspect.

But Poirot as a character is just as important as the quality of the plots. Superficially, it doesn't seem like there's any more reason to like Poirot than there is to like Philo Vance, but we still do. In large part, his comic appearance and mannerisms (such as his not-quite-perfect grasp of English) balances out his arrogance. Perhaps most importantly is that unlike Vance, he can be reasonably polite and sociable to those around him.

His appeal also ties back in with the quality of the stories in which he appears. Because these are so well plotted, his ability to solve each case generates a very real feeling that he is indeed a genius. He thus earns the privilege of being egotistical. "I have the habit of always being right," he once commented with typical false modesty, "but I do not boast of it." It all boils down to the readers' willingness to readily accept him as a real person, just as we do with Sherlock Holmes and Nero Wolfe.

The Poirot novels are usually told in the first person, with a Watson character narrating. Often, this is Captain Arthur Hastings, a retired Army officer with whom Poirot shares a flat in London for some years. In later books, mystery writer Ariadne Oliver (an alter ego for Christie) would sometimes take this role. Occasionally, the narrator would be a one-shot character, with circumstances setting them alongside Poirot for the duration of a single mystery.

In *Murder in Mesopotamia* (1935), the Watson is Miss Amy Leatheran, a nurse who had been hired to look after the wife of an archeologist working on a dig outside Baghdad. But the wife is soon murdered. Poirot, who was traveling through the area, is asked to investigate and he ends up using Amy as an assistant.

She sees his methods first hand as he employs his brains (his "little grey cells," as he calls them) and his "passion for order and method"* to seek out a solution. He gets people to talk to him, sometimes using

---

*DeAndrea, 278.

charm, sometimes exaggerating his difficulty with English to get someone to underestimate him. He gathers up various opinions of the murdered woman in order to establish motives, but it is a bit of deductive reasoning involving how the murder was committed that allows him to puncture an apparently perfect alibi. Amy hadn't thought much of Poirot when she first saw him, but she had an enormous respect for him at the end.

Agatha Christie grew a little tired of Poirot later in her career and gradually used him less often. She wrote *Curtain* in the 1940s, in which an aged and infirm Poirot solves one more case before passing away. She intended it to be published after her own death, but allowed it to see print in 1975, after the Poirot novel *Murder on the Orient Express* had been made into a successful film. (Christie died in 1976.) Poirot's last case was one of his best, with a conclusion that trumps even *The Murder of Roger Ackroyd* in pure shock value.

Poirot had appeared in a number of films both before and after *Murder on the Orient Express* and was very well represented by actor David Suchet in a British television series first produced in 1989. But, despite his popularity with American readers, the clever Belgian had only a brief career on American radio during that medium's Golden Age.

Orson Welles played a broadly comic (though still brilliant) Poirot in a 1939 episode of *The Campbell Playhouse*. "Who am I?" he rants at one point when the local constable doesn't recognize him. "Hercule Poirot — master detective. Possessed of the finest brain in Europe. Known in every continent; in every land; nay, in every city!"

This was a faithful if slightly rushed adaptation of *The Murder of Roger Ackroyd*, with Welles playing both Poirot and Dr. James Shepherd (who acts as Poirot's Watson). Listening to him switch back and forth between an English accent and a (not-quite-convincing) Belgium accent — often in the same scene — is almost as much fun as following along with the actual story.

Poirot got his own series on the Mutual network in 1945, with Harold Huber playing the role in a much more subdued manner. All of Poirot's traits are still there, including his egotism, but not to the degree where we would get too annoyed to spend time with him each week.

In this series, Poirot is moving to New York for reasons that are never made clear. The premier episode, "The Case of the Careless Victim," finds Poirot searching for "a bright, sunshining apartment of a reasonable quietness near the heart of the city." His search is interrupted, though, when he discovers a body in the hotel room next to his own.

The woman renting that room, Abigail Fletcher, is leery of Poirot at first. "I've read many detective stories," she tells him, "and none of them had a detective who looked like you."

But she soon learns how valuable it is to have Poirot involved when he deduces the victim had been killed in the room one floor above and moved to its new location, thus proving her innocence. "You deal with Hercule Poirot," *he* tells *her*, "who goes one step beyond the obvious." What follows is a well-constructed mystery with, yes, a very unlikely suspect turning out to be guilty. As a bonus for Poirot, the murderer's apartment is now free for him to rent. He also hires Abigail Fletcher as his secretary.

Huber is very good as Poirot, especially in the subtle surprise he expresses whenever he meets someone who doesn't recognize his name. Only eight of the more than forty episodes produced seem to have survived, but all are equally well-plotted and Huber seems to be enjoying himself throughout. It's easy to accept him as the same brilliant detective we first met in print.

Judging from the first episode, it seemed likely that Abigail Fletcher was supposed to have been a regular supporting character, but she doesn't appear in any of the other surviving episodes. Another character, police Inspector Stevens, does reappear, becoming Poirot's regular contact with the police.

If the series were to have a shortcoming, it is the decision to settle Poirot down in New York City. This might have been a decision by the network or the producers to make Poirot more identifiable with American audiences. But if so, this is weak reasoning. One of the fun aspects of the original prose is that Poirot is often traveling the world, stumbling into murder cases in unique locales such as an archeological dig in Iraq, a boat sailing down the Nile or a small village in England. With radio's inherently unlimited budget for travel expenses, confining him to a single location was needlessly limiting. Some characters are attached to a specific location — Sherlock Holmes in Victorian London or Philip Marlowe in Los Angeles — but Poirot had been designed to go anywhere he needed to be to solve a case. Also, getting him out of New York would have given the writers a chance to directly adapt some of Christie's original short stories. Still, what few episodes we have are quite good, so it's really not necessary to be too critical.

Huber returned as Poirot for a CBS series that ran in 1946–47. This was a fifteen-minute show that ran on weekdays and consisted of five-chapter stories. It is, in theory, a great format for Poirot, allowing for more complex mysteries and character development. But no episodes from this series have survived to have judgment passed on them.

As popular as Agatha Christie is with American audiences (not to mention most of the rest of the world — her works have been translated into over a hundred languages), it's amazing that Poirot wasn't more prominent in American radio. It's equally amazing that Miss Marple, a purely delightful creation, never got a series of her own on a U.S. network. Both characters have strong and unique personalities, while Poirot's brief time on radio demonstrated he could carry a series. But as well-traveled as Poirot was, even he couldn't get everywhere. A brief stop in New York to appear on radio before heading off to Europe or the Middle East was probably the best he could do for us.

Hercule Poirot on radio:
Mutual: 2/22/45–10/14/45
CBS: 4/1/46–11/21/47 (serial)
Poirot: Harold Huber

First prose appearance: *The Mysterious Affair at Styles* (1920), by Agatha Christie

Nero Wolfe

In very general terms, detective stories can be divided into two categories. There are those involving a brilliant detective, in which the protagonist uses deductive reasoning to identify the guilty party. This is the genre created by Edgar Allan Poe in "Murders in the Rue Morgue " and perfected by Arthur Conan Doyle in the Sherlock Holmes stories.

Then there's the American hard-boiled genre, developed by writers such as Dashiell Hammett and Raymond Chandler. Here the protagonists are cynical, hard-edged men more likely to beat information out of someone than ponder over obscure clues.

Of course, the two genres overlap to an extent. Sherlock Holmes was involved in a few fist or gun fights, while Hammett's Continental Op was capable of the occasional leap of deductive logic. But it was Rex Stout, when he introduced us to Nero Wolfe and Archie Goodwin in the 1934 novel *Fer-de-Lance*, who managed to perfectly meld the traditional with the hard-boiled.

Nero Wolfe is an enormously fat man who, if he had his way, would never leave his Manhattan brownstone. He lives by a strict schedule, eating meals (prepared by his gourmet chef Fritz Brenner) at exactly the same time each day. He spends a total of four hours each day in the greenhouse built on the roof of his home, where he tends the thousands of orchids he keeps there. Most of the rest of his day is taken up by reading, with occasional pauses for a glass of beer.

He's not really a recluse. He enjoys good dinner conversation, has a few select friends and will, on occasion, leave his home for an orchid show or to deliver a speech at a chef's convention. But for the most part, he'd be content if he never had to set foot outside his front door or otherwise interrupt his routine.

But his chosen lifestyle requires money. "I have no talents," he once said. "I have genius or nothing." So Wolfe puts his genius to work as a private detective, charging high fees for his services.

His assistant in this profession is Archie Goodwin. It's Archie who provides the hard-boiled half of the team, narrating the stories in "a clean, American vernacular that is a joy to read."* Archie does the footwork, searching for evidence, interviewing witnesses and suspects and reporting everything he's learned to Wolfe. Often his job is arranging to bring people to the brownstone for Wolfe to question personally.

It's important to note, though, that Archie is not just a collector of information, but a skilled detective in his own right, perfectly capable of making intelligent decisions. He freely admits he doesn't have Wolfe's genius, but he's still good at his job. It's this balancing of two men with different skill sets, rather than a simplistic boss-servant relationship, that give the stories verisimilitude.

Stout came up with some excellent plots. Novels such as *Prisoner's Base* (1952) and *The Golden Spiders* (1953) are as well-constructed as anything else in the mystery genre. But it's Wolfe and Archie — the way their personalities sometimes mesh together and just as often clash — that make the stories so much fun. Archie would often have to pester or trick the inherently lazy Wolfe into taking on a case when the bank balance dropped too low. Or he would have fun with his misogynist boss by telling him he was getting married and would be moving his wife into the brownstone.

Wolfe, on the other hand, would often get on Archie's nerves by not explaining his deductions, so Archie often didn't know what was going on until Wolfe gathered the suspects in his study and revealed the killer's identity.

On top of all this, Archie's cynical wit and Wolfe's love of obscure words (he commonly peppers his sentences with words like rodomontade, usufructs and subdolous) make both men fun to listen to.

Stout also injected an interesting variety of regular supporting characters into the stories. The most notable was police Inspector Cramer, who inevitably clashed with Wolfe, always suspecting that Wolfe and Archie were lying to him or concealing evidence to protect a client. This was true just often enough to keep Cramer perpetually suspicious and aggravated. His verbal clashes with the two private detectives are often highlights of the stories.

Other supporting characters do their share to carry the narratives along in an entertaining manner — and we get to know and like all of

---

*DeAndrea, 381.

them. Wolfe's very proper chef Fritz Brenner; private eye Saul Panzer (one of several operatives hired by Wolfe on a case-by-case basis when he and Archie need additional help); Cramer's subordinate Sgt. Purley Stebbins; reporter Lon Cohen (with whom Archie often barters to exchange information).

For the most part, Stout depended on the gradual unfolding of the mystery to generate suspense, but he was quite capable of introducing an element of immediate danger when the story required it. Perhaps the best example of this is from *Prisoner's Base*, when roughly halfway through the novel, Wolfe arranges a session in his study to interview various people involved in the case he's investigating.

Later that night, Archie is awakened by a phone call from Sarah Jaffey, a woman who had been at the session because she might have had pertinent information. She's lost her keys (the doorman had let her into her apartment) and wonders if she had left them at the brownstone.

Archie immediately guesses that the keys might have been taken by the killer, who might even now be in Sarah's apartment, waiting to do her in. In the days before cordless phones and call waiting, Sarah was now trapped where she is. If she hangs up, the killer (if he's there) will be free to do her in.

Archie tells her to say "Wait a moment, I'll check," put the phone down without hanging up and walk quickly out of the apartment, slamming the door loudly as she leaves so that Archie knows she's safe. He listens for several minutes without hearing the door. Then he races to her apartment, not knowing if she's dead or alive — not even knowing for sure if she had been in danger. It's a wonderfully suspenseful sequence.

Stout also had fun placing Wolfe in situations where the corpulent detective was forced to leave his home. Archie once tricked him into coming to a crime scene by pretending to get knocked out during a phone call. On another occasion, Wolfe was socially obligated to escort a visitor to a World Series game — at which, of course, some one was murdered.

In the 1955 novella "The Next Witness," Wolfe is in court, subpoenaed as a witness because he had been involved in the initial investigation. While waiting his turn on the witness stand, he deduces from someone else's testimony that the man being tried for murder is innocent. What's more, the testimony Wolfe is about to give would help convict the defendant.

Wolfe will not allow this, as much because it's an affront to his dignity than an affront to justice. He and Archie leave the courthouse. Knowing that a contempt of court warrant will soon be issued for them both, they can't go home. So Wolfe finds himself accompanying Archie as they ferret out the real killer. This includes a long drive to a small upstate town (Wolfe hates and distrusts automobiles) and spending a night in an apartment with no furniture truly adequate to properly accommodate Wolfe's bulk. But his irritation does not interfere with his genius and the murderer is soon identified. It's a good, solid mystery in terms of plot, made all the more enjoyable by Wolfe's chronic discomfort throughout the tale.

Nero Wolfe came briefly to radio on NBC in 1943, played by the ubiquitous Santos Ortega and later Luis van Rooten. Francis X. Bushman played Wolfe for the Mutual Network in 1946. The series with the most surviving episodes, though, is the 1950–51 NBC series starring Sydney Greenstreet.

Greenstreet's Wolfe was not quite Stout's Wolfe. He had a tendency toward fits of joviality that his literary counterpoint never exhibited. Though he was still reclusive, the radio Wolfe seemed less unwilling to leave the brownstone when necessary. The orchids were rarely mentioned. The truly disappointing change from the original prose came when most of the supporting characters were dropped — Inspector Cramer shows up a few times, but his clashes with Wolfe had less emotional energy behind them than in the books. Fritz and Saul are occasionally acknowledged in dialogue, but rarely appear, while several other characters vanish entirely.

So, as with Flashgun Casey, Nero Wolfe was made less interesting when he came to radio. But whereas Casey on radio was somewhat bland, Sydney Greenstreet's performance endowed his version of Wolfe with a distinctive and entertaining personality. He may not be the same Wolfe we read about, but he's still someone with whom we'll enjoy spending half-an-hour.

Actually, the standard half-hour format for radio mystery shows was probably the biggest detriment to a more faithful adaptation. So much of what makes Wolfe and Archie classic characters isn't necessarily a part of the actual plot of any one story. It's interesting to note, in fact, that Stout never wrote short stories featuring Wolfe — only novels and novellas. He always allowed room for interplay between his two protagonists and provided background information on Wolfe's preferred daily habits. The radio show simply had no time to do this. An hour-long format would have been a better fit for the characters. And, of course, there would have been more opportunity to include the supporting cast.

Also, no one was ever cast to play Archie on a regular basis — nearly every week, someone else would step into the role. Some of radio's best character actors, including Herb Ellis, Harry Bartell, Lawrence Dobkin and Gerald Mohr, took their turns in the part. Gerald Mohr, in fact, played Archie a week after playing a killer that Archie helped to catch.

Any one of these fine actors could have handled the part well on a regular basis and thus develop a lasting chemistry with Greenstreet. One source claims Greenstreet, concerned with the show's low ratings, chronically insisted that the actors playing Archie be replaced.* But whatever the reason, no one ever took Archie on permanently.

Despite these flaws, it was a good show. Greenstreet (a wonderful character actor) seemed to be having fun with the part and the scripts were well-written. In "The Case of the Party of Death," from February 1951, Wolfe is invited to a cocktail party by a woman who fears she will be murdered. He refuses to attend, of course, but delegates Archie to go in his place. His instructions include orders for Archie to call him after someone is murdered, provided that Archie hasn't himself been killed.

At the party, Archie meets two business partners, one of whom is accusing the other of stealing from him, and their two gorgeous but jealous wives. One of the men is indeed murdered — killed by poison when he drinks out of his wife's glass. Was the wife the intended victim? Wolfe knows, but he's not yet telling.

The next day, Wolfe has the surviving party-goers come to his office. He's already deduced the killer's identity and the method used to introduce the poison into the drink. He uses a reenactment of the last few minutes of the party to provide proof. He also anticipates and foils a suicide attempt after the guilty party is exposed.

Harry Bartell plays Archie in this episode and deftly handles both his interplay with Wolfe at the brownstone and his banter with the beautiful wives at the party. Wolfe's deductive thought process is properly explained at the climax.

Like the original prose, the radio series usually depended on the mystery alone to carry the plot along, but one exceptionally fun episode placed Wolfe and Archie in direct peril. "The Case of the Calculated Risk," from January 1951, featured Gerald Mohr in one of several appearances as Archie. The story begins with a man visiting Wolfe to say he plans to kill someone who wronged him, recounting the reason for this (his intended victim had cheated him financially), but without giving any real names so

---

*Thrillingdetective.com

that Wolfe can't simply stop him. He wants Wolfe to step in if he dies before killing his enemy.

When the man is murdered the next day, Wolfe and Archie methodically track down his old enemy and prove he's the killer. But before they can follow up, the killer confronts them at gunpoint in Wolfe's study. Wolfe gets his hand into his desk drawer, threatening to pull a gun. If the killer shoots him, Archie will have time to draw his own pistol. If he shoots Archie, Wolfe will get him. Wolfe's calm explanation of the situation and the banter between the two detectives while the killer becomes more and more desperate all makes for an extremely gripping climax.

Though the show was good and occasionally great, it's not really Stout's Wolfe and it suffers noticeably because of this. There was no reason the characters Stout created or the plot structures he used would not translate to radio with reasonable faithfulness. Unlike with the original Boston Blackie or Saint stories, there were no insoluble conflicts with the broadcast standards of the day.

Changes when a character is brought from prose to radio are inevitable. It's tempting to complain this time simply because Nero Wolfe is one of the great creations of detective fiction, on par with Sherlock Holmes and Hercule Poirot. You can mess with Boston Blackie, the Falcon or even the Saint without doing any real harm, but changing around a classic is never going to be a truly satisfying endeavor. All the same, the radio show gave us interesting protagonists and good stories, so perhaps it earned its own right to exist after all. This is something each individual Nero Wolfe fan would have to decide for himself.

Nero Wolfe on radio:
NBC Blue: 7/5/43–7/14/44
Wolfe: Santos Ortega, Luis van Rooten

Mutual: late 1945 (exact date uncertain)–12/15/46
Wolfe: Francis X. Bushman

NBC: 10/20/50–4/27/51
Wolfe: Sydney Greenstreet

First prose appearance: *Fer-de-Lance* (1934),
by Rex Stout

Sherlock Holmes

Sherlock Holmes is perhaps the most perfectly formed fictional character of all time. Everything about him — his habits, faults and eccentricities — all come together to create a person we think of as real, even when we know that he's not. Take any one habit or personality trait away from him and he ceases to be Sherlock Holmes.

Holmes is the world's first "consulting detective," using his incredible mind to deduce the solutions to obscure or complex mysteries. His work is pretty much his life; he has no interest in romance and he's not very sociable. Even the things he ostensibly does to relax, such as playing his violin, are often just additional methods to help him organize his thoughts. "My mind is like a racing engine," he once explained.

During the course of his long career, he solved murders, stopped blackmailers, broke up Professor Moriarty's criminal empire, recovered stolen goods and dodged assassination attempts. But it's not his success as a detective alone that makes him so memorable. Many of the sixty original novels and short stories, while serviceable mysteries, are far from brilliant in terms of their plots. It's the synergy of everything that makes Holmes who he is that raises the stories to true classical status.

We first meet Holmes in the novel *A Study in Scarlet*, which was published in *Beeton's Christmas Annual* in 1887. Narrated by John Watson, the former army doctor who rooms with the detective, the novel is a wonderful introduction to Holmes. We discover Holmes's ability to deduce numerous facts about people simply by looking at them. We find out that he is shockingly ignorant on many subjects, such as literature and astronomy, because these do not concern his business as a detective. And we get to tag along as we watch him track down a killer.

Holmes was an instant hit with the public and author Arthur Conan Doyle turned out a second novel titled *The Sign of Four*. Soon, he was churning out a series of short stories for *The Strand* magazine. Growing tired of the character, he tried to get out of being contracted to do a second series of stories by asking for too high a price, but this backfired when the editors at *The Strand* readily coughed up the money. So he ended that series with "The Final Problem," in which Holmes and his arch enemy, Professor Moriarty, plunge to their deaths together off Reichenbach Falls. But public outcry eventually forced Conan Doyle to reveal that Holmes had merely faked his death to avoid assassins. Eventually, two more novels and three more collections of short stories saw print.

All through the books, Holmes remains the same fascinating person, keeping odd hours, performing noxious chemical experiments in his rooms at 221B Baker Street and writing monographs on subjects such as identifying tobacco ash and decoding ciphers. Watson was his stalwart companion throughout, willing to help the detective at a moment's notice even after he (Watson) had married and moved out of Baker Street. How the good doctor's patients felt about this (he had set up a private practice) was never recorded.

The friendship between Holmes and Watson is yet another vital part of Holmes' character. Watson is intelligent and capable, but has little talent himself for deductive reasoning. He does, though, act as an effective sounding board for Holmes and is always dependable in dangerous situations. Also, the friendship gives us occasional glances at Holmes' basic decency. Every once in a while, wrapped up in logic and facts, Holmes would casually say something that would annoy or hurt Watson. But he would never hesitate to apologize to his friend when he became aware of this.

The best Holmes stories are those that present the most *outré* mysteries or those that give us some new insight into Holmes's character. In the novel *The Valley of Fear*, we learn that Holmes indulges in cocaine between cases to stave off boredom. Fortunately, Watson eventually weans him off the drug.

We learn about Mycroft Holmes, Sherlock's corpulent older brother, in "The Greek Interpreter." Mycroft is even smarter than Sherlock, but too inherently lazy to attempt detective work. He spends his time at the Diogenes Club, an exclusive institution whose members are forbidden to talk to one another. Mycroft works for the government in a seemingly minor capacity. In reality, as Sherlock once explains, "Again and again, his word has decided the national policy."

In "A Scandal in Bohemia," we discover that Holmes is not completely immune to a woman's charms, though it is Irene Alder's success in outwitting him rather than her beauty that sets her up as The Woman in his memory.

Most of the original stories (known to fans as the Canon) center around Holmes's mental gymnastics, but Conan Doyle could toss in a dollop of action or suspense from time to time. *The Sign of Four* includes an exciting nighttime boat chase along the Thames river. "The Red-Headed League" and "The Adventure of the Empty House" each puts Holmes and Watson on a stakeout to build up suspense. *The Hound of the Baskervilles*, arguably the best of the four novels, has an aura of spookiness lying over the story from start to finish.

But in the end, Holmes's genius is always at the forefront. Oddball cases such as "The Red-Headed League" stand out because of the Great Detective's ability to make sense of bizarre mysteries. Mr. Jabez Wilson had answered an advertisement for men with red hair. He had been hired for a nice sum of money to spend four hours each day at a specific location, copying the *Encyclopædia Britannica* in longhand. He's told this is all part of a league set up in the will of a red-haired millionaire. But then, after several weeks, the League's office was closed up without explanation.

Wilson comes to Holmes for advice. Before the case is closed, Holmes has deduced the real motive behind the League in time to put a stop to a crime. What make the story so much fun is that, odd as it all is, it all makes sense in the end — as Watson tells Holmes: "You reasoned it out beautifully. It is a long chain, and yet every link rings true." Not all Conan Doyle's mysteries are as cleverly constructed as that one, but as long as Holmes is there in the middle of it all, we are always entertained.

When Holmes came to American radio, he did so successfully primarily because one particular writer: Edith Meiser. A former actress and vaudevillian who turned to writing, Meiser had been introduced to Holmes when she was thirteen years old and had been in love with him ever since.*
In 1930, she sold the idea of a Holmes series to NBC.

Meiser's understanding of Holmes was perfect and her scripts, whether adaptations of the original stories or new adventures, unfailingly had Holmes sounding and acting like Holmes should. It was the start of a long and successful career for her — she was still turning out scripts for the Great Detective two decades later.

Meiser's contribution to the Holmes radio canon is extraordinary, but she eventually got some help. Writers such as Leslie Charteris (the creator

---

*Tollin, *Holmes*, 3.

of the Saint) and Anthony Boucher (who also wrote for *Ellery Queen*) also contributed authentic and intelligent scripts during the 1940s.

For the premiere broadcast, an adaptation of "The Adventure of the Speckled Band," William Gillette (famous for playing Holmes on stage for many years) came briefly out of retirement. This episode no longer exists in its entirety, but radio historian Jim Harmon reports that in one surviving scene Gillette, who was getting on in years, sounded too old and too American.*

Richard Gordon took over the role after the premiere. It was the beginning of a long, mostly continuous run for the detective on American radio, with at least seven actors taking over the lead role at different times. The show jumped back and forth between NBC, Mutual and ABC. It was never a huge ratings hit, but it was blessed by writers who knew enough to leave Holmes the way he was.

Meiser adapted many of the short stories at first, then serialized the novels. When she had burned through Conan Doyle's tales, she began to write original scripts. Professor Moriarty, who is mentioned in just of couple of the original stories and appears only in "The Final Problem," became a frequently reappearing villain. Cases mentioned in passing in the Canon, such as "The Case of the Giant Rat of Sumatra," were fleshed out in full. As the show jumped to different networks with different actors, it would often return to the Canon once again for fresh adaptations.

Throughout its run, the show used the same format. The show's announcer would stop by 221B Baker Street, where Dr. Watson was sitting comfortably beside a blazing fire. After exchanging pleasantries and pausing to allow the announcer to plug the current sponsor, Watson would then begin to relate one of Holmes's many adventures. When George Washington Coffee was the sponsor, Watson would have a pot of the stuff brewing over the fire.

Watson was initially played by Leigh Lovel, but half-a-dozen other actors cycled through the role over the years. The best known actors to play Holmes and Watson on radio came to the roles straight from the movies.

In 1939, Universal Pictures released two excellent Sherlock Holmes films starring Basil Rathbone as the detective and Nigel Bruce as Watson. Rathbone's crisp, energetic take on Holmes is spot-on and to this day, many fans still consider his performance to be the definitive one. (Jeremy

---

*Harmon, *Radio Mystery and Adventure*, 171.

Brett, who played Holmes on television in the 1980s, does give Rathbone a run for his money.)

Rathbone and Bruce began to play the duo on radio that same year. Though both actors were capable of blowing lines during the live broadcasts a little too often, Rathbone was still excellent as Holmes. The scripts continued to be first-rate and the production values were superlative.

Nigel Bruce as Watson has always been problematical, both in the films and on radio. It's his performance that has turned Watson into the bumbling comic relief he is now commonly perceived to be. Though his loyalty to Holmes is still strong, Bruce's Watson was something of a klutz and definitely not too bright. This carried over onto the radio as well.

In Conan Doyle's story "The Adventure of the Devil's Foot," Holmes unwisely experimented with a burning powder that had been used to commit a murder. When fumes from the powder threatened to overwhelm both Holmes and Watson, it was Watson that pulled himself together and dragged his friend to safety.

But in an otherwise faithful 1947 radio adaptation of that story, with Tom Conway playing Holmes and Bruce playing Watson, it is Holmes who smashes open a window to clear the room of the fumes. Poor bumbling Watson loses his moment of glory.

On the other hand, Bruce was a fine actor, giving us an affable Watson we can't help but like. This interpretation of the good doctor is the only significant downside to the series, but if we accept this Watson for what he is, it's not a serious problem.

Rathbone left the series in 1946. Tom Conway, who played the Falcon in film and would eventually play the Saint on radio, did a very good impersonation of Rathbone as he played Holmes through July 1947. John Stanley and Ben Wright both had brief turns in the role before the show finally left the airwaves in 1950.

Stories from original canon were adapted yet again in an exceptional series produced in Britain in 1954. Airing in the United States on NBC the following year and on ABC in 1956, the show starred John Gielgud as Holmes and Ralph Richardson as Watson. Orson Welles, who had played Holmes sixteen years earlier on *The Mercury Theater*, turned up as Professor Moriarty when "The Final Problem" was dramatized.

Arthur Conan Doyle got Holmes exactly right the first time around and he has been so well-represented on radio simply because writers such as Edith Meiser respected this. "I play the game for the game's own sake," Holmes once told his brother Mycroft as an explanation of why he does what he does. Fortunately, radio gave us yet another satisfying and entertaining medium in which to play the game along with him.

Sherlock Holmes on radio:
NBC: 10/20/30–5/26/35
Holmes: William Gillette (1 episode),
Richard Gordon, Clive Brook, Louis Hector
Watson: Leigh Lovel

Mutual: 1/1/36–9/26/36

NBC: 10/1/36–12/24/36
Holmes: Richard Gordon
Watson: Harry West

NBC, NBC Blue, Mutual: 10/2/39–5/27/46
Holmes: Basil Rathbone
Watson: Nigel Bruce

ABC: 10/12/46–7/7/47
Holmes: Tom Conway
Watson: Nigel Bruce

Mutual: 9/28/47–6/6/49
Holmes: John Stanley
Watson: Alfred Shirley

ABC: 9/21/49–6/14/50
Holmes: Ben Wright
Watson: Eric Snowden

NBC: 1/2/55–6/5/55

ABC: 5/1/56–9/4/56
Holmes: John Geilgud
Watson: Ralph Richardson

First prose appearance: *A Study in Scarlet* (1887),
by Arthur Conan Doyle

Mr. and Mrs. North

Pam and Jerry North began their fictional existence as characters in a series of short vignettes written by Richard Lockridge in the early 1930s. Appearing first in the New York *Sun* and later in the *New Yorker*, the stories were light domestic comedies that dealt with the not-too-serious troubles of a young married couple living in the big city. Compared to Nero Wolfe or Nick Carter, the Norths' life in New York City was downright sedate — no corpses or death traps were involved.

This changed dramatically in 1940, when the young couple suddenly developed the habit of frequently stumbling over dead bodies or otherwise becoming involved in murder investigations. In that year, Richard Lockridge's wife Frances tried her hand at writing a mystery. Richard suggested she use the Norths as the protagonists and the two ended up collaborating. *The Norths Meet Murder* became the first of over two dozen novels featuring the couple, with the series running until Frances' death in 1963.

The premier novel is a fine one — a very well-constructed, nicely paced mystery with fair clues. It begins as if the Norths were still in a domestic comedy, with Pam deciding to use a vacant studio apartment located above their own rooms to throw a party. We are quickly introduced to her quirky speech patterns; she has a habit of letting her words get just a little bit ahead of her thoughts and often seems to expect people to know what she's talking before she actually tells them what she's talking about. As a character in a later novel described it, "it was ... like trying to read a sentence in its entirety, not word by word." Pam comes across as a little bit scatterbrained, but we soon learn that she's possibly the smartest person around.

Pam brings Jerry upstairs to look the studio over and the tale suddenly veers into new territory when they find a corpse in the bathtub. It's an abrupt segue from light comedy to murder, but the abruptness works to give the moment a sense of real danger.

The police are called and homicide lieutenant Bill Weigand arrives to investigate. He's a bit thrown by Pam at first (Why did you go upstairs? Why, to show Jerry. To show Jerry what? Well, about where to put things. Put what things where? Oh, we were planning a party.). But he soon realizes she is very perceptive about human nature and quite capable of making an occasional deductive or intuitive leap. As the case progresses, he meets with the Norths several times, sharing information with them and collecting their opinions. When the investigation reaches a dead end, it's Pam who suggests having "a suspect party.... All the suspects and maybe some other people I owe [invitations] to ... and you can come and discover the murderer." Weigand, partially in desperation and partially because he's come to trust Pam, agrees to this seemingly ditzy plan.

The party does help expose the killer's identity, though not before he corners Pam in that same studio apartment. Weigand and his partner, Sgt. Mullins, arrive in the nick of time to save her. This is the first time in what will become a longstanding tradition — as smart as Pam is, she ends up needing rescuing quite a lot.

The novel works on several levels. Aside from the solid plot, Pam and Jerry North are genuinely charming people. Their verbal interplay isn't often laugh-out-loud funny, but it's always fun to read and always seems perfectly natural. They are completely believable as a couple who are in love and truly enjoy each other's company.

Bill Weigand, who becomes close friends with them, is also a well-drawn character. He's no Lestrade or Inspector Farraday, unable to cope with murderers without outside help. Instead, he's an intelligent and capable cop who simply realizes that Pam and Jerry are another valuable resource to use in an investigation. In *The Norths Meet Murder*, for instance, he and Pam both realize who the killer is at more-or-less the same time, having gotten there along separate paths of deductive reasoning. In *The Dishonest Murderer* (1949), Pam is wrong about the killer's identity and it's Weigand who comes to the correct conclusion.

Weigand's chief assistant is Sergeant Aloysius Clarence Mullins, who is perpetually annoyed by "screwy" cases that can't be solved by simply beating a confession out of a suspect. The two cops, one thoughtful and one rough-edged, play well off each other, giving the novels yet another entertaining "couple" to carry the plot along.

The novels also make good use of New York City, presenting a realistic look at what it was like to live there during the 1940s and 1950s.

Between the characterizations and the setting, the authors managed to build a world where it seemed perfectly acceptable that a young married couple would end up helping to catch killers in their spare time.

Later novels would sometimes feature the Norths discovering yet another body, but also used both their friendship with Weigand and/or public knowledge of their experiences to get them involved in other cases. In *The Dishonest Murderer*, for instance, Jerry (who's employed at a publishing house) is working with a retired admiral who has written a book about his wartime experience. The admiral's daughter, Winifred (Freddie) Havens, is engaged to a U.S. Senator. There's a wonderfully tense opening chapter, as Freddie and other characters becoming increasingly concerned when the senator is late to a party. Finally, they learn he's been found dead in an alley, inexplicably dressed in a bum's clothing.

For various reasons, Freddie is terrified that her father is guilty. Knowing that the Norths have been previously involved in murder cases, she goes to them for help. Weigand stops by their apartment at the same time and welcomes their involvement. Later, the admiral also asks them for advice.

In the meantime, another man is murdered. It's Freddie who discovers the body — much of the novel is told from her point of view — and she once again has reason to believe that her father is guilty. But neither Weigand nor the Norths suspect the admiral.

Pam, in fact, suspects that an old lover of the senator is guilty, having lured him to a seedy neighborhood by forging a letter from his black sheep brother George:

"So she writes this letter about George. Maybe she pretends she is George. She says she — George, that is — has to see the senator about something important. Suppose she — that is, George — says she, I mean he, of course, is in a jam and, for his own protection — I mean the senator's own protection — he — I mean George — has to have him..."

"You mean the senator?" Jerry said.

"All right," Pam said. "I'm just talking the way I'm thinking."

On this occasion, Pam deduces the method, but fingers the wrong suspect. Weigand is on the right track, though, arriving in time to save Pam and Freddie from the killer. It's another fine novel, once again balancing a good plot with excellent characterizations. The pacing is particularly good, as the plot jumps from one point of view to another — Freddie to Weigand to Pam and back again — in a way that helps build a high level of suspense by the climax.

It does have a few minor flaws. Many readers will see the twist at the end coming just a few pages sooner than the authors probably hoped. The admiral's clipped manner of speech (he doesn't seem to know what a pronoun is) is a rare failing at keeping the dialogue sounding natural. But Pam's charm, Weigand's good police work and Freddie's heartfelt distress over suspecting her father more than make up for this. As was true in other novels in the series, we come away satisfied with the resolution and with the hope that we'll some day get to have dinner with Pam and Jerry — providing, of course, that no one gets murdered before dessert is served. Unfortunately, if the Norths are present, that's all too likely.

An audition show for the Norths was recorded in 1941 in which the couple returned to their romantic comedy roots. This didn't catch on and when it came to NBC as a regular series a year later, Pam and Jerry were once again amateur detectives. Joseph Curtin was Jerry, while Alice Frost played Pam with vocal mannerisms that remind one of Gracie Allen. (Gracie had actually played Pam in a 1941 movie.) The show was a hit, running until 1947 on NBC, then continuing on CBS until 1954.

Mr. and Mrs. North deserved its success. If the thirty-minute format required somewhat simpler mysteries than were found in the original novels, they were still well-constructed stories with satisfying solutions. Curtin and Frost had an excellent chemistry, with Frost particularly skillful in balancing Pam's scatterbrained ambiance with a sense that she really is smart. Perhaps most importantly, we never doubt that Pam and Jerry are in love. They might bicker occasionally over Pam's desire to get involved in yet another mystery, but they obviously enjoy one another's company.

Each episode began with a brief bit of third-person narration, setting up the situation and introducing new characters. Then the narrator faded away, allowing character dialogue and sound effects to carry the rest of the story along. As with the original novels, the show often used Jerry's work as a publisher to bring the Norths into contact with victims and suspects.

In "The Opera Murder," from August 1944, we find out that they know famous opera singer Victor Stefano, who once considered publishing his memoirs. But now Stefano comes to them for help, convinced his wife is plotting to murder him.

Stefano is indeed killed. Lt. Weigand doesn't suspect the wife, though. Instead he's convinced that a woman named Sally Ford (who may have been having an affair with Stefano) is guilty and all the evidence does seems to point to her. But Pam has a hunch Sally is innocent. (Weigand at one point wonders why he bothers with clues when Pam is always voicing her hunches.) Pam is right, of course, eventually backing up her hunch with a nice bit of deductive reasoning.

That was a common conceit of the show — Pam would have a hunch, at first unsubstantiated, that always proved accurate. This was dramatically dangerous, since in a lesser show it would function as an awkward deus ex machina. But here it worked because Pam would eventually pick up on the clues necessary prove her right. Riding on the charm of the main characters, the show was able to make this conceit work on a regular basis.

When the show came to television in 1952, Pam and Jerry were played by Barbara Britton and Richard Denning, who eventually took over the roles on radio as well. Like Curtin and Frost, the couple played off one another with humor and charm, allowing the show to continue without a loss of quality. Britton's version of Pam seemed a little less inherently scatterbrained, but she was just as likable and just as believable.

Later episodes depended less regularly on Pam's out-of-the-blue hunches, but still gave listeners good mysteries with fair clues. The writers also recognized the need to surround the Norths with additional characters who were both individually entertaining and dramatically viable. A 1950s-era episode titled "Collector's Item," for instance, tossed a self-centered author, a snooty art critic and a henpecked art dealer into a plot that involved forgery and murder. Another episode, "Cry Foul," involves an ex-boxer who is still devoted to his former wife — even while she's attempting to frame him for murder. With the usual robust contingent of radio's character actors to fill these roles, the stories remained strong throughout the show's run.

For about six weeks in late 1954, *Mr. and Mrs. North* changed from a weekly show to a fifteen-minute daily serial. Unfortunately, most of the episodes from this run no longer exist. As with the serial episodes of Charlie Chan, modern listeners can hear enough of a particular story to realize it's quite good, only to be rudely cut off before the story ends.

The first five episodes of a serial adventure called "Nightwalk" begins when Pam and Jerry help a distraught woman wandering in the rain. Jerry, in fact, pulls her out of the way of a speeding car. They offer to take her home, but she runs away at the first opportunity. A postcard she leaves behind gives the Norths an address and Pam insists they investigate.

At that address, though, they find another woman stabbed to death. Over the course of the first two episodes, we are gradually and efficiently introduced to everyone involved. The woman they had met was Laura, who has only recently been released from a sanitarium. She's given to sleepwalking and has been convinced that her sister Evelyn (the dead woman) has been having an affair with Laura's husband. In fact, Laura is convinced she's guilty, even though she doesn't actually remember committing the crime.

Laura's husband and his business partner also have motives, though. Evelyn knew the two men are guilty of tax fraud and had been blackmailing them. On top of all this was the question of who had tried to run down Laura.

It's all nicely paced, with information fed to the listeners in doses just large enough to keep them coming back for the next episode. As the plot progresses, Pam, Jerry and Weigand all have their individual moments of sharp deductive reasoning, avoiding the trap of making a protagonist look smart simply by having everyone else look dumb. Extending the story over multiple episodes both allowed for an intriguingly convoluted plot and gave some nice opportunities for more personal interplay between the Norths.

But then, just as it's getting really good, the story comes to an abrupt end at a point where original recordings no longer survive. This is one of the inherent dangers of becoming an old-time radio aficionado, at least in regards to serialized shows. All too often, missing episodes mar a storyline beyond repair.

But we can take consolation in the continued existence of a small but representative number of self-contained thirty-minute episodes. Pam and Jerry translated quite well from prose to radio, because they remained the perfect married couple — witty, in love, and prone to stumble over corpses. There's really nothing else two people can reasonably ask for out of a relationship.

The Norths on radio:
NBC: 12/30/42–12/18/46

CBS: 7/1/47–4/18/55 (10/4/54–11/19/54 as serial)
Mr. North: Joseph Curtin, Richard Denning
Mrs. North: Alice Frost, Barbara Britton

First prose appearance (as amateur detectives):
The Norths Meet Murder (1940),
by Richard and Frances Lockridge

The Thin Man

Having taken a look at Pam and Jerry North, we now turn to Nick and Nora Charles, another husband-and-wife team with a talent for figuring out whodunit. By now, we can't help but wonder why the average married couple in real life doesn't concentrate more on being witty and solving crimes. Certainly it would make many of them more interesting. But one of the purposes of fiction is to help fill in these sorts of inexplicable gaps in reality. Nick and Nora certainly do their share in this regard.

Dashiell Hammett's novel *The Thin Man*, serialized in the magazine *Redbook* in 1933 and published in book form in 1934, is his last important work and different in tone from his earlier work. During the 1920s, he was almost inarguably the single most important figure in the development of the hard-boiled genre. His protagonists were tough, professional private detectives thrust into often very complex cases. Hammett's stark and unemotional prose carried the plots along swiftly and he often ended a story with a jarring twist.

The protagonist of *The Thin Man*, though, no longer needs to be tough and professional. Nick Charles has married a wealthy heiress and retired from the detective business, concentrating his time on gambling, parties and drinking far too much alcohol. His wife, beautiful brunette Nora Charles, is perfectly happy to let him spend her money and to join in the drinking. But when an opportunity to help investigate a murder arises, she insists that Nick get involved.

Not that *Nick* is eager to still catch bad guys. He at first tries to avoid a return to the detective business ("I'm too busy trying to see that you don't lose any of the money I married you for," he tells Nora). But newspaper stories exaggerate his involvement, which brings a gun-wielding thug to his hotel room late one night. Nick captures the thug (annoying his wife when he knocks her out to get her out of the line of fire, thus causing her to miss the good part) and realizes he's now involved whether or not he want to be.

Hammett maintains dramatic viability throughout all this by periodically reminding us that Nick is indeed a skilled detective. Many of the cops and underworld characters he meets know him — either personally or by reputation — and respect him. He understands the darker side of human nature and easily juggles the many confirmed truths and probable lies he collects, slowly building it all into something that makes sense.

The murder victim was the private secretary and probable mistress of Clyde Wynant, a wealthy and eccentric inventor who Nick had once met while he was still a detective. Wynant, the titular "thin man," has been missing for some time. Efforts to find him fail and soon there's another murder. Wynant seems the most likely suspect, but his ex-wife and two children also had motives. Wynant's family collectively defines the word "dysfunctional" and all of them lie to Nick in various ways for various reasons.

Nick eventually fingers the killer. He then happily retires from the detective business once more, telling Nora, "All this excitement has put us behind in our drinking." The tipsy couple disappear from literature as Hammett, sadly, largely ended his career as a writer. *The Thin Man* is far from his best work, but it's still a lot of fun to read. It's a good mystery and Nick and Nora are undeniably charming.

MGM kept Nick active as a detective by adapting *The Thin Man* into a film in 1934. The movie version starred William Powell as Nick and the painfully beautiful Myrna Loy as Nora. The film's plot is reasonably faithful to the book, telling the story with efficient economy, but its main strength is the chemistry between Powell and Loy. The two are perfect together, trading quips effortlessly as they easily convince anyone watching the movie that they are hopelessly in love. (The best line: A cop finds a pistol hidden in their hotel room and asks, "Don't you know about the Sullivan Act?" "Oh, that's all right," replies Nora. "We're married.")

The movie was a hit and a sequel, *After the Thin Man*, was released two years later. Four more "Thin Man" movies (the "Thin Man" nom de guerre was eventually if nonsensically applied to Nick) were produced by 1947. The plots gradually become a little sillier as the level of comedy increased, but all are still reasonably good mysteries made all the more entertaining by Powell and Loy. Powell's version of Nick, like Hammett's, was a skilled detective who was just as comfortable associating with the denizens of a sleazy speakeasy as he was with high society. Loy was a perfect foil, always insisting he get involved in a case, then worrying about him whenever this seemed to place him in danger. It was one of those rare instances of perfect casting, turning what would have been a forgettable series of B-movies into classy productions that can still engage the imagination two generations later.

When *The Adventures of The Thin Man* came to radio in 1941, it — like *Boston Blackie* and *Charlie Chan*—was informed more by the movies than the original prose. The series ran off and on over all the major networks until 1950, but kept Himan Brown as the producer-director throughout its run. Brown knew a good thing when he saw it and instructed the stars to sound as much like Powell and Loy as possible, fooling many listeners over the years into thinking that it was indeed those two actors playing the roles regardless of what the announcer claimed. Les Damon, Les Tremayne, David Gothard and Joseph Curtin took turns as Nick. Nora was played straight through by Claudia Morgan.

Unfortunately, less than a dozen episodes of the series seemed to have survived, but those few are all quite good. Claudia Morgan seemed to work equally well with any of the different Nicks, giving the couple the same sort of loving synergy that Powell and Loy had brought to the screen and coming as close as the 1940s would allow to hinting at a healthy physical relationship. (The standards of the era sometimes seemed absurdly strict — as in shying away from just saying that a married couple is sleeping together. But, on the other hand, those standards did guard against the level of tasteless excess that often infests popular culture today. The feeling of sincere romance in Nick and Nora's relationship was heightened by the need to imply rather than graphically show physical intimacy.) The mysteries they investigated weren't as solidly plotted as they might have been — but the show was played as much as a comedy as a mystery, so this is forgivable.

An episode from 1944 begins when a pretty but naïve young woman comes knocking on the Charles' door late one night. Her name is Joan Winslow and she calmly announces she is planning on murdering an unwanted suitor, then asks Nick's advice on how to get away with it. "Can I pass as a femme fatale?" she asks. "Well, you'd be sort of a femme fatale junior grade," he answers. "Maybe I can stab him in the back and claim self-defense," is her nonsensically casual answer to that. Soon fed up with her ramblings, he puts her over his knee and spanks her, then sends her home, confident he's knocked any foolish ideas out of her head.

A little later, the prospective murder victim calls Nick, only to get shot before he can do more than express a concern that his life is in danger. Nora thinks this serves him right for calling them in the middle of the night, but the couple head over to the victim's home regardless. They find him dead, along with enough evidence to mark him as a blackmailer.

A woman named Olga calls and tells Nick she has information about the murder. Nick goes to see her while Nora heads off to see Joan. Nick ends up bashed over the head by Olga, while Nora is tackled by Joan's somewhat confused football-player boyfriend, who sports the unlikely nickname of "Plunger."

Nick eventually manages to get all the suspects together in the same room. To protect her boyfriend, Joan tries to confess to the murder; she knows Plunger's father was one of the blackmail victims and she thinks Plunger did it. But Nick knows by now who is guilty and uses a clever lie to get at the truth. The killer pulls a gun, but is tackled by Plunger before anyone is shot.

The episode ends, as most of them did, with Nick explaining his deductive reasoning to Nora. He adds that he told a lie to trap the killer, but then "any experienced husband knows how to tell the right fibs at the right time."

It's all great fun and it's a pity so few episodes are still available. Nick and Nora charmed their way across the original novel, the movie screen and the radio air waves. Countless male fans of all three media have fallen at least a little bit in love with Nora, while Nick always remained a believable protagonist.

Why *can't* real-life married couples be more like them?

The Thin Man on radio:
NBC: 7/2/41–12/23/42

CBS: 1/1/43–12/26/47

NBC: 6/22/48–9/22/48

Mutual: 10/28/48–1/20/49

ABC: 6/23/50–9/1/50

Nick Charles: Les Damon, Les Tremayne,
David Gothard, Joseph Curtin
Nora Charles: Claudia Morgan
First prose appearance: *The Thin Man* (1934),
by Dashiell Hammett

The Fat Man

"In the past eighteen years," the overweight detective once said, "I've been getting my fun out of chasing crooks and tackling puzzles.... It's the only kind of sport I know anything about."

Samuel Dashiell Hammett created his detective character in 1923, using him in a series of short stories and novellas published mostly in *Black Mask* magazine. Hammett (a former Pinkerton detective) brought a stark realism to his tales, using a sparse and unsentimental prose that still remains gripping over eight decades later. He had a talent for building complex but believable plots in the space of just a few pages, then dropping in some of the best and most unexpected plot twists ever devised. It was hard-boiled detective fiction at its absolute best.

Hammett's creation is never named. He's come to be known as the Continental Op because he worked for the San Francisco branch of the Continental Detective Agency. This is more than just a conceit of Hammett; it serves to emphasize that the Op lives primarily for his work. There is, in fact, very little in the stories that indicate he has any significant life outside his work. There's an occasional reference to a poker game at his apartment or a visit to a boxing match, but the Op is first and foremost a detective.

Nor is there ever any indication that he wants anything else out of his life. He hunts crooks not because of moral concerns over good and evil, but because he's good at it and he likes it. Close friendships, romance or hobbies are all secondary to this. Another character once describes him as "A monster. A nice monster, an especially nice one to have around when you're in trouble, but a monster just the same, without any human foolishness like love in him."

Physically, he seems an unlikely detective. Forty years old and twenty pounds overweight, he's in no danger of being mistaken for Nick Carter.

But he's smart, tough and determined; the reader has no trouble accepting him as a skilled detective.

Some of the later Op stories were interconnecting novellas that Hammett later re-wrote slightly and published as novels. The best of these was *Red Harvest* (1929), in which the Op travels to the city of Personville, commonly known as Poisonville because it is an utterly corrupt place. Several different mobs own the local government and the police department, allowing them to openly run a variety of rackets.

The Op cleans up the town by using lies and half-truths to convince the various crime bosses that they are being betrayed, thus gradually turning them against one another. It's a dangerous game and he must himself dodge a few bullets along the way. By the denouement, the mobs are broken largely because they kill each other off. It's a wonderfully constructed plot, forming one of the best crime novels ever written.

Presumably, the average citizen of Personville was oppressed by the mobsters and happy to see their town free again, but this is merely an assumption as we never actually meet any of them. We only encounter the crooks and dirty cops. Nor does the Op ever seem to think about the innocent citizens one way or the other. He's no Knight Errant striving to serve a higher good. Instead, he does what he does simply because it's his job.

In "The Whosis Kid," a short story from 1925, the Op is taking in the fights one evening when he spots a gunman (known as the Whosis Kid) who specializes in stick-ups. Despite the fact that he's got the night off, the Op decides to follow the gunman purely on speculation. He ends up in the middle of a gang of crooks who are busy double-crossing each other over some stolen jewels. But even when things get really dangerous he "counted on coming through all in one piece. Few men *get* killed. Most of those who meet sudden ends *get themselves* killed. I've had twenty years of experience at dodging that. I can count on being one of the survivors of whatever blow-up there is. And I hope to take most of the other survivors for a ride."

He does turn out to be one of the survivors, but only barely. The climax involves the Op and the Kid stalking each other in a pitch-dark hotel room.

Typical of Hammett's best tales, it's a tight, well-written story. The Continental Op is a consummate professional throughout. There's never any sense of emotional involvement from him, but there doesn't need to be. Sufficient emotion to generate drama comes from the characters around him. He stays above all that as he puts in yet another day's work.

The Continental Op kinda, sorta came to radio in 1946. *The Fat Man*, which premiered on ABC and ran on that network until 1951, claimed in the opening narration to feature "Dashiell Hammett's fascinating and exciting character," though it does not identify which specific character.

Like the Op, the protagonist of the show is an overweight private eye. But the similarities end there. It seems to be a case where Hammett let the network use his name, then took the money and ran, leaving producer Ed Rosenberg to do whatever he wanted.

Rosenberg didn't do half-bad. The show's protagonist is Brad Runyon, an obese P.I. who tips the scales at around 240 pounds. Listeners were reminded of this in the teaser at the beginning of every episode: "There he goes, into that drugstore ... he's stepping on the scale. Weight—237 pounds. Fortune—danger!" Veteran character actor J. Scott Smart played Runyon, providing first person narration in a drawling monotone that seemed to somehow emphasis his obesity. (Smart was fat in reality, allowing him to play Runyon in a 1951 movie.)

Unlike the Op, Runyon did not work for an agency, but operated out of his own small office. The cases he was involved in leaned towards the hard-boiled, but also allowed him to show off more traditional deductive skills as well. Individual episodes were not as tightly plotted as Hammett's best stories, but Smart's performance endows Runyon with enough intelligence and rough charm to bull his way through to the climax each week. It wasn't unusual for Runyon to end up shooting the villain at the end—"The only inoculation against a confirmed criminal," he says in one episode, "is a strong fist and a fast trigger."

In an episode titled "The Crooked Horse," from 1946, a woman comes to Runyon's office. "[She] wasn't beautiful," Runyon tells us, "but there was a straightforwardness about her that spelled brains." The woman is staying at a nearby hotel. The previous night, she had heard the soft pop of a silenced gunshot from the room next door, then saw a dead body through the keyhole. But when the hotel clerk checked the room, it was empty. No one had believed her story.

Runyon checks out the supposed murder room. Picking up on various small clues, he comes to believe that a man was indeed murdered, but also realizes his client was not telling him the whole truth. He confronts her and she admits to being a government agent. Runyon can't know with certainty if this is true, but opts to trust her for the time being. "Maybe I'm a sap. Okay, I'll play blind."

The murder victim was a foreign agent who was supposed to meet a colleague and take possession of an important secret formula. The murderer was most likely an agent from yet another country, also after the formula.

Runyon soon figures out who the victim's contact was and where the body was hidden. But the contact is also murdered before he can be confronted. Runyon must not only find the killer, but the missing formula as well. He finally does get everything sorted out, ending things in a confrontation with the killer by firing a well-placed pistol shot.

The episode includes a great bit near the end. Runyon calls his usual contact at the police station and tells him he's in a hotel room with a dead body. "What, again?" replies the cop.

It's a nifty episode and the show on the whole was entertaining. Runyon's narration is well-written, providing the audience with information quickly and clearly enough to allow for a lot of story in the space of a half-hour episode. The plots of most episodes include some nice twists and turns, while the clues are always there for all of us to hear. Because of good writing and good acting, we can accept the obese Runyon as a smart detective and a really tough guy.

Had it involved any real attempt to adapt Hammett's work, *The Fat Man* would have been disappointing. Runyon and the Continental Op may both sport a belly that sags over their belts a little too much, but they are really two different personalities and the stories they tell are far apart in theme and style. Thus, *The Fat Man* doesn't disappoint a fan of the original prose the way *The Adventures of Nero Wolfe* might. Despite the use of Hammett's name, the connection with the Op stories is just too tenuous. The only possible way to judge *The Fat Man* is on its own merits. And taken on its own, it did pretty good.

The Fat Man on radio:
ABC: 1/21/46–9/26/51
Brad Runyon: J. Scott Smart

First prose appearance: "Arson Plus" (1923),
by Dashiell Hammett (writing as Peter Collinson)

Sam Spade

San Francisco–based private eye Sam Spade is, in many ways, a dislikable guy. When his partner, Miles Archer, is murdered one night, he seems almost disinterested. We soon learn that he was having an affair with Archer's wife — not because he really liked her, but because he was contemptuous of the crude and dull-witted Archer. He comes across as a cold-blooded, calculating personality who plays people against one another, using lies and half-truths without qualm.

But all the same, readers of Dashiell Hammett's classic 1929 novel *The Maltese Falcon* inevitably end up rooting for Sam. This is in large part because he's surrounded by a pretty rotten lot of villains throughout most of the novel. Next to them, he doesn't seem so bad.

But it's mostly because we gradually come to see that Sam has his noble side. He has a sense of justice — a code that requires him to bring in his partner's killer. Never mind that he didn't like or respect Archer in the least. Never mind that his course of action might mean handing the woman with whom he is falling in love over to the police. "When a man's partner is killed," he explains, "he's supposed to do something about it." And he does, mostly by staying one step ahead of the various bad guys even before he himself knows what's going on.

The Maltese Falcon is quite properly considered a classic of the hard-boiled genre because it gives us a fascinating protagonist in Sam Spade, then drops him into a convoluted, intriguing plot. As the book opens, Sam is visited by a beautiful redhead named Wonderly, who asks Sam and his partner to retrieve her younger sister. The sister, she claims, has run off with a dangerous gunman named Floyd Thursby.

Archer trails Thursby, only to be murdered. Thursby is killed as well before the night is over. It soon turns out that Miss Wonderly isn't really named Wonderly — she goes through another alias before Sam learns her name is Brigid O'Shaughnessy. Her sister doesn't exist and her true motivations are unclear. Despite this, it is soon obvious that she and Sam are attracted to one another. Well, Sam at least is attracted to her. How much we can believe about Brigid's true feelings is open to question.

Other strange people begin to look up Sam, often with the threat of violence as they at first assume that he knows a lot more than he actually does. The supporting cast rapidly grows, introducing us to the gaudy homosexual Joel Cairo; the garrulous fat man Casper Gutman ("Talking's something you can't do judiciously unless you keep in practice," he explains at one point); and the arrogant young thug Wilmer, who isn't nearly as tough as he thinks he is.

Initially, Sam has no idea what's going on, but employs a cool professionalism and a quick tongue to keep in the midst of things until he has it figured out. Everyone is after a rare statuette of a falcon, coated with black lacquer but made from pure gold. Gutman has pursued it for years and now it has found its way to San Francisco after having been stolen from its previous owner in Constantinople. Gutman and Cairo are competitors, with Brigid (who may know where the falcon is) seemingly caught in the middle.

In the meantime, another body turns up, this time in Sam's office. The police are demanding more answers from him than he is ready to give. Gradually, Sam puts everything together, including some firm conclusions concerning who has shot whom.

Along the way, we find out some interesting things about Sam. He doesn't carry a gun and doesn't usually depend on violence to get the job done. He does have a quick temper aimed at anyone who takes a swing at him, but keeps his emotions well hidden in most other situations.

The only person we see him show real friendship towards is his loyal secretary, Effie Perine. Effie is more than likely a little bit in love with Sam, often going above and beyond any reasonable secretarial duties at his request. She agrees to hide Brigid O'Shaughnessy at her home at one point. When Sam later calls her in the early morning and asks her to run an unusual errand, she does so without question. But Sam isn't just using her — several times, most notably when the normally reticent detective actually apologizes after speaking sharply to her, we get hints that he really does consider her a friend.

Perhaps the incident that tells us the most about Sam comes when he tells Brigid about a case he worked on years before. A married man had disappeared without a trace, leaving a wife and two children behind. Several years later, Sam runs across him in another city, remarried and living under another name. The man, Sam discovered, had one day been nearly killed by a falling beam. Suddenly struck by how arbitrary life was, he had left everything behind and wandered the country for a time. Then he settled down and married again, picking a new wife very much like his old one. "But that's the part I always liked," Sam explained. "He adjusted himself to beams falling, then no more of them fell, and he adjusted himself to them not falling."

All through the Falcon case, Sam Spade adjusted himself to falling beams with great aplomb, constantly adapting himself to rapidly changing situations. The various convolutions in the plot eventually wrap around and tie together. Everything is explained; various killers are exposed; and Sam shows us that we shouldn't be "...too sure that I'm as crooked as I'm supposed to be." Sam's speech at the denouement, explaining his code of ethics to Brigid, is a classic moment in detective literature, providing a character template that has been used by many other writers over the years since Hammett's heyday.

One of the more interesting aspects of *The Maltese Falcon* is its moral balance. Sam's virtues don't cancel out his faults. One major decision he makes alienates him from Effie. Also, his cavalier treatment of Archer's widow is not excused or forgotten — Sam may have solved the case, but he's left on the last page of the novel with a lot of emotional messiness he can no longer avoid. Ironically, it's this acknowledgement of Sam's sins and their consequences that help keep the reader sympathetic to him.

Another of the novel's notable traits is the lack of reliance on action to carry the story along. In his Continental Op stories, Hammett often tossed his protagonist into a fist fight or gun fight. But with Sam Spade, he takes a different approach. *The Maltese Falcon* is indeed violent, but that violence is often lurking in the background. The murders all take place "off stage." Sam slugs Joel Cairo at one point and later does the same to Wilmer, but he depends more heavily on his wits than on his fists. The story is very dialogue-heavy, but it never drags. Hammett keeps the tension high throughout, using both his ear for natural-sounding dialogue and his sense of realism to carry the plot along. Ambiance becomes more effective and more purely exciting than gunfire.

The Maltese Falcon was published towards the end of Hammett's career as a writer. Sam was popular enough to reappear in a trio of short stories, all of which were good but fairly standard mysteries. He vanished when Hammett stopped producing fiction in the 1930s.

But you can't keep a good detective down. Within a dozen years of its initial publication as a serial in *Black Mask* magazine, *The Maltese Falcon* had been adapted into a movie three times. The first two adaptations were lousy, but the 1941 version with Humphrey Bogart is nearly perfect and a classic in its own right.

Then Sam vanished again, but only for a few years. In 1946, *The Adventures of Sam Spade* made its debut on radio. But by that time, he was a somewhat different man.

Many of the qualities that made the private detective such a powerful character in the original novel would have worked against him in a continuing series. And this wasn't due just to the broadcast standards of the day — eventually, Sam's less admirable traits would drain away any sympathy or respect the audience might otherwise have for him.

So Sam Spade on radio became, as radio historian John Dunning wrote, "a hard-knuckled master of street-level whimsy and sarcastic comeback."* The show was, to a degree, a parody of the hard-boiled genre. But at the same time, the plots were solid and progressed with a reasonable degree of logic. It was a fascinating balancing act, treading a thin line between comedy and mystery while still remaining dramatically viable.

Credit for this goes to producer/director William Spier, as well as writers Bob Tallman, Jo Eisinger and, later, Gil Doud. Several of the early episodes were adaptations of short stories by Hammett, but the creative staff was essentially putting their own stamp on the character right from the beginning. The radio show was filled with funny one-liners, snappy dialogue and quirky but still believable characterizations. This was combined with straightforward storytelling, mixing it all into a format that (like all good parodies) poked fun at its source material while simultaneously honoring it. When Tallman and Doud, suffering from creative burnout, left the show in mid–1949, other writers were able to maintain the same qualities.

But it wouldn't have worked at all without Howard Duff in the lead role. It was yet another of those instances of perfect casting that is sometimes vital to a show's artistic and commercial success.

Duff gave such a rapid-fire delivery of his lines that it's amazing he had time to take enough breaths during a broadcast to remain conscious. It superficially comes across as a very broad portrayal of a stereotypical private eye — the sarcastic and perpetually broke tough guy who keeps a glass of bourbon in his desk drawer. But Duff infuses the character with

---

*Dunning, 13.

enough energy and charm to carry it past mere stereotype. Supported by the strong scripts provided by Tallman, Eisinger and Doud, the radio Sam Spade became a classic character of the medium.

Loyal secretary Effie Perine was still there as well, a little more airheaded than in the novel, but still secretly in love with Sam. She was played by Lurene Tuttle, whose comedic sensibilities and chemistry with Howard Duff were yet additional factors in the show's success. Effie existed primarily as a plot device — Sam would arrive back at the office after finishing up on a case and dictate a report to her. This structure allowed Sam to provide first person narration, but it also allowed for enough interaction with Effie, usually taking place just before and just after Sam recounts his latest adventure, to help develop her into a likeable and oddly believable character.

An episode from December 5, 1949 begins, as usual, with Sam calling Effie. "You've heard of pulling a rabbit out of a hat," he tells her, "well, I've pulled one out of a pickle."

"Don't you want to talk about it, Sam?" she asks.

"Frankly, no, but it's expected of me. Sharpen a carrot, throw me some rabbit punch, get the hutch ready, for I'm about to hippity hop through the door with the lowdown on the Flopsy, Mopsy and Cottontail Caper."

It all began, Sam soon recounts in his report, when he arrived at his office one morning to find someone else sitting at his desk. This was a fast-talking private eye from Chicago named Fritz Crockett, who had recently lost his license and had decided to make a fresh start in San Francisco. Fritz already has the confused Effie ordering extra furniture and now he attempts to impress Sam by recounting unlikely adventures involving disguises and music-hall accents.

Sam is soon ready to just kick Fritz out, but the prospect of a paying job — already arranged by Fritz — changes his mind. The job involves guarding a small, jeweled crown that is to be worn by someone at a swanky costume party. Sam and Fritz are to do the job in disguise. The disguises consist of a pair of large rabbit costumes. Sam is apoplectic, but the $100 fee overrides his sense of dignity.

Their client is the host of the party, Mrs. Montignue, who tells them to bring the crown down from its safe in an upper room at the proper time. While waiting, Sam meets a girl dressed in a skimpy Parisian dancer costume, who inexplicably knows that he is a detective. He also meets Mr. Montignue, who is dressed as a giant pickle.

When the time to retrieve the crown arrives, he learns that Mrs. Montigue already gave the safe combination to someone in a rabbit suit, thinking it was either Sam or Fritz. Running upstairs, the two detectives and their client find an empty safe and a groggy Mr. Montigue, who explains that someone in a rabbit suit "dragged me into a room and made me take off my pickle."

"The Montignue's party," Sam narrates, "not only had a Flopsy and a Mopsy, but it also had a thieving Cottontail." By this time, the thief had changed from a rabbit to a pickle and had made a getaway.

Sam spots the girl in the dancer costume also leaving and, on a hunch, decides to ditch his own rabbit suit and follow her. He trails her to the back room of a French restaurant, finding Mr. Montignue and another man already there.

This leads to a confrontation with the thieves that includes an explanation of motives and an offer to pay off Sam. Sam won't betray a client, so someone pulls a gun on him. He's disarmed (unlike his prose counterpoint, the radio Sam habitually carried a pistol) and he seems helpless.

Fritz bursts in at that moment, sporting an absurd disguise and confusing everyone for several seconds until his false mustache falls off. Fritz gets slugged, but Sam uses the distraction to jump the gunman and get his weapon back.

The case is wrapped up after Mrs. Montignue forgives her husband and decides to donate the crown to a French historical society. (The crown once belonged to Josephine.) Sam gets rid of Fritz by recommending that he be given the job of escorting the crown across the Atlantic.

As Sam ends his report, Effie comments that she'll miss Fritz. But Sam dismisses him with the remark, "Let him get his own program."

This particular episode was sillier than most, but it represents just how effectively the show melded comedy and mystery. Howard Duff once remembered, "We did some outrageous things sometimes ... [producer] Bill Spier had quite an antic sense of humor. I thought they went too far quite a few times, but it was basically a fun time for all of us."*

Because of the skill with which the stories were constructed, it was fun for those listening as well. Even when a broadly defined comedic character like Fritz and the idea of Sam Spade in a rabbit suit were thrown into the story, the plot itself still unfolded in a logical and satisfying manner. Howard Duff could tap away at the "fourth wall" between himself and the audience by hinting that Sam knows he's a character in a show without spoiling anything from a pure story point of view.

A more typical episode might be "The Lazarus Caper," from 1948,

---

*Grams, *The Adventures of Sam Spade*, 49.

in which a man named Timothy Lazarus asks Sam to bring him back from the dead. Seven years earlier, Lazarus and his wife had tried an old insurance scam: they'd taken out a large policy on his life, then he had disappeared. His wife would wait the requisite seven years, have him declared legally dead and collect the money. He, in the meantime, had used a plastic surgeon in Mexico to change his appearance. The two would eventually re-unite somewhere out of the country.

But Lazarus's wife Emma has remarried and now refused to acknowledge her original husband. She has apparently out-scammed him. Her choice of a new husband, though, had been unwise — Sam recognizes him as a seedy medical doctor who had ties with gangsters.

Lazarus still loves Emma and wants Sam to establish his identity even if it means jail time, all in hopes of winning her back. Sam, in turn, takes the job in hopes of collecting a reward from the insurance company.

Sam tries to obtain Lazarus' old dental records, but someone has switched them. A secretary from the dentist's office turns up dead and Sam is nearly killed himself. He soon figures out who is behind it all and sets a trap that drops the killer into the hands of the police. Lazarus and Emma reconcile, but are immediately separated again when they are sent to jail for insurance fraud.

The episode ends with Sam, suffering from the after effects of having earlier been drugged, falling into an exhausted sleep. Effie is left to frantically wonder what to do with the twenty-four cartons of coffee Sam had asked her to order, which were now all leaking onto the office floor.

The story had strong hard-boiled sensibilities that included fast-paced plot exposition, allowing the story to cover a lot of ground in just half-an-hour, as well as a lack of sentimentality regarding the supporting characters. But it also had the charm and humor that Howard Duff and Lurene Tuttle brought to every episode. It is a prime example of just how much fun and engaging a good radio show can be.

The Adventures of Sam Spade suffered a severe setback in late 1950, when Dashiell Hammett and Howard Duff both ran afoul of the House Un–American Activities Committee. Duff was dropped from the roll and Steve Dunne was brought in as a replacement.

Dunne did a credible job, but the role was owned by Duff and the show was never quite the same. The sponsor, Wildroot Cream Oil, soon opted to drop the show (and any connection with Dashiell Hammett) anyway. Sam Spade left the airways in April, 1951.

But a good number of recordings of many individual episodes survive today, giving us a real treasure trove of old-time radio. Neither fictional villains like Casper Gutman nor real-life villains like Joe McCarthy have ever managed to best Sam Spade. He out smarted the lot of them.

Sam Spade on radio:
ABC: 7/12/46–10/4/46

CBS: 9/29/46–9/18/49

NBC: 9/25/49–9/17/50
Sam: Howard Duff

NBC: 11/17/50–4/27/51
Sam: Steve Dunne

First prose appearance: *The Maltese Falcon* (1929), by Dashiell Hammett

Philip Marlowe

"I'm a romantic, Bernie," explains Marlowe to a friend in the novel *The Long Goodbye*. "I hear voices crying in the night and I go to see what's the matter. You don't make a dime that way."

Los Angeles–based private eye Philip Marlowe sums himself up quite effectively in that brief bit of dialogue. He didn't mind making money, but that was never his primary motivation. He is, essentially, a modern day knight, striving to help those in need. His armor might not be shining any more, its luster dimmed by tobacco smoke and gunpowder, but his sense of honor always remains intact.

Raymond Chandler's first hard-boiled story, "Blackmailers Don't Shoot," appeared in *Black Mask* magazine in 1933. The protagonist was a tough, smart-mouthed P.I. named Mallory — a sort of embryonic Marlowe. Chandler continued to write short stories and novellas for the pulps through 1938, changing his main character's name several times but always keeping the same personality type. Each of his protagonists had a rough exterior, but an innate sense of right and wrong. All of them were driven to help those weaker then they were. In 1944, Chandler wrote an essay titled "The Simple Art of Murder," in which he explained "Down these mean streets a man must go who is not himself mean, who is neither tarnished nor afraid." This was an idea that would culminate in Philip Marlowe.

Chandler did not produce fast enough to survive in the pulps, where a writer had to sell many stories at relatively low rates to earn a living. So, in 1939, he turned almost exclusively to novels. He cannibalized plot elements from several of his short stories to produce *The Big Sleep*, the first of six novels featuring Marlowe. (An unfinished seventh novel, *Poodle Springs,* was completed by Robert B. Parker in 1989.)

All the Marlowe novels are classics, though the earlier ones are arguably the best. All feature complex plots that twist and turn in multiple directions before all the loose ends are more or less tied up at the end. It wasn't unusual for one or two of those loose ends to still be dangling free when a Marlowe novel ends, but the plots in Chandler's best works are really secondary to theme and atmosphere. He shows us a bleak, corrupt world, infested with people who have chosen to prey upon one another. But this is balanced out by Marlowe, who provides the novels with a moral center.

Smart-mouthed and outwardly cynical, Marlowe opened up shop as a private detective after losing his job as an investigator for the D.A. "I was fired," he explains to his client in *The Big Sleep*. "For insubordination. I test very high on insubordination...."

But he is definitely someone you want on your side when you're in trouble. "You don't know what I have to go through or over or under to do your job for you," he tells his client. "I do my best to protect you and I may break a few rules, but I break them in your favor. The client comes first, unless he's crooked. Even then all I do is hand the job back and keep my mouth shut."

In this case, Marlowe's client is General Sherwood, a wealthy old man whose two daughters are running a little too wild. One of the daughters, Carmen, is possibly being blackmailed and the General hires Marlowe to look into it.

It isn't long before Marlowe finds Carmen, naked and incoherently drunk, in a room with a murdered man. He delays reporting the murder in order to get Carmen dressed and take her home. Soon, a couple more bodies turn up. Marlowe manages to gather up enough evidence to point the police at the killer without bringing the Sternwood name into it. The General pays Marlowe five hundred dollars.

But Marlowe is not himself satisfied and he's unwilling to accept a fee for a job he doesn't feel he's adequately completed. There are still some unanswered questions, mostly revolving around a man named Rusty Regan, a former bootlegger who had married Sternwood's older daughter Vivian. Regan had apparently run off with the wife of a local mobster. Though any connection to the blackmailing and murders that had already been uncovered seemed tenuous, Marlowe continues to look into the matter. Besides, he knew that Sternwood had liked Regan and was hurt by his son-in-law's abrupt disappearance. Finding Regan would help the old man. Marlowe's compassion, as it always does, edges past his cynicism.

Along the way, we also learn that Marlowe is educated and intelligent, working through complex chess problems in his spare time. He doesn't seem to have much of a personal life beyond this — like Hammett's Continental Op, his life is pretty much his work. But the Op took satisfaction in his work in a very objective manner, without overt concern for anyone's personal feelings. Marlowe is more subjective and much more empathetic towards his clients.

There's another murder and Marlowe himself is kidnapped and forced to kill a mob thug while escaping before everything comes to a head. The novel ends with a great twist involving Regan's actual fate. Later novels in the series were just as complex and just as atmospheric.

Chandler wasn't the first to use the rapid pacing and sharp dialogue that was already stereotypical of the genre, but he was better at it than just about everyone else. His ability to establish atmosphere or describe a character quickly and effectively is virtually unmatched. A 1938 story titled "Red Wind" is a prime example of this, providing us with what might possibly be the single best opening paragraph in American literature:

> There was a desert wind blowing that night. It was one of those hot dry Santa Anas that come down through the mountain passes and curl your hair and make your nerves jump and your skin itch. On nights like that every booze party ends in a fight. Meek little wives feel the edge of the carving knife and study their husbands' necks.

The protagonist in "Red Wind" was originally named John Dalmas, but this story was later reprinted with Marlowe replacing Dalmas. (Several other early Chandler stories were also reprinted as Marlowe stories.) When Marlowe came to radio in 1947, the first episode was an adaptation of this story.

During its initial run as a summer replacement series on NBC, Marlowe was played by Van Heflin and the scripts included several more adaptations of Chandler's short stories. By now, network radio producers were beginning to realize just how well the hard-boiled genre worked in that medium. The brisk pacing that fit the genre so well fit into a thirty minute time slot just as perfectly.

It took skill to do it right. The dialogue might be coming fast, but it still had to be clear enough to the listeners to allow them to follow the plot. The reader of a novel or short story proceeds at his or her own pace and can jump back to re-read a sentence if necessary. A radio listener had to grasp it all right away. The right combination of good writing, directing and acting was essential, otherwise we'd be left with an incoherent mess.

The Adventures of Philip Marlowe had the good writing and directing right from the start, but it didn't at first have the right actor in the lead role. Van Heflin was excellent in movies such as *Shane* and *3:10 from Yuma*, but on radio (at least in the few surviving episodes from his run as Marlowe) he came across a little too flat. The scripts were good, by Marlowe didn't seem to have much personality.

When the show came to CBS in 1948, radio veteran Gerald Mohr took over the lead. Mohr's deep, distinctive voice meshed perfectly with the wise-cracking dialogue and *Philip Marlowe* became on of the best of radio's hard-boiled offerings.

The producer-director this time around was Norman Macdonnell, one of radio's sharpest storytellers. Macdonnell's staff of writers, most notably Katherine Hite, were also among the best in the business. When the show premiered in September 1948, "Red Wind" was again chosen to kick things off. That opening paragraph was just too cool to ignore.

For the rest of the show's two-year run, most episodes were from original scripts. But Macdonnell, Mohr and the writers consistently did justice to Chandler's creation. The half-hour format meant the radio plays could never have the complexity of the original novels, but the idea of a modern day knight walking the mean streets of Los Angeles was kept intact. Marlowe dealt with thugs, grifters, killers, and double-crossing clients, but he himself remained a good guy throughout.

The opening was perhaps a little too corny. "Get this and get it straight," says Marlowe. "Crime is a sucker's road, and those who travel it end up in the gutter, the prison, or the grave." Chandler was rarely that unsubtle, but Mohr always delivered the lines with enthusiasm and the overall quality of the show makes it all the more forgivable.

An episode titled "Eager Witness," from 1949, is typical of the series. Marlowe, as always, provides first-person narration, telling us right up front that "This started with a man on trial for his life and an A-1 citizen eager to testify. But there it was interrupted. And it wasn't until I found a corpse in a bubbling bath, gunplay in the woods and lots of blackmail that the real eager witness had a chance to talk."

Marlowe is testifying at the murder trial of a smooth gambler named Earl Jurnigan, who is accused of murdering an elderly horse trainer named Curt Hopper. The case against Jurnigan seems air-tight until a prominent businessman named Leonard Gaines testifies that Jurnigan was at his home the night of the murder.

There is no apparent reason why the respectable Gaines would lie and it's likely Jurnigan will be acquitted. But Hopper's daughter Gail hires

Marlowe to prove Gaines is indeed a liar. Gail had already done some amateur detective work on her own, discovering that Gaines is being blackmailed by his ex-wife Debbie over the contents of a letter, though there is no obvious connection to the murder trial.

Marlowe takes the case after a hit-and-run driver tries to run down Gail. ("Well, that will keep things from getting dull, won't it?" he comments.) That night, he checks into the San Fernando valley health spa where Gaines is scheduled to meet Debbie. Marlowe's vivid description of the run-down spa and the elderly clerk at the desk ("Mr. Sharpe — a misnomer if I ever heard one.") demonstrates just how skilled the creative staff of the show was, taking perhaps thirty seconds to paint an effective word picture of the setting and then quickly getting back to the story. This, in turn, allows the listener to understand the logistics behind the brisk action that soon follows.

Debbie is murdered before meeting with Gaines — Marlowe finds her in one of the spa's bubbling hot springs with a knife in her back. Soon the spa is infested with suspects. Gaines is present, as is a thug who works with Jornigan and Debbie's boyfriend Eugene Mowry. Marlowe is obligated to clobber the thug and later trade shots with someone in the woods before he's able to figure it out — a complex plot involving adultery, several levels of blackmail, double-crosses, triple-crosses and a seemingly innocuous clue that turns out to be the key to everything.

For a thirty minute show, it was a relatively complicated plot, but crisp writing and Mohr's solid performance as Marlowe keeps the story moving along without ever leaving an attentive listener behind. It's a prime example of why radio is such a wonderful storytelling medium — it forces the listener to pay attention, but rewards him by fully engaging his imagination and providing him with satisfying, well-constructed stories.

What's more, *The Adventures of Philip Marlowe* did justice to its source material. The individual radio episodes lacked the depth of the novels, but it's still easy to think of Gerald Mohr's Marlowe as the same guy we're reading about in *The Big Sleep* or *The Long Goodbye*. The radio show may simply be telling us of less important cases Marlowe handled in-between the events of the novels, but they are still worth our time and attention. Philip Marlowe was a product of the 1940s and 50s, but knights in shining armor will always be relevant.

Philip Marlowe on radio:
NBC: 6/17/47–9/9/47
Marlowe: Van Heflin

CBS: 9/26/48–9/29/50

CBS: 7/7/51–9/15/51

Marlowe: Gerald Mohr

First prose appearance: *The Big Sleep* (1939), by Raymond Chandler

Michael Shayne

A sailor named Davis Dresser was caught up in a fight in a Mexican bar one evening. Stunned by a blow from a bottle, he was carried to safety by a large, craggy Irishman with red hair. The redhead may very well have saved Dresser's life, but he also provided the future writer with the inspiration for one of the most commercially successful private eye characters ever created.

In 1939, using the pen name Brett Halliday, Dresser wrote *Dividend on Death*, the first of what would eventually be seventy-seven novels and three hundred short stories featuring a redheaded Miami-based tough guy named Michael Shayne. Dresser wrote or co-wrote fifty of the novels. After he retired, other writers (still using the Halliday nom de plume) continued producing books. In 1956, the *Mike Shayne Mystery Magazine* began a nearly thirty-year run, providing an outlet for all those short stories.

Shayne was superficially a pretty generic private eye character — a tough-talking loner who didn't take any guff and often barreled his way through an investigation with swinging fists and a belligerent attitude. The last Shayne short story was published in 1985 — forty-six years after his debut. But in many ways, Shayne himself hadn't changed at all. He was still quick with either a verbal retort or a right cross. He still shouldered his way into rooms and apartments to snap questions at suspects and reluctant witnesses. He still played fast and loose with the law, making up with the cops in the end by handing over yet another murderer.

Though Shayne's adventures never reached the same level of literary excellence as did Spade and Marlowe, they still have their own unique energy. To quote writer L.J. Washburn, who wrote some of the later Shayne novels: "[The stories were] a cross between hard-boiled private eye, screwball comedy, and fair-play detection."* In the early novels, Dresser stepped away from the usual P.I. stereotype by giving Shayne a wife. The detective met the beautiful Phyllis Brighton in his first recorded case and was married to her by the time the third novel, *The Uncomplaining Corpse*, was published in 1940.

Phyllis was a great character — completely in love with her man and more than willing, regardless of a lack of either qualifications or experience, to step in to help him on a case. She did just that in *The Uncomplaining Corpse*. The book begins when a man named Arnold Tripp approaches Shayne to get his help pulling off an insurance scam. Tripp wants Shayne to arrange for someone to pretend to steal some valuable jewelry.

Shayne contemptuously turns Tripp down. Later, Tripp's wife Leora comes to see Shayne and he discovers that she thinks he was being hired to investigate some threatening letters she received.

Soon after, Shayne runs into an ex-con named Joe Darnell. Darnell's trying to go straight and get enough money to marry his girl, but he can't find steady work. Shayne impulsively decides to help him out. He tells Darnell to pretend to go through with the fake robbery at Tripp's house, collecting the $1,000 in cash Tripp would leave as payment. But Darnell would leave the jewelry box he was supposed to steal behind, thus preventing Tripp from carrying out the insurance scam.

It was a somewhat less than legal idea, but Shayne saw it as a way to help a friend and annoy a crook. It all goes wrong, though. That night, when Tripp sees Darnell standing over Leora's strangled corpse, he shoots and kills him.

To the cops, it looks like one of Shayne's operatives had committed a vicious crime. In danger of losing his license and convinced that Darnell did not kill Leora, Shayne dives into the investigation. There's no shortage of suspects — Tripp; his two greedy and selfish children from a previous marriage; Leora's ex-con brother, recently released after serving time for manslaughter; a man with whom she had been having an affair who was now romancing her step-daughter. All had a motive. All had opportunity.

Phyllis knows how deep into trouble her husband has sunk. Without telling him, she hooks up with Leora's ex-lover, hoping to vamp him for information. By the time Shayne finds out about this, neither Phyllis nor the ex can be found anywhere. Later, the man turns up dead and Phyllis ends up in jail as the main suspect.

*thrillingdetective.com

To Shayne, this is actually good news. As long as she's behind bars, she's safe. But this also leads to some increased friction involving Shayne's friend, Miami detective Will Gentry. While Phyllis is still in jail, Gentry finds out Shayne has lied outright to him about certain aspects of the case. For a time, Gentry's convinced the private eye is sacrificing his own wife for a chance to collect a large fee. Because of this, Shayne feels more alone than he ever had in his life. "He had played a lone game in the past, but there had always been that good inward feeling that he had one friend who was backing him to the limit and beyond." But now, he was truly on his own.

He works well on his own, though, turning up some evidence that seems to point to one particular suspect. But Shayne withholds this from the cops, even going as far as faking evidence in order to set up a situation where he can convince several of those involved in the case to pay him off. "This promised to be the sort of photo finish he enjoyed — split-second timing with lives hanging in the balance while he sat back and pulled the strings." With the primary suspects gathered together, he uses a bit of deductive reasoning to identify the real killer — all after pocketing the cash several of the suspects had brought him. The killer is arrested, Phyllis is set free, Shayne keeps his license, his reputation and the money.

It's a very well-constructed plot, with frequent twists and an effective denouement. Shayne's loving relationship with his wife is a nice balance to the brutal persona he often adapts when he's working. The strained relations with Gentry added tension and the line of deductive reasoning Shayne follows to the killer is sound.

For several years, Shayne remained happily married as he handled complex cases and always looked (with more successes than failures) to collect nice fees along the way. Sadly for the couple, Shayne's popularity would soon doom his young wife.

In 1940, Dresser sold the movie rights for Shayne to 20th Century–Fox. The successful series of B-movies that followed, with Lloyd Nolan as Shayne, presented the detective as unmarried. This led Dresser to kill off Phyllis in the books. A new love interest in the form of Shayne's new secretary, Lucy Hamilton, soon appeared. But unlike Phyllis, Lucy never managed to get Shayne to the altar.

To an extent, the later books in the series became more standard detective fare, but Dresser's energetic style and sound plots were still above average. Even after Dresser retired in 1958, the various ghost writers that took over usually handled the character well. When Mike finally went down for good in 1985, he went down swinging.

Michael Shayne first came to radio on the Mutual network in 1944, with Wally Maher in the lead role and Louise Arthur (later replaced by Cathy Lewis) as his assistant Phyllis Knight.

The Mutual show was canceled in 1947. Mike returned to radio in a syndicated series in 1948, starring Jeff Chandler. Most surviving episodes come from this series, in which Chandler handles the tough-guy role with cool self-confidence. The books had been written in the third-person, though always from Shayne's point-of-view. The radio show took advantage of Chandler's firm, distinctive voice and returned to the traditional first-person narration more typical of the hard-boiled genre. For reasons unknown, Shayne was moved from Miami to New Orleans.

Built on the strength of Chandler's performance, the show gave its listeners the sort of solid, fast-moving plots that always served the genre well. Each episode began with Shayne narrating a particularly dramatic or dangerous event set late in the story — his car was sliding off a wet road or he'd be in the middle of the fight with a large, peg-legged thug. After the credits, the story would backtrack to the beginning and explain exactly how Shayne got into that situation.

"Wandering Fingerprints," from 1949, began with Mike telling us, "She closed my office door behind her, started walking slowly towards me. Her lips looked warm; her eyes looked cool. Matter of fact, everything about her looked awfully good to me. Except for one thing — that big, black gun she was pointing at my belt buckle."

When the story jumps back to the beginning, Shayne is meeting a potential client named Ziegler at a bar. Ziegler claims to have invented a process that lets him transfer fingerprints from one surface to another. He wants Shayne's help in using this process to blackmail people. Mike tells him to get lost, but Ziegler seems confident the private eye will eventually agree.

The next day, police Inspector LaFevre arrives in Shayne's office, telling him his fingerprints were found in a home that had been robbed the day before. When Shayne claims that can't be true, LaFevre calmly tells him "Fingerprints are sort of a hobby with us."

Fortunately, Shayne has an alibi for the time of the robbery. But Ziegler was actually expecting that — he didn't want Shayne in jail, but rather helping him set up his blackmail ring. If Shayne continues to refuse to help, his fingerprints will turn up at a murder scene. Ziegler claims he has already successfully framed a man named Metcalfe, who is currently on trial for murder.

Shayne tries to tell LaFevre about the fingerprint transfer process, but the cop just thinks he's nuts. So Shayne checks into the Metcalfe case. He quickly discovers that Metcalfe really is guilty of murder.

Suspecting that Ziegler was lying about the fingerprint process, Shayne confronts a woman he believes to be Zeigler's partner. But he learns she too is being blackmailed into helping the crook.

That allows Shayne to deduce how his prints had been planted at a crime scene and track down Ziegler's real confederate. Shayne goes to the confederate's apartment and confronts him, but Ziegler is there as well and gets the drop on the detective. Then LaFevre arrives, just in time to save the day — the cop had done some investigating on his own and found his own lead to Ziegler.

The presence of the girl was not really necessary to the plot, but pretty girls were expected in private eye stories and she was sandwiched into this one without it becoming too obvious a contrivance. Otherwise, the story was good. The ending, with the antagonistic cop proving to be capable and arriving just in time to save Shayne, provided a nice irony. LaFevre was adroitly played by Jack Webb, who demonstrated his own skill at handling the hard-boiled genre both here and as the lead in several other detective shows before eventually moving on to the more straight-laced *Dragnet*. Other surviving episodes from the syndicated series (about thirty exist) are also good.

The syndicated show ran for two years. An ABC series ran briefly in 1952–3, with Donald Curtis as Mike, but none of these seem to survive. That's too bad, but syndicated series with Jeff Chandler was in all likelihood the best of the lot anyways. It followed the same conventions as other hard-boiled detective shows in both theme and structure, but (as was true with Sam Spade and Philip Marlowe) a strong, distinctive lead actor and good writing gave it an individual flavor. In both books and radio, Mike Shayne may not have been quite in the same league as Spade and Marlowe, but he managed to come pretty darn close.

Michael Shayne on radio:
Mutual: 10/16/44–11/14/47
Shayne: Wally Maher

Syndicated: 1948–1950
Shayne: Jeff Chandler

ABC: 10/14/52–7/10/53
Shayne: Donald Curtis
First prose appearance: *Dividend on Death* (1939), by Davis Dresser (writing as Brett Halliday)

The Shadow

It could be argued that the Shadow doesn't qualify for inclusion in this book. After all, he did appear on radio *before* he appeared in print. But he is here for two very good reasons. First, his initial appearance as an established character with an active role in a story (as opposed to simply acting as a narrator) was in print. Second, the Shadow is simply too cool to be left out.

In 325 issues of *The Shadow Magazine*, he was a mysterious figure who remained hidden in the darkness until the moment when he pounced upon criminals and madmen, twin automatics blazing. He had a veritable army of agents planted around New York City, gathering information or themselves joining in direct battle when needed. He was a master of disguise, employing several different secret identities. He climbed sheer walls with the aid of specially designed suction cups and took to the air in his gyrocopter, pursuing evil no matter where it tried to hide.

On radio, the Shadow was a wealthy man-about-town who could use the power of his mind to render himself invisible. He used telepathy and caused others to hallucinate, favoring these mental powers over the use of firearms. He had just one assistant, the lovely Margo Lane, who alone knew he was the Shadow. Still a figure of mystery, his abilities and methodology were significantly different from his pulp magazine counterpart.

But before he was any of these things, he was just a voice. The Shadow was first heard in 1930, hosting *Street & Smith's Detective Story Hour*. This show dramatized tales out of *Detective Story* magazine — its purpose was purely to sell more copies of that particular periodical.

The Shadow was initially played by James La Curto, but Frank Readick soon took over the role. With a sinister voice and the world's creepiest laugh, Readick was the most memorable part of *Detective Story Hour*, acting as narrator and occasionally jumping in during the story to be the voice of conscience, echoing inside the mind of a killer.

In fact, Readick was so good at this he ended up selling the wrong magazine. The executives at Street & Smith Publications soon learned that newsstand venders weren't being asked for *Detective Story*, but for "that magazine with the Shadow" or simply "the Shadow magazine."

If people wanted a Shadow magazine, Street & Smith was perfectly content to give them one. Editor-in-chief Frank Blackwell brought in writer Walter Gibson to create a character to match the voice.

Gibson had ghost-written stories for famous magicians such as Houdini and Blackstone. He was familiar with the tricks of stage magic himself. This, plus his experience writing for magazines such as *True Detective*, was all mixed together with the sound of Frank Readick's laughter to create one of the best and most popular characters to come out of the pulp era.

The premier story, from April 1931, is titled *The Living Shadow*. It begins with a young man named Harry Vincent standing at the edge of a bridge in New York City. He's lost both his money and his girlfriend, so he now contemplates suicide. But the Shadow suddenly appears out of the fog and offers him another choice. "I will improve your [life]," the Shadow explains. "I shall make it useful. But I shall risk it, too.... This is my promise: life with enjoyment, with danger, with excitement.... Life, above all, with honor."

Harry accepts, becoming one of the Shadow's agents. Immediately, he's hip-deep in a case involving secret codes and stolen jewels.

This first story tells us nothing about the Shadow's background or true identity. We discover he has remarkable physical and mental prowess; that he is an expert in disguise; and that he has a knack for being in just the right place to perform last minute rescues. But the air of mystery around him remains thick.

It soon appears that the Shadow is really wealthy dilettante Lamont Cranston. But in the third novel, *The Shadow Laughs*, we find out that he only borrows that identity whenever Cranston is off globetrotting. This briefly causes the real Cranston some consternation when he returns to New York, wondering why so many people remember him being somewhere he wasn't. But the Shadow pays him a midnight visit to explain and Cranston becomes a willing part of the deception.

It wasn't until *The Shadow Unmasked*, published in 1937, that we learn the Shadow is really Kent Allard, a flying ace who fought in the Great War. Allard had supposedly been killed when he crashed his plane in a

Guatemalan jungle years before. Somewhere in that jungle, he found great wealth and secretly returned to civilization to begin his private war on crime.

His agents were important soldiers in that war. Harry Vincent continued to appear frequently in the novels, living in a hotel room (all expenses paid) and remaining available whenever the Shadow called him to duty. Clyde Burke was a newspaper reporter who covered the police beat. Cliff Marsland had done time for a crime he didn't commit, but his reputation as a crook made him useful for undercover work. Burbank seemed to live at his telephone switchboard, serving as a contact between the agents and the Shadow. Moe "Shrevvy" Shrevnitz drove a cab. Margo Lane, who originated on the radio show, eventually showed up in the novels. There were at least a dozen others.

The Shadow himself had a wide range of skills. Clad in a dark cloak and slouch hat, he was able to blend into any handy patch of darkness and effectively become invisible. He was an expert with firearms and in unarmed combat. He could disguise himself as just about anyone and mimic voices perfectly. He could pick locks and made use of sleight-of-hand tricks. He often put other magician's tricks to work getting out of the many death traps in which he frequently found himself. He was just plain cool.

The Shadow magazine was soon a best-seller, inspiring a wave of pulps featuring specific characters. Walter Gibson was originally told that Street & Smith would need four novels a year, as the magazine would only be sold quarterly. Soon, he was told it would be a monthly. Soon after that, he found out it would be *twice* a month. That meant twenty-four novels a year.

Gibson proved up to the challenge, managing not only to meet this schedule, but often stay six months ahead. He eventually wrote 283 of the Shadow novels, for a total of about 15,000,000 words. In his prime, he was able to bang out 15,000 words a day on a manual typewriter, often stopping only when his fingertips began to bleed.

Still, to cover their bets, Street & Smith eventually brought in another writer, Theodore Tinsley, to produce four stories a year. Regardless of who the actual author was, the byline in each issue would always read "From the Private Annals of the Shadow, as told to Maxwell Grant." Grant was a house name used to provide a sense of continuity to the magazine despite multiple authors.

Tinsley's stories were usually pretty good, but it was Gibson who defined the Shadow and his mythology. Gibson thrust his character into one wild adventure after another, pitting him against thugs, spies, maniacal killers and master criminals. Despite the speed at which he wrote, Gibson's plots are solid and packed with gun fights, chases and rescues that all unfold in a logical manner. The events of the novels are described in clear, straightforward prose that never wanders off unnecessarily. Excitement and mystery are mixed together in equal measure, often keeping us guessing as to exactly what the heck is going on until we get to the last page.

The Shadow's opponents are always interesting and appropriately dangerous. *Gangland's Doom* found the Shadow in Chicago, breaking up the mob that was responsible for the death of one of his agents. In *Hands in the Dark*, he matched wits with a gang of crooks who were following obscure clues to a cache of hidden loot. *The Romanoff Jewels* took him to the Soviet Union, battling spies and traitors. *The Black Hush* is one of several novels with a science fiction element: the villains are robbing banks with the help of a ray that creates pitch darkness. *Zemba* is set in Paris, where the Shadow and a master spy plot and counterplot against one another, leading up to what may be the single best twist ending ever.

To a degree, the stories were formulaic, but Gibson varied the details enough to keep them fresh almost every time. His background in magic, for instance, allowed him to come up with an incredible variety of death traps and an equal number of clever ways to escape from them. Action sequences might take place atop a skyscraper, in a tunnel being dug under a bank, in a factory amidst vats of molten steel or aboard a ship caught in a violent storm.

The Shadow magazine ran until 1949. Toward the end, it had become a quarterly publication once more. Walter Gibson had moved on and a writer named Bruce Elliot was churning out very poor quality stories. When The Shadow vanished from the newsstands, it was pretty much an act of mercy. But over on the radio, the Shadow had by that time been on the air for a dozen years, with another half-decade of life left in him.

The Shadow continued in his role as narrator until March of 1935, still played by Frank Readick for most of that run. During the 1931–32 season, the Shadow was also given the job of narrating *Love Story Hour*, which dramatized tales out of Street & Smith's *Love Story* magazine. No recordings of this show seem to have survived, which might also be considered an act of mercy. It's difficult to imagine this was anything but a bad idea.

Eventually, Street & Smith began to push the idea that the Shadow become the actual hero of the show, based on the character from the magazine that was selling so well. The sponsor, Blue Coal, was happy with the show the way it was. The resultant disagreement briefly silenced the Shadow's eerie laughter as he went off the air.

Finally, a compromise was worked out. Blue Coal would sponsor the new format, while Street & Smith agreed to return to the Shadow-as-narrator if this change didn't go over with the audience.

Edward Hale Bierstadt was assigned to write the first script. He read a number of the Shadow novels and met extensively with Walter Gibson. Street & Smith editor John Nanovich was also involved in the creative process.

Bierstadt liked what Gibson was doing and wanted to keep the same aura of mystery around the unusual protagonist. But there were a lot of elements to the Shadow's mythology that would not transfer easily to radio. There is, sadly, no detailed record of the ideas and thought processes involved in the Shadow's evolution from pulp to radio, but it's easy enough to deduce why many of the changes were made.

The Shadow's ability to assume different identities would have been difficult to pull off on radio — it would have required using multiple voices for the same character and would have often confused even attentive listeners. The Shadow's relatively large number of agents, identifiable on radio by their voices alone, presented a similar problem.

In fact, much of the Shadow's complex mythology was problematic. Had the show been formatted as a serial, it may have been possible to keep the character closer to his pulp roots. But for a half-hour show consisting of self-contained episodes, a lot of elements had to be dropped or simplified.

So the Shadow became Lamont Cranston on radio, giving up both his other identities and the idea that he was just borrowing Cranston's life. Most of the agents disappeared. In an early draft of the first script, Harry Vincent appeared as the Shadow's assistant. But by the time the Shadow was back on the air, Harry had been replaced with the "lovely Margo Lane." This provided a clear difference in the voices of the protagonists and provided Cranston with a romantic interest.

The biggest change was dropping the Shadow's slouch hat and cape in favor of giving him the ability to literally become invisible. As the opening narration of each episode explained: "Years ago in the Orient, Cranston learned a strange and mysterious secret: the hypnotic power to cloud men's minds so they cannot see him."

Police Commissioner Weston, a regular supporting character in the novels, also made the move to radio. Weston and Cranston were friends. Though often annoyed by Cranston's urge to play amateur detective, Weston allows Cranston to tag along on investigations. He has no idea, though, that Cranston is really the Shadow, carrying on investigations of his own.

The other character brought over from the pulps is Shrevvy, the cab driver. An active agent of the Shadow in the novels, Shrevvy is regulated to comic relief on radio. His main shtick, aside from being a little dense, is repeating phrases within the same sentence: "I was gonna ask you to do a favor for me; I was gonna ask you." Or "Which is the residence we're looking for; which is the residence?" Shrevvy never really clicked as comic relief—he's more annoying than funny. But when he appears, it's usually only for a minute or two before we get back to the good parts.

Orson Welles was given the title role, while Agnes Moorehead played Margo Lane. *The Shadow* premiered on the Mutual network on September 26, 1937. Titled "The Death House Rescue," it was about a man awaiting execution for a murder he did not commit. Suspecting his innocence, the Shadow pays him a visit and uses mental telepathy to pull a possible clue out of his subconscious. Tracking down the real killers, the invisible Shadow terrifies them sufficiently to force them to confess.

Welles and Moorehead both gave strong performances in the lead roles both in this initial broadcast and in subsequent offerings They were backed up each time by clever scripts and good production values. The best episodes used the Shadow's strange powers and the often bizarre plots of the villains to overlay an aura of spookiness over the detective show format. In "Death from the Deep," a modern day pirate uses a submarine to wreck havoc on the high seas. In "White God," a mad scientist sets up shop on a South Seas island and builds a giant magnet to rip airplanes out of the sky. In "Firebug," the Shadow matches wits with a psychotic arsonist.

All these stories fairly drip with melodrama, but it's amazing how well they hold up decades later. What saves them from becoming high camp is the skill with which they were done. With both good acting and good special effects, the potentially absurd scripts become enthralling, suspenseful stories still quite capable of creeping out listeners today. Certainly the listeners at the time were more than happy with what they were hearing. *The Shadow* would run for sixteen years, often as one of the most highly rated shows on the air.

Welles left the show in 1938 to head up *The Mercury Theatre on the*

Air. Bill Johnstone, a veteran radio actor who had played the wrongly accused man in "The Death House Rescue," took over the role, giving both Cranston and the Shadow a very effective and authoritative voice. Bret Morrison replaced Johnstone for a year in 1943–44. John Archer was the Shadow in 1944–45. Then Morrison returned to play the part until the show went off the air in 1954. Margo, in the meantime, was played Moorehead, Marjorie Anderson, Marion Sharkely, Laura Mae Carpenter, Lesley Woods, Grace Matthews and Gertrude Warner.

In the early years, the Shadow occasionally made use of powers other than invisibility. In both "Message from the Hills" and "Power of the Mind" he received telepathic messages from another character. Another episode had him generating hallucinations in the mind of a killer. In later episodes, these other abilities were forgotten and the Shadow was left with invisibility as his sole power.

But invisibility is a pretty nifty power. It is, in fact, the perfect power for a radio superhero, where the audience can't see him anyway. The wonderful opening narration explained it best: The Shadow was "never seen, only heard — as haunting to superstitious minds as a ghost — as inevitable as a guilty conscience."

Cranston used his power together with his skill at deductive reasoning to hunt down crooks. Often, it seemed as if the menace he was battling might be supernatural, but there was always a "rational" explanation. A vampire draining his victims of blood turned out to be a greedy doctor selling the blood on the black market. When a vacationing Cranston and Margo visit a Western ghost town, they seem to really encounter supernatural beings — until the Shadow manages to smoke out the gang of thieves who are faking the ghosts.

A couple of classic episodes used sound effects to generate spine-chilling moments. "The Voice of Death" was about a mad scientist who transplanted vocal cords between different species, creating a pack of killer dogs that emitted the cute meows of kittens before attacking. In "The Laughing Corpse," the murderer does in his victims with a poison that forces them to laugh so hard they soon suffocate.

Poor Lamont and Margo couldn't turn a corner without stumbling over yet another case of weird villainy. One bad guy uses a trained gorilla to kill, while yet another uses a trained panther. A madman sick of all the noise in New York City plants bombs set off by tuning forks, triggered when someone made a sound at just the right pitch. A midget criminal posing as a child arranges to get adopted by a rich family. In the "Return of Carnation Charlie," an executed murderer apparently comes back from the dead to seek vengeance. In "The Little Man Who Wasn't There," the crimes of an apparently invisible thief convince Commissioner Weston that the Shadow has turned evil. "The Shadow Challenged" also features a criminal who seems to be invisible — this time played by former Shadow Frank Readick.

Inevitably, the show began to run out of steam. The quality of the scripts dropped, with the plots becoming formulaic and the villains becoming more mundane. The spooky aura so important to the Shadow was lost to overfamiliarity.

But even the later shows often have wonderfully suspenseful moments tucked away inside them. *The Shadow* at its best is a prime example of just how vivid storytelling on the radio could be. We believe a man could turn invisible. We believe a trained panther is stalking victims in Central Park. We believe a giant magnet is pulling airplanes out of the sky. We believe that madmen and killers are all around us; that horrible death in countless forms is only the prick of a hypodermic away. And we are, by golly, better off because of this.

The Shadow (as a definable character) on radio:
Mutual: 9/26/37–12/26/54
Lamont Cranston/The Shadow: Orson Welles,
Bill Johnstone, Bret Morrison, John Archer,
Steve Courtleigh (6 episodes in 1945)

First prose appearance: *The Living Shadow* (1931),
by Walter Gibson (writing as Maxwell Grant)

The Avenger

Naturally, Street & Smith Publications wanted to replicate their success with the Shadow. In 1933, they began to publish *Doc Savage*, featuring a hero who had been raised from childhood to achieve physical and mental perfection. The plots drew more commonly from science fiction conventions than the Shadow. Doc was much less disposed to kill, depending on his seemingly endless array of gadgets and inventions to subdue the bad guys without resorting to deadly force. Written by Lester Dent, using the house name Kenneth Robeson, the Doc Savage stories are inventive, energetic tales that kept the magazine going for 181 issues.

In 1939, Street & Smith gave Richard Henry Benson, known to the underworld as the Avenger, a try in his own magazine. Benson was one part Shadow and three parts Doc Savage, drawing elements from each in an attempt to recreate the commercial success of those two characters. This didn't succeed—*The Avenger* only ran twenty-four issues, with each issue featuring a novel-length story. Later, Benson was demoted to a backup feature in *Clues Detective* magazine before finally vanishing from the newsstands.

But the Avenger was more than just a carbon copy of his more famous literary cousins. The stories were published under the "Kenneth Robeson" byline, but were actually penned by veteran pulp writer Paul Frederick Ernst. Ernst knew how to construct a good pulp adventure story, linking fight scenes and death traps one after another alongside a plot that moves fast enough to cover over its own flaws. Along the way, he managed to give Benson and his agents their own unique personalities. Among fans of pulp fiction, the Avenger is fondly remembered and, in the 1970s, the original stories were reprinted in a series of paperbacks.

Richard Benson has a macabre origin. A wealthy and successful engineer, he was on a passenger plane with his wife and young daughter.

Returning from a trip to the bathroom, he discovers his family is now missing. What's more, everyone else on the airplane denies they were ever aboard.

Eventually, Benson finds out they were dropped out a trap door by criminals who had mistaken them for someone else. In the meantime, the emotional shock of the incident deadened the muscles in Benson's face and turned the skin a ghastly white.

This enables Benson to reshape his skin like putty, making him by default a master of disguise. He forms "Justice, Inc.," dedicated to helping the innocent and stopping the nefarious plans of the guilty. Over the course of the first few issues of *The Avenger*, he recruits a small band of agents, each of whom has his or her own area of expertise. Benson's inventive genius also supplied them with an array of useful gadgets, such as bullet-proof clothing, gas pellets and tiny two-way radios. Benson also carried a pair of commonplace devices: a silenced pistol he christened Mike and a throwing knife named Ike.

The mysteries Benson and his companions encountered were inevitably bizarre. In "The Sky Walker," a madman with a sonic disintegrator and an invisible airplane attempts to blackmail a city. In "River of Ice," a criminal uses a surgical technique to turn victims into robotic slaves as he seeks to loot the huge gold-laden tomb of a pre–Ice Age civilization. Occasionally, an adventure might be slightly more mundane, but there was always a science fiction element thrown in somewhere along the way.

As he investigated these cases, Benson would use both his intelligence and his fighting skills to see them through. The other members of Justice, Inc. were strong characters as well and all get their moments to shine during the course of the series. In fact, the stories were innovative for their time by including a black couple in the group. Josh Newton and his wife Rosebel were portrayed as intelligent and capable, with the others treating them as equals. For a 1940s-era pulp, this is downright astonishing.

Every story saw the good guys avoid death traps and assassination attempts as they gradually figured out what the latest band of criminals were up to. One or more of them would inevitably get captured at some point. In fact, Benson often allowed himself to get captured as a way of finding out more about his opponents, confident of his ability to affect an escape later on. There were fist fights, gun fights, car chases and plane crashes.

In many ways, it was not significantly different from the dozens of other adventure and mystery pulps that inundated the newsstands at the time. But it was always fun to read, which is all a pulp magazine story was ever meant to be.

Richard Benson came to radio in a series produced by New York station WHN in 1941. At least one of his agents from the prose, Fergus "Mac" MacMurdie, followed him to this new medium. No episodes from this series survived, though, so we have no way of knowing how faithful they were to the original stories.

Odds are there were some changes. Benson's emotionless yet pliable face is a neat visual that works great on a magazine cover or when described in print, but not something that would come across effectively on radio. It would have been interesting to know if this early series found a way to handle this or just changed the premise.

When the Avenger returned to radio in a 1945–46 syndicated series, he was no longer Richard Benson. Instead, he was Jim Brandon, a biochemist who had developed a "diffusion capsule" that turned him invisible. He also slapped together a "telepathic indicator," that allowed him to pick up random thoughts.

This incarnation of the Avenger was an almost literal carbon copy of the Shadow. Each episode starts with the Avenger, like the Shadow, telling us that "crime does not pay." The Avenger has an attractive female companion, Fern Collier, who is the only person who knows his secret identity. And, of course, he has the power to turn invisible. He even has an antagonistic relationship with a police inspector, reminiscent of Lamont Cranston and Commissioner Weston.

James Monks does a good job as Jim Brandon and Helen Adamson is very spunky as Fern, but there's no originality to the show at all. It copies *The Shadow* in every key way, including the melodramatic feel to the individual plots.

In the premier episode, "High Tide Murders," a smuggler is using several jewelers in town to fence his goods. When they start demanding more money, the smuggler lures them to a seaside cabin and drops them through a trap door at high tide, allowing the tide to carry their bodies away.

Brandon picks up a telepathic death cry. Later, when one of the bodies washes up, a piece of evidence indicates the man was a jeweler. Brandon and Fern investigate. Brandon eventually uses tidal charts to figure out where the body was originally dumped into the ocean. In the meantime, Fern is captured by the smuggler. As the Avenger, Brandon arrives at the seaside cabin in time to save Fern. The smuggler, shooting wildly to try to kill his invisible adversary, falls through his own trap door.

It's a perfectly good story, but replace Brandon with Cranston and Fern with Margo Lane and you have a Shadow episode without changing anything else. It's really too bad — the pulp stories managed to inject a level of individuality into a derivative character. The radio show, though, was a pure copycat without any individuality at all.

The Avenger on radio:
WHN, New York: 7/18/41–11/3/42
Richard Benson: unknown

Syndicated: 1945–46
Jim Brandon: James Monks

First prose appearance: *Justice, Inc.* (1939), by Paul Frederick Ernst (writing as Kenneth Robeson)

The Green Lama

By 1940, the pulp magazines had given their readers masked vigilantes, super-scientists, Western lawmen, private eyes, G-Men, spies, Foreign Legionnaires, space men and jungle men. It probably wasn't all that surprising when a Buddhist priest action hero also joined the ranks.

The Shadow had led the way, opening the door for the idea that a regular series featuring a specific character could alone grasp the readers' imaginations and thus keep magazine sales numbers high. One particular publishing firm, the Frank A. Munsey company, was looking for such a character — someone unusual enough to perhaps steal some readers away from the highly popular Shadow.

So the Green Lama was born, first appearing in the April 1940 issue of *Double Detective* magazine. Like the Shadow, he had a secret identity and recruited a team of agents to assist him in his personal war against crime. The Lama would also imitate the Shadow in that he would often employ magician's tricks to outwit the bad guys. The radio version of the Shadow had learned how "to cloud men's minds" in the Orient; the Green Lama acquired many of his unusual skills while studying Buddhism in Tibet.

Though derivative in many ways, the Green Lama has his own personality and his stories have their own unique flavor. Writer Kendell Foster Crossen (using the pen name Richard Foster) dropped the Lama into fast-moving plots involving murder, kidnapping, espionage and corruption. These stories did exactly what pulp stories were supposed to do. They provided their readers with an hour or two of escapism.

The Green Lama's real name is Jethro Dumont, a wealthy New Yorker who, after ten years in Tibet, returns home to fight for justice and protect the innocent. He's particularly well-qualified to do so. His skills include an intimate knowledge of pressure points and nerve centers on the human body. He can, for instance, tap you on the top of your skull and thus temporarily paralyze both your arms. He's also pretty skilled with his *kata*, a long silk scarf that he often uses to disarm gunmen or garrote a villain unconscious.

Unlike the Shadow, Dumont doesn't carry a gun or use deadly force. His unusual skill at hand-to-hand combat means he doesn't have to. He does, though, supplement his fighting skills in one peculiar way. By drinking a solution of radioactive salts, he temporarily gains the ability to administer electric shocks by touching his opponents. How he avoids radiation poisoning is conveniently never discussed.

No one knows Jethro Dumont is really the Green Lama. In fact, his secret identity is *so* secret that not even the author of his stories knows for sure. One of the conceits of the character was that the Lama's true identity was never overtly revealed, with writer Richard Foster adding occasional footnotes stating his belief that Dumont *probably* was the Lama, though we couldn't know for sure. But then, both men are Buddhist priests and Dumont seems to show up wherever the Lama does. If the Lama investigates a case in Hollywood, for instance, Dumont turns up there on vacation.

It was actually a contrived idea that never really added anything to the stories — it was so painfully obvious that Dumont *was* the Green Lama that there was no chance of generating any real sense of mystery in this area.

But the other ideas behind the Lama — his unusual fighting skills combined with sharp detective instincts — more than made up for this. He had a fun supporting cast as well. By the end of his first adventure, he had recruited a reformed mob gunman named Gary Brown, a beautiful socialite named Evangl Stewart and a brilliant doctor/scientist named Harrison Valco. This small but diverse group proved to be capable assistants, able to handle themselves in dangerous situations and rescue the Lama from certain death at least as often as he had to rescue them. Eventually, Gary and Evangl married and left the vigilante business, but the Lama had by then recruited yet another pair of agents.

Then there was the mysterious woman named Magga, who popped up (always in disguise) in unexpected places, providing the Green Lama with vital information or assistance in escaping a death trap. Motivated by her own sense of justice (and, implicitly, by her love for the Green Lama), she remained a complete mystery to the readers as well as the other protagonists. Though used as something of a deus ex machina at times, she was also a fun character.

All this was tied together with a solid sense of continuity. Supporting characters, locales, and the occasional bad guy would carry over from one story into the next, helping to build a believable, self-contained world in which the Green Lama could operate.

For instance, the story "The Wave of Death," from the July 1940 issue of *Double Detective*, picked up right where the previous story left off. The Lama, Gary and Evangl were in California after having just broken up a baby-stealing and phony adoption ring. The Lama learns that a local scientist named Rogers Fenimore has invented a new and deadly weapon. Japanese spies are out to get this weapon.

The Japanese are based on a fishing boat posing as the crew, but several traitorous Americans are also helping them. An FBI agent is murdered under odd circumstances. Another half-dozen feds are gunned down while guarding Fenimore. The scientist is kidnapped, but not before he burns the plans to his invention. There is a working prototype, but Fenimore has hidden this.

The Green Lama and his agents follow up several leads, but the Lama is mistaken for a spy and arrested by the FBI. Fortunately, a friendly police officer (someone the Lama had aided during the baby-stealing case) arranges for his escape. He tracks down the prototype and rescues Gary and Evangl from assassins.

Finally, he learns of the fishing boat. So has Magga, who has been carrying out her usual role throughout the story of turning up with important information at irregular intervals. Magga is captured and is about to have her throat slit when the Lama storms aboard the boat. Using his electric touch, he takes out a number of the Japanese. He's badly outnumbered, though, and only Gary's timely arrival and expert marksmanship saves the Lama, Magga, and Fenimore. Gary, unlike his boss, has no objections to firearms (though, to be fair, he did shoot to wound rather than kill).

It's not a perfect story, depending a little too much on Magga's convenient arrivals and a few minor coincidences to carry the plot along. But the action — especially the fight aboard the fishing boat — is done well and the various plot elements are brought efficiently together at the climax.

The Green Lama had a run of about three years, with a total of fourteen novella-length stories, before his pulp career came to an end. In the meantime, he appeared in comic books as a more traditional superhero, wearing a stream-lined green costume as he gained the ability to fly and fire energy beams. But when he finally made the jump to radio in 1949, he backpedaled a little toward his pulp magazine roots.

The Green Lama ran on CBS for just eleven episodes during the summer of 1949. The show was produced and directed by Norm Macdonnell, who also headed up quality programs such as *Gunsmoke*, *Philip Marlowe*, and *Escape*. It's no surprise, then, that *The Green Lama* sounded pretty good as well.

On radio, the Lama was still Jethro Dumont, but he no longer had a secret identity. Everyone knew Dumont was the Lama. In fact, the premier episode, "The Man Who Never Existed," quickly established that Dumont is famous for his crime-solving abilities. It was a conceit that allowed the show to quickly establish its premise and move on with the story without wasting any time at all.

Dumont was played by Paul Frees, one of the finest radio actors and voice artists of the 20th century. His deep and authoritative voice gave the Green Lama a level of credence that might have otherwise been lacking in its unlikely premise. Ben Wright, another radio vet, played his Tibetan servant Tulka. (In the pulps, Dumont's servant had been named Tsarong. This was probably a bit too much of a tongue-twister for radio.) Skilled actors such as Lawrence Dobkin, William Conrad, and Georgia Ellis played the various killers, bystanders, and victims.

At the beginning of each episode, Tulka explains that Dumont is known as the Green Lama because of "his great wisdom and powers of concentration." These powers come in handy, allowing him to pretty much magically summon up clues from time to time. He also seems to be able to call up occasional bursts of super-strength. In one episode, for instance, he single-handedly topples a three-ton mechanical dinosaur that was about to trample him. Unlike his pulp counterpart, though, he did not guzzle radioactive salts to give himself more power. In a post–Hiroshima world, this just wasn't quite as believable as it used to be.

Only four or five of the original episodes still survive. The premier episode, "The Man Who Never Existed," began with Dumont getting a call from an old friend, an archeologist named Hendricks. Hendricks asks for help, but his call is cut off before he can give details.

Soon, Hendricks's body turns up. Dumont identifies the body, but further checks by the police can't verify this. There seems to be no official record at all of Hendricks' existence.

In the meantime, a Mayan artifact originally found by Hendricks is stolen from a local museum. Using his powers of concentration, Dumont is able to call up a mental image of the artifact and thus learns it has been taken to Mexico. He follows it there, encountering several potential suspects along the way.

Dumont is able to eventually figure out what's going on, rescuing the innocent and bringing the guilty to justice. An explanation tying together the disparate plot elements is provided at the climax.

It was all very solidly written. The use of a mystic ability to pull a clue out of thin air might have been a cheat, but that ability is an inherent part of the character and Dumont also uses logical deductive skills to balance this out.

The several other surviving episodes are also good. Jethro Dumont never did manage to steal away the Shadow's fans, either in the pulps or on radio. But he entertained his share of readers and listeners nonetheless. Those ten years in Tibet weren't completely wasted.

The Green Lama on radio:
CBS: 6/5/49–8/20/49
Jethro Dumont/The Green Lama: Paul Frees

First prose appearance: *The Green Lama* (1940),
by Kendell Foster Crossen (writing as Richard Foster)

Fu Manchu

Sometimes, a writer comes up with an idea for a villain so memorable that it's difficult to invent a hero interesting enough to make a worthy opponent. This was the case with Fu Manchu, the "Devil Doctor." Fu Manchu is "tall, lean and feline, with a brow like Shakespeare and a face like Satan." He's a master criminal whose primary goal is the overthrow of Western civilization. To this end, he employs countless human assassins, poisonous plants, animals, and insects as well as hideous death traps in all shapes and sizes. Fending off old age and natural death through the use of an elixir of his own invention, he sows a trail of murder and destruction that stretches across decades.

Fu Manchu was created by Arthur Sarsfield Ward (using the pen name Sax Rohmer) in 1912 and the character is still relatively well known today. On the other hand, few people outside fans of the original stories will remember the name Denis Nayland Smith, the longsuffering British agent who battled against the criminal mastermind. We may root for the good guy when we read one of Rohmer's stories, but Fu Manchu is the person we really remember afterward.

To a modern reader, the Fu Manchu saga shows its age in a couple of ways, most notably by the racial stereotyping so common in the early stories. Fu Manchu wasn't alone in his quest to destroy Western civilization. Pretty much every single Chinese (and most, if not all, other Asians) were in on the plot with him. The white race had to be on constant guard or the "Yellow Peril" would overwhelm them. Though Rohmer lightened up considerably in later novels, his early work can be a very in-your-face example of how prevalent and acceptable racism was in Western society at that time.

But, if a reader places these attitudes in historical context and accepts the stories for what they are, then they are still exciting and entertaining adventure yarns. Rohmer was a great writer, able to generate equal doses of excitement, suspense and horror as he rapidly unfolds the plot.

The first series of Fu Manchu stories was serialized in the British magazine *The Story-Teller* beginning in October 1912. *Collier* magazine began running it for American readers the next spring. Rohmer used a Holmes/Watson approach for the heroes. The narrator is Dr. Petrie, who is recruited by his old friend Nayland Smith to assist in the battle against Fu Manchu. In these early stories, Fu is an assassin for a secret society called the Si-Fan. He's in England knocking off specific people, either as part of a plot to subtly weaken Western governments or because they might know a little too much about the Si-Fan. Right off the bat, we get an eerie sequence in which a rare poisonous centipede, drawn to its target by an equally rare scented oil, kills Fu Manchu's first target and nearly gets Smith. Smith and Petrie follow up clues to an opium den, where they narrowly avoid the first of many death traps.

Most of the rest of the stories involve Smith and Petrie, helped by Inspector Weymouth of Scotland Yard, hurrying from one potential victim to the next, doing what they could to foil various bizarre assassination attempts. They also receive surreptitious help from Karamaneh, a slave girl belonging to the Si-Fan who has fallen in love with Dr. Petrie. It's love at first sight for the girl — Smith explains this is "characteristically Oriental"— but Petrie soon grows fond of her as well.

A particularly gruesome death trap, involving fast growing fungi spores that drive men mad before suffocating them, takes out several Scotland yard bobbies, but the main protagonists manage to stay alive. Finally, they catch Fu Manchu. But in the meantime, Fu has used a peculiar poison to turn Weymouth into a raving lunatic. He agrees to administer the cure and does so, but uses that action to generate an opportunity to escape. The book ends with Smith leaving England in pursuit of his nemesis.

The stories were extremely popular and soon compiled into a novel, titled by American publishers *The Insidious Dr. Fu-Manchu*. The sequel began a run in *Collier* in 1914 and appeared in book form as *The Return of Dr. Fu Manchu* in 1916. As with the first book, its origin as a serial makes it very episodic, but each episode is great fun. Both Fu Manchu and Smith are back in England. This time, Fu's assassination attempts involve cats with poisoned claws, a snake hidden in a walking stick, and a small, enormously strong primate that is never clearly seen.

The climax revolves what must almost unquestionably be the single creepiest death trap ever — a compartmentalized cage that forces you to watch while you are consumed a portion at a time by starving rats. With the help of Karamaneh, Smith and Petrie escape. Fu Manchu is apparently killed, by his body isn't recovered.

Later Fu Manchu stories followed the same pattern, with Rohmer sometimes waiting years before returning to write more of the master villain's adventures. Fu becomes the head of the Si-Fan, but his daughter, Fah lo Suee, turns up as a supporting character and spends a lot of her time trying to do him in and take over the secret society. The last book, *Emperor Fu Manchu*, was published in 1959, the same year Arthur S. Ward died. In this entry, Fu Manchu is no longer a straight-out villain—he's now determined to save China from Communism and reestablish the old Imperial government. He uses the corpses of Burmese assassins brought back to a zombie-like existence as one of his main weapons. It's no wonder the Devil Doctor was always more memorable than the capable but relatively average Denis Nayland Smith.

Fu Manchu attempted to conquer Western airwaves on several different occasions during the Golden Age of Radio. The first time was on a show called *The Collier Hour*, an hour-long program that would dramatize several stories from *Colliers* during each episode. Between May 1929 and May 1931, *The Collier Hour* did a trio of twelve-part adaptations of Rohmer's stories. Arthur Hughes starred as the Devil Doctor, but none of these episodes survive today. How faithful they were to the original or how effective they were in a new medium is now lost to the ages.

John C. Daly took over the role of Fu Manchu in 1932–33 for a half-hour series on CBS, with Charles Warburton as Nayland Smith. Harold Huber later replaced Daly as Fu. Once again, no episodes are known to survive, though the first broadcast was an adaptation of "The Zayat Kiss," the very first Fu Manchu story. It's probably safe to assume that all or most of the other episodes also drew directly from the original stories. According to radio historian Martin Grams, Jr., the cast wore full costumes while recording the show in front of an audience. Grams also notes that the director, G. Fred Ibbett, was known for making sure the sound effects were realistic.* In all likelihood, the show was a lot of fun.

It wasn't until 1939 that someone finally produced a Fu Manchu series that survives today. *The Shadow of Fu Manchu* was a syndicated fifteen-minute serial that starred Ted Osborne as Fu Manchu. Hanley Stafford was Nayland Smith and Gale Gordon, best known for his excellent work in comedic parts on both radio and television, was Dr. Petrie.

---

*Grams, *"In the Shadow of Fu Manchu,"* 2.

Forty of the one hundred-fifty-six episodes produced survive, but old-time radio fans are fortunate in that thirty-nine of these make up one complete storyline. The last remaining episode is a random selection from much later in the series. There are rumors that additional episodes from later in the series may exist somewhere, though none of these form complete storylines.

The surviving storyline is an extremely faithful adaptation of the first two novels. The episodic nature of the novels made them near perfect for a radio serial, providing built-in cliffhangers as Smith and Petrie raced around England dodging death traps and foiling murder plots. In fact, the radio show matches the source material perhaps more faithfully than any other show analyzed in this book. The protagonists face the exact same dangers while reciting dialogue often taken verbatim from the original prose. In the original, Nayland Smith was always explaining his deductions or identifying Fu's latest nasty animal or insect. This also transferred nicely to radio, allowing the characters to believably use dialogue to pass information on to the audience. There are a few instances in which a character would be describing what he saw for no good reason other than to let the audience know, but these were rare. Overall, the show worked for the exact same reason Rohmer's books work — it wrapped a feeling of spine-chilling menace around a sense of adventure.

All this was supported by good production values and acting. For the first few episodes, Osborne's supposed Chinese accent is a bit hard to understand, but someone apparently noticed this and his line readings soon became much clearer. Stafford and Gordon have a nice rapport as Smith and Petrie, while actress Paula Winslowe manages to generate empathy as Karameneh. Edmund O'Brien played Inspector Weymouth and spits out an extremely chilling laugh during the sequence in which Fu Manchu has driven him insane.

Excellent sound effects are a vital component to the serial. A lot of unusual sounds, representing everything from a coughing ape to muffled drums to a horde of rats, are needed at different times. The sounds used are all good — they are appropriately unearthly when they needed to be and added to the feeling of danger necessary to make the story viable.

Fu Manchu never did manage to overthrow Western civilization. Instead, he became a part of its cultural history. It would probably annoy him to know this, but there's nothing he could do about it now — except maybe drop one or more of us into a cage full of poisonous fungi or starving rats. But *The Shadow of Fu Manchu* is a great show and it's well worth the risk of inviting the Devil Doctor's wrath for an opportunity to listen to it.

Fu Manchu on radio:

NBC Blue: 1929–31 (serial: heard as part of *Collier Hour*)
Fu Manchu: Arthur Hughes

CBS: 9/26/32–4/24/33
Fu Manchu: John C. Daly, Harold Huber

Syndicated: 1939–1940
Fu Manchu: Ted Osborne

First prose appearance: "The Zayat Kiss" (1912), by Arthur Sarsfield Ward (writing as Sax Rohmer)

Molle Mystery Theater

The host of *The Molle Mystery Theater* was "criminologist Geoffrey Barnes," a connoisseur of mystery and detective stories. Each week he would briefly introduce the story we were about to hear, reminding us along the way that *Mystery Theater* "presents the best in mystery and detective fiction." Ironically, the actor playing Barnes, Bernard Lenrow, actually was such a connoisseur in real life. It was Lenrow who picked the stories that were dramatized on *Mystery Theater*, consistently demonstrating in his selections that he was not just well-read, but also had extremely good taste. One assumes he didn't just play himself as host because "criminologist" sounds better in that context than "actor."

The Molle Mystery Theater (sponsored by Molle Shave Cream — hence the name) ran as a half-hour show on NBC beginning in 1943. It presented a fair number of stories original to radio, but also depended heavily on adaptations of both classic and modern mystery short stories to fill up its schedule. The show concentrated on stories that featured some sort of twist, shock or surprise at the end. Other than this, the tales chosen for adaptation jumped from one end of the mystery genre to the other. There were traditional whodunits, such as "Fifty Candles," based on a story by Charlie Chan's creator Earl Derr Biggers. The series delved into hard-boiled territory with stories by Raymond Chandler and Dashiell Hammett. Chandler's story "Spanish Blood," re-titled "Murder in City Hall" for the radio show, was popular enough to be repeated twice.

Other stories had a supernatural twist to it. Robert Louis Stevenson's "The Bottle Imp" follows a Hawaiian native named Keawe as he buys a strange glass bottle for fifty dollars. The bottle supposedly contains a demonic imp capable of granting wishes. The catch is he must sell the bottle for less than he bought it before he dies, or he will be condemned to spend eternity in hell.

Keawe wishes for his dream house in Hawaii and gets it, though he is appalled by the method through which it comes to him. He sells the bottle and later falls in love. But circumstances threaten his happiness, so he must seek the bottle again to get another wish. By now, though, it has changed hands several times and is selling for just one penny, apparently making it impossible to sell again if he does buy it. By the time the story reaches its climax, there have been a few more good twists. There's also a strong moral backbone to the tale in the form of characters willing to accept eternal damnation to save a loved one.

The radio play modernized the story and moved it to New York City. To fit the eventful story into a half-hour time slot, the action was simplified — the cost of the bottle is already down to three cents when the story opens and the protagonist is already married. The most significant change is the condition of the curse that comes with buying the bottle. Now it must be sold at a loss within a fortnight, or the owner will go insane.

This is actually an understandable change to make for a radio drama, giving the curse a sense of urgency that works quite well within the confines of the time slot. The original story depended on interactions between the characters (most significantly, on Keawe falling in love) to build tension. In the radio play, with its streamlined plot, there isn't time for this. Instead, the modified curse is used to more directly drive the events of the story along. The end result is very good, though the absence of the 19th century South Seas setting and the Hawaiian characters does take away some of the story's unique ambiance.

Most adaptations on *Mystery Theater* were more faithful to their sources. Agatha Christie wrote both a short story version and a stage play of "Witness for the Prosecution," turning out a story that was tailor-made for radio. Most of the action in the story is dialogue-driven, as the protagonist (the lawyer defending a murder suspect) either interviews people or cross-examines witnesses during the trial.

As originally written, "Witness for the Prosecution" has a wonderful twist at the end, then adds yet another even better twist on top of that. The radio play, despite Americanizing the setting and characters, retains all this faithfully, keeping the double surprise at the end intact. There is one additional twist near the end original to the radio play, most likely put there to satisfy the network censors. (What would have dissatisfied them cannot be discussed here without spoiling the ending.) But this was skillfully added and didn't detract from the impact of the finale at all. Christie's yarn is just as good on radio as it is in print or on stage.

Robert Bloch's classic horror story "Yours Truly, Jack the Ripper" is about a man named Sir Guy Hollis who is convinced that Jack the Ripper still lives, even though (at the time the story is set) nearly sixty years had passed since the Whitechapel murders. That would mean the Ripper must be an old man, but Sir Guy is convinced that the murderer is nevertheless still young — that his (or her) brutal murders are a sacrifice to the dark gods as payment for immortality. Sir Guy credits the Ripper with nearly a hundred more murders in the decades since his London killing spree.

This story was originally published in 1943 in *Weird Tales*, a pulp magazine that specialized in horror and fantasy. Thus, most readers are expecting Sir Guy's theory to be proven true. Robert Bloch, perhaps the best horror writer of the 20th century, manages to give us an absolutely wonderful shock at the end despite our expectations. "Yours Truly, Jack the Ripper" is superbly atmospheric and terrifying.

The radio play is an almost word-for-word transfer of the prose, working nearly as well on the air as it did in print. But here the faithfulness of the adaptation brought an odd problem with it — the staggering finale is reached with a good five minutes of airtime left to fill. An inevitably anticlimatic epilogue to the story was added, filling up the rest of the time slot and probably satisfying the network censors (who would have once again had reason to object to the original ending as it stood). It's one of *Mystery Theater*'s finest episodes, but only if you turn it off at the right moment.

Other authors used on *The Molle Mystery Theater* included Aldous Huxley, Somerset Maugham, Edgar Allan Poe, and Cornell Woolrich. In 1948, the show gained a new sponsor (Sterling Drugs) and a new format. Gone were the adaptations of short stories; in their place were original stories featuring Inspector Hearthstone, an "implacable manhunter" working for the London Police. When Hearthstone was spun off into his own series, *Mystery Theater* brought us the adventures of Los Angeles homicide detective Mark Sabre. Both these new characters were okay, but *Mystery Theater* never regained the quality it once had. Going up against writers like Chandler, Poe and Bloch, poor Hearthstone and Sabre never stood a chance.

The Molle Mystery Theater provided five years of good radio drama, with a fair number of episodes surviving today. It presents us with a prime example of just how well matched the short story was with the half-hour radio anthology show. All that's required to get started is picking the right stories to tell. Bernard Lenrow certainly picked well; whatever persona he chose to assume as the show's host, he really did have undeniably good taste.

Molle Mystery Theater:
NBC: 7/7/43–6/25/48
Host: Bernard Lenrow

Part II

Adventure

Tarzan

Edgar Rice Burroughs found success as a pulp writer in 1912, when his classic science fiction novel *Under the Moons of Mars* was serialized in *All-Story* magazine. In that novel, which was eventually followed by ten sequels, Burroughs had used Mars to create the perfect fantasy world, believably mixing together airships and super-scientific devices with monsters, sword fights and beautiful princesses in need of rescue. He demonstrated himself to be a master of exciting prose and tense narrative pacing.

But it was later that same year that Burroughs created his most famous character. This particular hero would remain on Earth for his entire career, but the world he inhabited was no less of a creation of fantasy than Burroughs's version of Mars. Tarzan of the Apes would roam across much of Africa, encountering many more lost civilizations than one would have reasonably suspected could exist. He fought evil humans, lions, panthers, apes and the occasional dinosaur. He was captured quite often, but always managed to escape. He left Africa a few times, accompanying an expedition to the savage underground continent of Pellucidor and spending part of World War II in Asia stalking Japanese soldiers. But he always returned to his jungle home and to Jane, his beloved but somewhat neglected wife.

The idea of a man being raised by animals was hardly new, going back at least as far as the myth of Romulus and Remus. Rudyard Kipling had given us Mowgli, the boy raised by wolves, just a few decades before Tarzan. But Tarzan struck a chord, becoming (along with Superman and Sherlock Holmes) a character who is instantly recognizable by every member of Western civilization and by a fair percentage of the rest of the world. One is tempted to theorize about all sorts of psychological or sociological reasons for this, but the main reason is that Tarzan is really, really cool. He's the ultimate in wish-fulfillment, living exactly the life he wants to and always acting competently and without fear in any situation.

Tarzan of the Apes was published in its entirety in the October 1912 issue of *All-Story*. The tale begins with Lord and Lady Greystoke aboard ship, en route to one of Britain's African colonies. Before they reach their destination, the crew mutinies against the ship's sadistic captain and the Greystokes are marooned on a remote section of the African coast. They are left tools and weapons, though, and they manage to build a cabin and survive for about a year. Their son is born in that cabin.

But Lady Greystoke dies after childbirth and her husband is killed soon after by one of the large, savage apes that inhabit the area. Their infant son survives when he is "adopted" by Kala, a she-ape whose own son had recently been killed. She names the boy Tarzan, which means "White Skin" in the apes' primitive language.

What follows is an example of perfect storytelling, as Burroughs creates a coherent life style for a nonexistent species of carnivorous ape and describes how Tarzan survives and ultimately thrives as a member of the tribe. He becomes incredibly strong and agile, able to hold his own in a fight with his fellow "apes" and eventually becomes leader of the tribe.

Burroughs needed to provide young Tarzan with at least a little bit of education and comes up with a brilliant solution to this problem. Tarzan eventually discovers his parents' cabin. He finds a hunting knife and soon figures out how useful it is in a fight. More importantly, though, he finds books, including a children's alphabet book and a large dictionary. Over the years, he laboriously deduces the meanings of the letters, teaching himself to read and write English even though he has never heard the language spoken. Eventually, a tribe of cannibals migrates into the area. Observing them (and frequently stealing from them), he learns to use a bow and arrow.

When Tarzan is a young adult, a group of Americans is stranded at the same spot on which his parents were marooned. The group includes the beautiful Jane Porter, with whom Tarzan quickly falls in love. He watches over the group, keeping them safe. He often leaves them helpful notes, but they fail to equate the jungle man who pops out of the foliage with whomever is leaving the notes. After all, the jungle man doesn't speak English.

After a number of adventures, Tarzan rescues a French naval officer named d'Arnot from the cannibals. d'Arnot teaches Tarzan French and English and the two travel to civilization together to find Jane. The book ends, though, with Tarzan learning that Jane has already promised herself in marriage to someone else. True love wins out in the 1913 sequel, *The Return of Tarzan*. After numerous adventures and Tarzan's first encounter with a lost civilization, he and Jane are finally free to marry.

Burroughs would return to the jungle lord again and again throughout his career as a writer, eventually turning out a total of twenty-four Tarzan books. He wanted to kill poor Jane off early in the series in order to leave Tarzan free to roam the jungle, but magazine and book editors forbade this. Instead, Tarzan became the world's most inattentive husband, wandering around having adventures for months at a time, while Jane, with apparently infinite patience, waited for him at their bungalow.

Many of the later novels followed the same formula. Tarzan would stumble across a lost civilization. Often, he'd be held prisoner for a time, giving him a chance to learn the local language and gather background information about his captors. Then he'd get involved in overthrowing a despotic ruler, saving a victim about to be sacrificed, or just trying to escape violent death in general.

None of the later Tarzan novels have the archetypal feel of the first, but all are entertaining adventure stories. Despite the formula, each book has its own ambiance. The various civilizations the ape man encounters are varied and interesting — Burroughs had a talent for building make-believe societies, with each having its own consistent internal logic.

He encountered the denizens of Opar, a remnant of Atlantis, on several occasions. In Opar, the women are beautiful but the men have devolved into little more than apes. In *Tarzan, Lord of the Jungle*, he stumbles across the descendents of Crusaders who had gotten badly lost while marching to the Holy Land. In *Tarzan and the Lost Empire*, he's captured by one of two warring cities that are left over from the collapse of the Roman Empire. Here, Tarzan is tossed into an arena to fight in gladiatorial combat.

Through all of this, Tarzan uses his intelligence, courage and enormous fighting skills to come out on top. Often, there is a secondary hero — an explorer or safari member — who is free to fall in love with whatever princess/lost heiress/slave girl is in need of rescuing.

Burroughs was an early pioneer of modern merchandising and soon there were numerous Tarzan movies and an excellent comic strip initially drawn by Hal Foster. It wasn't surprising that Burroughs would take advantage of radio as well to promote the ape man and turn a little more profit.

Tarzan first came to radio in 1932 as a syndicated fifteen-minute daily serial. In general terms, the serial was faithful to the original novel, but gets off to an even quicker start. It opens with the Greystokes already marooned. A few episodes later, after they are killed and their baby is adopted by Kala, the serial skips over Tarzan's childhood completely. We jump almost straight to the arrival of Jane Porter and her party.

It's actually understandable that writers for a medium that depends heavily on dialogue wanted to quickly get to the part of the story involving verbal interaction between characters. The trouble with the rushed approach is that it sometimes led to awkward plot holes. For instance, the adult Tarzan is using a bow and arrow. When he sees Jane and the others, the third-person narrator tells us he is "studying the first of his fellow man he has ever seen."

This begs the question of where he got his bow. A few episodes later, the existence of the cannibal tribe is suddenly revealed, explaining Tarzan's bow but discrediting the statement that he had never before seen another human being. One gets the impression that the writers were making up their version of the story as they went, using the novel for a general guide but not worrying quite enough about the details.

Despite a few instances of sloppy story construction, the serial is good. The first 77 of the 286 episodes produced still exist and tell a fun, fast-moving story. The uncredited narrator does a fine job as he excitedly gives us blow-by-blow descriptions of Tarzan's frequent battles against humans, apes, lions and pythons. Until Tarzan has a chance to learn English, the narrator also lets us know what the ape man is thinking. When other characters show up in the jungle, the serial uses a narrative technique that Burroughs effectively utilized in his novels — shifting the point of view from one scene to another at cliffhanger moments in order to build up suspense. The sound effects accompanying all this are richly atmospheric.

A bit of nepotism may have been at work when the main parts were cast. Jane is played by Burroughs' daughter Joan. Her husband, Jack Pierce, plays Tarzan. But both were pretty good in their roles. In the serial, it's Jane who teaches Tarzan English and Pierce has the ape man swiftly but logically improves his language skills in stages over several episodes. When he is able to communicate, he sounds appropriately confident and authoritative.

At the end of the last surviving episode, Tarzan, Jane and several other characters are still in the jungle, dodging both cannibals and pirates. The remaining episodes seem to have covered the events of the first two novels, since actors are credited with having played characters from *The*

Return of Tarzan. But somewhere along the line, Burroughs became dissatisfied with the show and production ceased.

In 1934, with Burroughs exerting more creative control, a thirty-nine part serial titled *Tarzan and the Diamonds of Ashur* was produced. Carlton KaDell effectively portrayed an intelligent but fearless Tarzan. The story, which Burroughs reused for his 1938 novel *Tarzan and the Forbidden City*, finds Tarzan and his friend Paul d'Arnot escorting an expedition looking for a missing explorer. The explorer is said to have found the lost city of Ashur, which is reputed to be the location of the priceless Father of Diamonds. A rival expedition, interested only in the diamond, is also looking for Ashur.

This made for a large cast of supporting characters, something that radio drama usually shied away from to avoid confusing the audience. But both this serial and its 1936 follow-up, *Tarzan and the Fires of Tohr*, use a neat trick that allows us to keep track of everyone. The various characters represented a polyglot of nationalities and each had a strong accent. The individual French, German, Swedish, Chinese, and Irish accents identified each character for us, so we never lose track of who is who.

Multiple characters allow the serials to frequently use the shifting point-of-view technique to generate suspense. The occasional deaths of a few of the supporting characters, including sympathetic ones, also help in this regard.

Both serials are extremely well-plotted and represent Tarzan's finest hour on radio. Burroughs's input into the productions kept Tarzan faithful to his print counterpart and presented us with interesting and internally consistent lost cities. The only weak point is an unavoidable one for a radio series: the ruling casts of both Ashur and Tohr all just happen to speak English. But justifications (albeit slim ones) for this are provided in the stories, so this is easy to forgive.

Once again, a third-person narrator is used to describe much of the action, including Tarzan's hand-to-hand fights with everything from lions to a dinosaur. The overall plots grow quite complex, with the action sequences interwoven with political intrigue, human sacrifice, treachery and characters with hidden motives. These stories are carried coherently through thirty-nine episodes each and come to satisfying conclusions. They are models of precise storytelling and remain a joy to hear today.

But Tarzan left the airwaves at the conclusion of *The Fires of Tohr* and didn't return for fourteen years. In 1950, a half-hour syndicated show, with each episode a self-contained story, was produced. In 1952, these were broadcast again on CBS.

Tarzan is believably played by Lamont Johnson, though he isn't as authoritative in the role as Carlton KaDell had been in the 1930s. The stories cover everything from the ape man being shanghaied by pirates in "The Pirates of Cape Bandeira" to his having to fight a genetically engineered monster in "Tarzan and the Lypagor." Ivory smugglers and slave traders were pretty common. One episode, "The Arena of Death," adapted part of Burroughs' 1932 novel *Tarzan and the City of Gold* into a self-contained story.

It's all perfectly satisfying with solid plots and strong production values. But a Tarzan fan can find himself spoiled by the two mid–1930s serials, with their convoluted plots and intricately described lost civilizations. It is within adventures such as these that the Lord of the Jungle really belongs.

Tarzan on radio:
Syndicated: 1932–34 (serial)
Tarzan: James Pierce

Syndicated: 1934 & 1936 (two 39-part serials)
Tarzan: Carlton KaDell

Syndicated: 1950–51
Tarzan: Lamont Johnson

First prose appearance: *Tarzan of the Apes* (1912),
by Edgar Rice Burroughs

Escape

Escape was never a huge commercial success. Airing on CBS from 1947 to 1954, it jumped back and forth between a total of eighteen time slots. It almost never had a sponsor and it often disappeared from the network's schedule for months before returning. It seems as if the network executives, whenever they had a spare half-hour of airtime to fill, would just casually toss *Escape* in that direction.

But if this author was forced to pick one show from radio's Golden Age as the single best ever produced, it would be *Escape*. Making use of the best directors, writers, sound effects men and actors in the medium, the show presents us with breathtakingly good stories. *Escape* concentrated on stories of high-adventure. Most episodes were adaptations of short stories, with an occasional novel thrown in. (A few original scripts were produced as well.) Rudyard Kipling, Poe, H.G. Wells, Joseph Conrad, and Stephen Crane were among the more famous authors used. Less famous but still excellent stories by writers such as Roald Dahl or James Warner Bellah made for equally enthralling radio. *Escape* turned to legend a few times as well, recounting the adventures of both Robin Hood and Sinbad.

When the show first aired, William N. Robson was the producer-director. Robson was one of CBS's most talented house directors, having done excellent work in past years on shows such as the *Columbia Workshop* and the wartime anthology series *The Man Behind the Gun*. He was known as an authoritarian — if he wanted something done a certain way, then you'd by golly better do it that way. But the quality of his work during his long career indicates pretty clearly that his way was darn good.

In 1948, Norman Macdonnell took over the show. Macdonnell also headed up *The Adventure of Philip Marlowe* and later would run *Gunsmoke*— two more of the best radio shows ever. Whether it was Robson or Macdonnell in charge, *Escape* was in good hands.

These men were backed up by talented writers such as Les Crutchfield, John and Gwen Bagli, Gil Doud, and Kathleen Hite. Some of the busiest and best character actors in radio appeared regularly on the show, including William Conrad, Paul Frees, Parley Baer, Vic Perrin and John Dehner. By the late 1940s, these cast and crew members had many thousands of hours of experience in radio storytelling between them. In nearly every episode, their talents all meshed together perfectly.

Rudyard Kipling's "The Man Who Would Be King" was used on the premier episode. In this classic story of conquest, friendship and hubris, we follow along with a pair of 19th century mercenaries who have decided to set themselves up as kings of a remote country located near Afghanistan. A week later, the story was "Operation Fleur-de-Lis," about an OSS agent organizing a Resistance cell in occupied France. Jack Webb played the lead role in this one, which was presented in a matter-of-fact, almost emotionless style similar to what Webb would eventually use on *Dragnet*. It was a style that gave the denouement, involving the execution of a traitor, a lot of emotional impact.

These first two stories shared the common theme of high adventure, but otherwise were very different in plot and style. This was the key to *Escape's* artistic success: the tone for each individual episode was tailored to its specific plot. "Operation Fleur-de-Lis" emphasizes the emotional detachment a soldier must maintain to perform his often ruthless duty. "Command" and "Wild Jack Rhett" were intelligent Westerns with excellent characterizations. "Blood Bath" was a tale of betrayal and survival set in the South American jungle, with piranhas, vampire bats and pythons proving less dangerous than man's greed. "The Vanishing Lady" is heavy with melodrama, while "A Tooth for Paul Revere" is whimsical and "A Shipment of Mute Fate" is awash in pure dread. "Plunder of the Sun" is one of many tales dealing with a search for hidden treasure. Finales were happy or sad, straightforward or ironic, depending on what was most appropriate that week. Because *Escape* was an anthology show with no continuing characters, listeners never knew whether a sympathetic character would still be alive at the end. Story was everything.

Escape knew how to use words and music to grab its audience right from the start. Most episodes opened with either William Conrad or Paul Frees, with their deep, distinctive voices, asking the questions "Tired of the everyday routine? Ever dream of a life of romantic adventure? Want to get away from it all? We offer you ... Escape!" Moussorgky's *Night on Bald Mountain* then swelled up, while Conrad or Frees hinted at the coming adventure. "You are seated around a green felt table with a dozen desperate men," we are told; or "You are trapped in the dank darkness of a ruined plantation house"; or "You have shipped aboard a South Seas schooner, with the ghost of its dead captain in command." It was an introduction designed to personalize each story. It might have sounded contrived, but avoided this simply because it was done so well.

The adaptations were extremely faithful to the source material, with the most common change being to make the protagonist a narrator if he wasn't already. This added to the sense of danger and immediacy within the story and gave whatever actor was playing the lead in a particular episode a chance to shine.

Richard Connell's powerful story "The Most Dangerous Game" is written in the third person. But it is told entirely from the point of view of Rainsford, the big game hunter who is himself hunted for sport by a madman. Thus, when it was adapted for *Escape* in October 1947, scriptwriter Irving Ravetch was able to convert Rainsford into the narrator without having to alter the plot or the flow of the action in any significant way. Paul Frees was excellent as Rainsford, bringing across both fear and determination in equal measures as he describes his flight through the jungle and his desperate attempts to outsmart his opponent. Hans Conried was equally good as the insane but intelligent General Zaroff. The net result was a believable hero, a scary villain, and an extremely exciting story.

"Three Skeleton Key," by George G. Toudouze, is one of the creepiest stories ever written. The setting is a remote lighthouse located on a small island off the coast of Africa. Three men, one of whom narrates the story, perform the usually uneventful duty of tending to the light. Then one day a derelict ship smashes into the island. Thousands of large, starving rats swarm ashore. The men lock up the lighthouse, but these are ship's rats, able to climb. Within minutes, the rats literally coat the outside of the place, trapping the men inside. If the rats gain entrance, the men will be stripped to the bone in minutes.

This is a story which, if you read it while alone at home, will literally have you checking under your bed for rats before you go to sleep that night. The radio adaptation, written by James Poe, was perhaps even creepier, so thick with claustrophobia and tension that it's amazing the sound is still able to drip out through the stereo speakers.

Most of the changes made to the story for radio were minor. The names of the narrator's companions, Itchoua and Le Gleo, are changed to the less tongue-twisting Louis and Auguste. The protagonist/narrator gives us a brief tour of the lighthouse before rats arrive, so we are able to understand the action later in the story. Otherwise, the events of the story unfold much as they do in the original prose. The ending is quite significantly changed, but in a way that allows the use of a specific sound to provide a satisfying resolution.

Sound effects man Cliff Thorsness won an award for his contribution to "Three Skeleton Key," crunching berry baskets and rubbing a wet cork on glass to simulate the squeaking of the hungry vermin. The story was first broadcast in 1949, but was so popular it was repeated several times. (A repeat on live radio was not a recording of the first broadcast, but rather a brand-new performance.) For a March 1950 repeat, Vincent Price stepped in as the protagonist and did a magnificent job. If *Escape* is the best radio show ever, that broadcast of "Three Skeleton Key" is almost inarguably its best single episode.

Another man versus animal story, "Leiningen vs. the Ants," was also good enough to warrant several repeats. The changes made to it provide yet another example of how well the creative staff of *Escape* understood radio drama.

The original story, by Carl Stephenson, starts with a visit by a government official to the title character's South American plantation. The official warns Leiningen of an approaching horde of ants, urges him to evacuate, then himself leaves. The rest of the story, told in the third person, recounts Leiningen's increasingly desperate efforts to fight off the ants.

On radio, the government official remains at the plantation after delivering his warning and thus provides first-person narration. Otherwise, the play (written by Robert Wright) follows Stephenson's story closely. Leiningen, arrogant but also brave and resourceful, uses a moat and a gasoline-filled ditch to attempt to divert the ants away from his land. Despite everything he does, the ants continue implacably forward.

Finally, the only hope for Leiningen and his men requires that someone run across ant-covered ground and open a dam's water valve in order to flood the plantation. Leiningen himself makes the attempt. At this point, when the plantation owner personally takes action rather than directing others, the official's narration fades and Leiningen tells the story directly.

Adding the official to the plot is what makes it work so well on radio. Had Leiningen narrated the entire story, his pride and arrogance would have overshadowed his other traits, making him too distasteful a person to work as the protagonist. Instead, we perceive him through someone else's eyes, giving us a more balanced view. This doesn't make him completely likeable, but it does make us root for him. The official's first-person narration thus serves the same purpose as the prose story's third-person narration. Of course, William Conrad's excellent performance as Leiningen, mixing hubris with courage and intelligence, reinforces all this.

Escape did take a few missteps, usually on the rare occasions when the writers tried to crunch an entire novel into their half-hour time slot. *Beau Geste* rushes through the plot so quickly it's likely to give its listeners nose bleeds. On the other hand, a two-part adaptation of George Stewart's science fiction novel *Earth Abides*, about a plague that wipes out most of mankind, is one of *Escape*'s best efforts.

Overall, though, the show is at its best when it sticks to short stories. A short length doesn't matter as long as the story is well-told. *Escape* certainly tells stories well, taking us to jungles, Western towns, alien planets, aboard derelict ships and down fog-shrouded streets. Wherever it takes us, we're sure to have fun when we get there.

Escape:
7/7/47–9/25/54
(with many gaps during which is was not on the air)
Voice of *Escape*: William Conrad & Paul Frees

Part III

Westerns

Hopalong Cassidy

By the time the 20th century rolled around, the mythology that defines the popular view of the American West had already been firmly established. Even while the historical West was being fought over and settled, the dime novels of the 19th century were introducing the public to stereotypes such as the laconic cowpoke, the shifty gambler and the fast draw. Dime novels were not concerned with the brutality and tragedy — nor even with not-uncommon instances of true nobility — that often typified the West. Instead, they distilled everything down to simple formulas involving clearly defined good guys and bad guys. Even the eventful and often fascinating lives of historical figures such as Buffalo Bill Cody and Kit Carson were set aside. Dime novels featuring the adventures of these men turned them into super action heroes as they killed enough outlaws and Indians to depopulate the West several times over. Legend trumped fact pretty much before anyone even had a chance to write the facts down.

During the Civil War and for a decade or two afterwards, westerns and frontier stories were the most popular genre among readers of dime novels. Eventually, the detective story overtook the western in sales, but cowboys and six guns never fell out of favor. By the 1900s, writers such as Owen Wister, Zane Grey, and Max Brand would begin producing westerns of real literary quality, but even then their works were based more on the myth than the reality.

One contemporary of Grey and Brand was Clarence Mulford. Mulford lived in Brooklyn, but that didn't stop his imagination from ranging westward and, in 1906, he began to write a series of short stories featuring an exuberant and likable young cowboy named Hopalong Cassidy.

Hopalong, so nicknamed because of a slight but permanent limp, could usually be found working at the Bar 20 ranch. Along with the other members of the Bar 20 crew, he rode and fought his way across the West in what eventually become a lengthy series of short stories and novels published between 1906 and 1941.

Hopalong is a fun character. Mulford describes him as "a combination of irresponsibility, humor, good nature, love of fighting, and nonchalance when face-to-face with danger. His most prominent attribute was that of always getting into trouble without any intention of doing so." When he rides into a Mexican town to visit an old girlfriend, for instance, he'll discover the now-chubby gal is married and has a very jealous, knife-wielding husband. Hoppy has to disarm the husband and face down a mob before making his exit.

Soon after that, Mulford tells us, "There was that affair in Red Hot Gulch, Colorado, where, under pressure, he had invested sundry pieces of lead in the persons of several obstreperous citizens and then had paced the zealous and excitable sheriff to the state line."

But it's all in good fun, something that Mulford emphasized with breezy prose like the above examples and with characters who seemed to be able to enjoy themselves even in the midst of a blazing gun battle. Mulford dropped his characters right down in the middle of the mythological West, where a man "must tolerate no restrictions of his natural rights, and he must not restrict; for the one would proclaim him a coward, the other a bully." It was a point of view that often resulted in drawn revolvers and a high body count, but Hoppy, Buck Peters, Red Conners, and the other men of the Bar 20 always came out on top.

Mulford's stories don't hold up as well today as do the best works of Zane Grey and Max Brand, but they're still entertaining. The original set of stories were collected and published in the book *Bar 20* (1907). Throughout the book, Hopalong ambles casually from one adventure to another, taking part in a deadly fight against some hands from a rival ranch who had killed a friend; helping run down some renegade Indians; taking time off from the ranch to prospect for gold and defend his claim against outlaws; returning to the Bar 20 in time to join in a large-scale battle between the ranch hands and a gang of rustlers; and finally participating in a shooting contest — so effectively showing off his skill with a six gun that he scares away a gunman who had been intending to do him in. Mulford's casual writing style ambles along in pleasant rhythm with his protagonist. His action sequences, often involving lengthy and detailed descriptions of gun battles, effectively punctuate the individual stories.

None of it had anything to do with the historical West, but there was no requirement for it to do so. Many writers over the last century have produced excellent fiction set in an historically accurate Old West, but

Mulford's enthusiastic storytelling worked because it was set in the fabled West that came to us from the dime novels.

Hopalong Cassidy waited until 1948 to come to radio and, as we've seen in several other instances, he did so via the movies. When producer Harry Sherman was filming *Hopalong Cassidy Enters* in 1934, he at first cast the tall and strong-featured actor William Boyd as a bad guy. But Sherman then made the best decision of his career when he opted instead to give Boyd the lead.

Boyd's heroic version of Hoppy was incredibly successful. In this incarnation, Hoppy no longer indulged in alcohol and tobacco. His speech patterns changed dramatically. Mulford's character spat out such lines as "I just kicked yore marshall out in th' street, an' I'll pay yu th' next call. If yu rambles in range of my guns yu'll shore get in th' way of a slug." But the movie Hoppy used proper grammar and pronunciation. He didn't hesitate to use a gun if forced to, but he didn't leave anywhere near as thick a trail of corpses behind him as did the original. He was polite and respectful to women, but never did anything more than once kiss one of them on the cheek (and even this was considered by many fans to have been going too far). If Mulford had set his stories inside a myth, the movies were in turn set within a mythological version of that myth. The movie Hopalong lived in the same version of the Old West as did Roy Rogers, Gene Autry and the Lone Ranger.

Mulford once referred to the movie Hopalong as "an absolutely ludicrous character," but he was wrong.* Hopalong Cassidy had, in fact, become a role model for his growing legion of young fans. William Boyd recognized this and followed suit in his own personal life. Prior to 1934, he had been something of a mess, drinking and cheating his way through four marriages. After he began to play Hoppy, he cleaned up his own act. He quit drinking and his fifth marriage lasted for the rest of his life.

It is perhaps this sincerity — a real recognition of his responsibility to others — that helped make him so appealing as Hopalong. But whatever the reason, Hoppy's popularity was enormous. The first movie was released in 1935. By the end of the 1940s, there had been sixty-five more. Each of the films, rarely running more than sixty-five minutes, involved Hoppy and a couple of his Bar 20 companions foiling the machinations of yet another gang of outlaws, smugglers, or killers. One wonders when they had time to do any actual ranching, but its best not to dwell on such

---

*Sampson, 190.

things. Children packing the theaters on Saturday afternoon never questioned it and they certainly never got tired of it.

During the 1940s, William Boyd acquired the rights to the Hoppy films. In 1948, he teamed up with producers Walter and Shirley Wright to record episodes for a half-hour syndicated radio series. In the meantime, he sold the rights to the films to the fledgling medium of television and produced an additional fifty-two half-hour TV episodes.

The result, aside from making Boyd a multimillionaire, was a pop culture sensation. Hopalong Cassidy had never been more popular. When Boyd appeared in character at a Brooklyn department store, 85,000 people showed up to see him. When the first Hopalong Cassidy lunch box was made in 1950, sales for Aladdin Industries (the company that made the box) jumped from 50,000 units a year to 600,000.

Amidst all this frenzy, the radio show ran for two years in syndication and then two more years on network radio — first on Mutual, then on CBS. Hopalong rode onto the airways without missing a step. The show, like the movies, was formulaic but still enormous fun, depending largely on Boyd's steady and occasionally boisterous portrayal of Hopalong to carry things along. Production values were high and if the writing wasn't exceptional, it was solid.

The one regular supporting character had also been imported from the movies. Comic sidekick California Carlson, played by Andy Clyde, pretty much tailed after Hoppy wherever he went. In terms of suspending disbelief, comic relief characters often run into the problem of being pretty useless in any practical sense. One can't help but wonder exactly why the hero lets him tag along. But California was competent enough (if only barely) to be dependable in tight situations, so it was believable (if only barely) that Hoppy was willing to tolerate him as a partner. More importantly, the two men were friends. The idea that a brave and resourceful man keeps his less-effective partner around for the sake of friendship alone is appealing and perfectly in character for Boyd's version of Cassidy. Besides, California was someone Hoppy could talk to and, through this conversation, pass expository information along to the audience.

Many episodes played on an aspect of Hopalong that had been used effectively in a number of the movies — he was a skilled detective as well as a cowboy. Individual stories were often western-mystery hybrids, giving the show a flavor all its own. The premier episode on the Mutual network in 1950 is a good example of this. Hoppy and California receive word that an old friend, Kit Kelly, had been working a rich gold mine and had managed to thus far keep the mine's location a secret. But Kit's partner had been murdered and Kit himself was holed up at the mine, unable to safely leave.

Kit's wife Sally was living in a nearby town. The sheriff was missing and Sally suspected local gunman Luke Berry of killing her husband's partner. When Hoppy and California arrive in town, they witness Luke dying in a gun battle with the town doctor, Doc Seldon.

With Luke dead, Sally now feels it's safe to travel to the mine herself and bring her husband back to town. But Hoppy suspects something is up. Doing a little detective work, he discovers that Seldon and Berry had faked the gunfight. Berry was still alive (the missing sheriff took his place in his coffin) and the two crooks planned on using Sally as a judas goat to draw Kit out of hiding, kill him and jump his claim. Hoppy turns the tables on them by sending California to capture Berry, then tricking Seldon into a confession.

This was typical of Boyd's version of Hopalong, depending far more often on his brains rather than his guns to get the job done. Boyd's concern with the image he presented to his young fans caused him to tone down the violence on both the radio and TV shows, but good writing (as well as Boyd's sincere, straightforward portrayal of Hoppy) turned this restriction into a strength.

One can't help but wonder what might have happened if Mulford's version of Hopalong Cassidy had run across Boyd's version out on the open range. Chances are they would have ridden together for a day or two, but then eventually gotten on each other's nerves. They might very well have come to blows, but it would be difficult indeed to predict which of them would come out on top.

Hopalong Cassidy on radio:
Mutual: 1/1/50–9/24/50

CBS: 9/30/50–23/15/52
Hopalong: William Boyd

First prose appearance: *Bar 20* (1907), by Clarence Mulford

The Cisco Kid

The short stories of O. Henry are usually remembered for their twist endings. "The Ransom of Red Chief," for instance, involved a pair of kidnappers who snatch a child so ill-behaved and obnoxious that they end up paying the kid's dad to take him back. "The Gift of the Magi" was about a poor husband who sells his watch (a family heirloom) to buy a set of expensive combs for his wife as a Christmas gift. The wife, in the meantime, cuts her luxurious hair and sells it to buy a watch chain for her husband.

In 1907, O. Henry published "The Caballero's Way," a Western about a young outlaw named Goodall, more commonly known as the Cisco Kid. The Kid "had killed six men in more or less fair scrimmages, had murdered twice as many (mostly Mexicans), and had winged a larger number whom he modestly forbore to count."

In addition to his tendency to shoot people, Cisco has a reputation for being a *caballero*—a ladies' man—treating members of the fairer sex with "gentle words and consideration. He could not have spoken a harsh word to a woman." His true love is a beautiful Mexican girl named Tonia Perez. Cisco often hides out at Tonia's home near a small border settlement. But his love affair goes awry when a Texas Ranger named Lieutenant Sandridge arrives at the Perez home looking for Cisco.

"Never before had Tonia seen such a man. He seemed to be made of sunshine and blood-red tissue and clear weather." Sandridge was equally taken with the young girl and the two almost immediately begin plotting a way to ambush and kill Cisco. But the Kid is hiding nearby and overhears their plans.

His nature will not allow him to take direct revenge against Tonia. Instead, he employs a ruthless trick, forging a letter to Sandridge. The letter, ostensibly from Tonia, convinces the lawman that the Kid is planning on escaping the territory disguised in one of Tonia's dresses. This results in Sandridge mistakenly gunning down the poor girl, giving the Kid his revenge while still preserving his reputation as a *caballero*.

Written in Henry's typically affable prose, it's a good story, though not among the author's best. Certainly there was nothing about the character of the Cisco Kid that marked him as a potential hero. But hero he became. He reappeared first in a silent film in 1914, then eventually becoming the star of a series of B-movies produced in the 1930s and 1940s, played by Cesar Romero and Duncan Renaldo. By that time, Henry's original character had been pretty much tossed aside. The ruthless Caucasian killer had been replaced by a Mexican Robin Hood, riding across the American southwest in his endless quest to help the innocent. Why did they even bother calling him the Cisco Kid? The only apparent reason was that the name sounded cool.

When Cisco came to radio in 1942, he was played by Jackson Beck (the future Philo Vance). Beck is best remembered amongst old-time radio aficionados for his superb work as the announcer and narrator on *The Adventures of Superman*, but he could also do a wide range of accents. If his Spanish accent as Cisco falls a little short of sounding authentic, it was still a sincere effort. (Beck once stated that he "was careful not to be offensive."*) Perhaps most jarringly false thing about Cisco's dialogue involved the writing rather than the acting. If you made a drinking game out of the number of times Cisco used the word "hombre" in a sentence, you'd be dead of alcohol poisoning by the end of any one episode.

It was on radio that Cisco joined forces with Pancho, a fat and not-too-bright comedic sidekick, played by Louis Sorin. Pancho is pretty much the poster child for useless comic relief. Speaking in a voice almost identical to the voice Mel Blanc would later use for the cartoon character Speedy Gonzalez, Pancho nonsensically referred to himself in the third person, told bad jokes, obsessed about food and only rarely did something constructive. He also joined Cisco in saying "hombre" far too often.

Still, the same justification that applies to Hopalong Cassidy and California Carlson can be applied to Cisco and Pancho. The two are best friends, enjoying one of Pancho's purposely bad jokes at the end of each episode as they rode off to a new adventure. Pancho would tell the Kid about the robbery on the clothesline, where two clothespins held up a shirt. "Oh, Pancho!" was Cisco's inevitable rejoinder. "Oh, Ceesco!" replied Pancho. The show would fade out as the two men laughed uproariously.

*Nachman, 207.

It was corny, but it really did give the audience a sense that the two men were sincerely fond of one another.

The plots were relatively sound, though very formulaic. Cisco and Pancho were publicly known as outlaws (for reasons never given) and were often blamed for whatever crime had recently been committed whenever they arrived in a new town. They would have to elude a posse while tracking down the real killers, bank robbers, or smugglers. Along the way, Cisco would inevitably befriend a beautiful young woman, usually eliciting a breathless "Oh, Ceesco" from her by the end of the episode when he finally got around to kissing her.

The show ran on the Mutual network until early 1945. The Cisco Kid movies remained reasonably popular in the interim (with the character of Pancho jumping from radio into the films) and the Kid returned to radio in 1946 for a brief run on Mutual. In 1947, it became a syndicated show and remained on the air until 1956.

These later shows starred Jack Mather as Cisco and Harry Lang as Pancho. Mather and Lang both managed reasonably good accents. Mather played Cisco with a balanced mixture of authority and good humor. Pancho became at least a little bit useful, able to do his part in an occasional gunfight. (He still kept the annoying habit of referring to himself in the third person.) The scripts improved as well, depending less often on Cisco and Pancho being mistaken as outlaws. In fact, local sheriffs began to frequently show gratitude when they showed up in town, knowing they were there to help.

During the course of any one episode, Cisco would get into at least one fistfight and at least one gunfight, demonstrating his prowess in both forms of combat. When gunplay was unavoidable, Cisco would lift a trick from the Lone Ranger's playbook and shoot the gun out of his opponent's hand, rarely if ever using deadly force.

How Cisco and Pancho support themselves is never mentioned. They travel from place to place pretty much on a whim, involving themselves in whatever trouble they happen to stumble across. "We have no plans, senorita," Cisco explains to a lady in one episode. "We seldom make plans. We ride where and as the spirit moves."

In an episode from 1953, the spirit moved them to visit an old friend's ranch. But they found the ranch now being used by outlaws as a base. These bad men had recently ambushed and killed the sheriff and the deputy from the nearest town in order to rescue their leader, Chuck Madrone.

Madrone had murdered the owner of the ranch and now planned to ride into town to kill the owner's brother, Joe Daggitt, for testifying against him. Cisco and Pancho arrive in time to throw Madrone out of Daggitt's store, mistaking him for a mere bully. Soon afterwards, they learn of who Madrone really was. Madrone, in the meantime, has rounded up his gang and is returning to town.

Cisco recruits a few local men and positions them to defend a pass leading into town. As the locals and the outlaws exchange bullets, Cisco and Pancho climb above the gang and get the drop on them, shooting away their guns and forcing them to surrender. But Madrone has sneaked away and made it to town. Cisco gives chase, capturing the outlaw leader after a wild fist fight.

Cisco steals a kiss from Daggitt's daughter (earning him the typical "Oh, Cisco!"), then he and Pancho ride off to their next adventure, laughing at yet another of Pancho's abysmal jokes.

The Cisco Kid, especially in its later incarnation, was a fun show, well-crafted in terms of story and production values. Its primary appeal, though, came from the idea that two friends could have a good time riding across the Old West, righting wrongs and kissing pretty girls. It had nothing to do with the original prose story other than the name of the protagonist, but what the hey. It *was* a cool-sounding name.

The Cisco Kid on radio:

Mutual: 10/2/42–2/14/45
Cisco: Jackson Beck
Pancho: Louis Sorin

Mutual: 1946

Syndicated: 1947–1956
Cicso: Jack Mather
Pancho: Harry Lang

First prose appearance: "The Caballero's Way" (1907), by O. Henry

Part IV

Science Fiction

Buck Rogers

In 1926, publisher and editor Hugo Gernsback founded *Amazing Stories*, the first magazine dedicated solely to tales that had often been characterized as "scientific romances." Typified by the works of H.G. Wells and Jules Verne, these were the stories about the space travel, robots, death rays, time machines and all the other incredible inventions that the future seemed sure to give us.

Actually, the word science was often a misnomer when used to describe these stories. Outside of Jules Verne, few if any authors working within the genre really cared whether the fantastic plot elements they used might someday be possible. It didn't matter whether you could, in real life, build a steam-powered mechanical man, breathe on the surface of Mars, or find a dinosaur on a remote South American plateau. But you could do it in a work of fiction and make it sound really good. This illusion of scientific plausibility was an important part of maintaining dramatic viability within the genre. Besides, in a world where seemingly miraculous inventions like the telephone and the airplane were rapidly becoming common-place, building a robot or taking a trip to Mars didn't seem too far out.

Gernsback needed a standardized term for the genre. He briefly considered "scientifiction"—possibly the most annoying word ever—but fortunately settled on "science fiction." At first, he used a lot of reprints—stories by Wells, Verne, Burroughs and other well-established authors. Gradually, though, the supply of originals stories began to catch up with the demand. Thus, in 1928, the world was introduced to the hero who would eventually become known as Buck Rogers.

Philip Francis Nowlan's novelette *Armageddon 2419 A.D.* was printed in *Amazing Stories* in 1928. Its sequel, *The Airlords of Han*, was published the following year. Like most of what appeared in Gernsback's magazine, it was an adventure story driven along by its plot elements, eschewing in-depth characterizations in order to concentrate on the action and a lot of really nifty gadgetry.

The story begins in 1927, when a mining engineer named Anthony Rogers is trapped deep in a mine by a cave-in. A strange gas puts him in suspended animation and when he awakens, he discovers that 492 years have passed.

He finds no sign of civilization outside the now ancient mine and wanders around for several weeks before meeting someone. This turns out to be the beautiful Wilma Deering, who is jumping through the forest with the aid of an anti-gravity belt while blasting away at the men pursuing her with a pistol that fires explosive rockets.

Rogers, understandably, opts to help the pretty girl and saves her life. She accepts his story about suspended animation with remarkable aplomb, then provides him with information on the world of the 25th century.

America, it turns out, has been conquered by an Asian race known as the Hans. Using airships and disintegrator rays, the Hans had broken the back of American society. Now the Hans live in cities scattered about North America, while the surviving Americans live in the wilderness, gathering into groups known as "gangs." Wilma is a member of the Wyoming gang. The men pursuing her had been members of a rival gang that had been collaborating with the Hans.

She takes Rogers back to her gang and he soon becomes a part of that society. It quickly turns out that his knowledge of long forgotten military tactics can be used to help step up the fight against the Hans. Before long, Rogers becomes one of the leading military figures of the 25th century. From here, the book becomes a fairly straightforward war story, with Nowlan having fun inventing the tactics used by the two opposing sides based on their respective technologies.

The Hans, for instance, have control of the air. But their huge airships operate using "repellor rays" that literally lift them into the air and hold them up high enough to be out of the range of American weaponry. Rogers invents the tactic of firing rockets into the repellor rays and allowing the ray to carry the projectile up into the airships, destroying their engines and knocking them out of the sky. He later uses the rocket guns to reintroduce the concept of the artillery barrage. His experience in World War I has taught him that hand-to-hand combat is inevitable in battle, so he trains his troops in bayonet tactics.

The Americans have also learned to access another dimension and mine an element called inertron, which both defies gravity and provides a shield against Han disintegrator rays. Several gangs come up with different designs of inertron armor for their ground troops — the best one is probably a bell-shaped shell of the stuff, counter-weighted with another metal to keep it from simply floating away, that covers a soldier completely. He sees out through a periscope and operates a small rocket gun turret mounted on the top of the shell.

But the Hans react to the change in American tactics. They develop a convoy system for their airships that allows them to protect each other from ground attack. When the Americans begin flying inertron-sheathed rocket planes, the Hans begin playing their disintegrator rays around the enemy planes rather than right at them. This causes a vacuum as the air disintegrates, which in turn generates enough turbulence to crash the planes.

It's all great fun. It might not have anything to do with real science, but Nowlan was self-consistent within the rules he created. His action scenes are all done well; these include a ground battle against a traitorous gang, a commando raid on a Han city to steal information and a dogfight between a rocket plane flown by Rogers and a Han airship.

Nowlan's characterizations are very, very basic. Rogers is ridiculously casual about being thrust five centuries into the future. He and Wilma's inevitable romance is handled so perfunctorily that it could be dropped from the story entirely without anyone really noticing. But the main point of the story is to generate excitement through both the action and all the gee-whiz gadgetry to which both the good guys and the bad guys have access. And those writers responsible for bringing the premise to other media never forgot this.

Anthony Rogers's journey to radio did not involve a rocket plane or anti-gravity belt, but rather a side trip through the pages of a newspaper comic strip. Someone working for the John F. Dille newspaper syndicate took note of Nowlan's stories and thought the premise might work well as a daily comic. Nowlan was hired as writer and Dick Calkins was brought on as artist. But John Dille didn't think "Anthony Rogers" sounded quite right for a space opera hero. So Rogers was given the nickname Buck. And he's been Buck ever since, no matter what medium he appeared in.

The strip had a long, successful run. At first, it adapted the original prose stories, but once America was free again, Buck became a rocket ship pilot. Trips into outer space and to other planets (nearly all of which were inhabited) in our solar system became a normal part of Buck's life.

When Buck came to radio in 1932, he brought Wilma with him, along with several characters created for the strip. These included reoccurring villains Killer Kane and Ardala Valmar, but most important was the brilliant scientist Dr. Huer. Huer's role was stereotypical of brilliant scientists in many stories from the genre — he existed either to provide plot exposition or to invent something necessary to carry the story along. Often he did both at the same time. Did the writers need to explain to the audience just how Huer's new mechanical mole machine worked? Well then, Huer would explain it to Buck while the rest of us listened in. Then Buck, Wilma and Huer could get started with their underground exploration — with the various dangers and adventures that this would entail. It was an effective (if unoriginal, even in 1932) storytelling methodology.

During his time on radio, *Buck Rogers in the 25th Century* was marketed towards children and usually used the serial format. The original 1932–1936 show on CBS and a later run on Mutual were broadcast on weekday evenings, ending each fifteen-minute episode in a cliffhanger. Self-contained thirty-minute episodes aired on Saturday afternoons in 1940. 1946–47 saw a return to the weekday serial format, still broadcast on the Mutual network.

Over the years, Buck was played by Carl Frank, Curtis Arnall, Matt Crowley and John Larkin. Adele Ronson and Virginia Vass played Wilma and Edgar Stehli was Dr. Huer.

But though Buck survived everything from disintegrator rays to being marooned on desolate planetoids, he (like the heroes of so many radio serials) eventually fell victim to the all-too-common plague of lost recordings. Most of the surviving episodes come from the 1939 run and no complete storylines seem to survive. There is enough there, though, to allow us to come to some conclusions about the show.

Writer-director Jack Johnstone once admitted that he liked inventing super scientific gadgetry.* This is demonstrated even in the small sampling of episodes we have. The original rocket pistols and inertron belts are still there, but they are joined by Thermal Radiation Projectors, Flexo-Impervium metal, Electro-Hypno Mentalo-Phones, Sub-Cosmic Radio Units, Non-Recoil Energy Projectors and Molecular Expansion Beam Projectors. Many of these were invented by Dr. Huer, who managed to keep churning out new stuff despite spending so much time explaining to Buck exactly what it all did.

**Harmon*, 77.

In fact, it seems that the good doctor might have spent a little *too* much time explaining things. In several of the surviving episodes, he spends large chunks of time expositing on how a particular invention worked in far more detail than we needed to have in order to follow the story. Jack Johnstone was one of radio's great writers and directors, helming quality shows like The *Adventures of Superman* and *Yours Truly, Johnny Dollar*, but on Buck Rogers he would, from time to time, allow his enthusiasm for writing technobabble get the best of him.

Despite this, the show moved along at a nice pace and told some fun stories. In one story, Dr. Huer has invented the Gyro Cosmic Relativator, which would allow a rocket ship to accelerate instantly to its top speed. Buck and Wilma intend to take a ship equipped with the Relativator on a test flight. But Black Barney, a reformed space pirate, takes the ship up first to spare them the danger.

Unfortunately for Barney, the villainous Killer Kane has escaped from prison and sneaked aboard. Holding Barney at rocket pistol point, he forces the ex-pirate to land in the ruins of ancient Philadelphia. Meanwhile, Kane's lovely but evil partner Ardala has stolen a Psychic-Restriction Ray from Dr. Huer's lab. She meets Kane in the ruins of Philly and they use the ray to brainwash Barney into serving them. Barney then flies to the city of Omaha, where he cons the local leader out of some powerful weapons by claiming he's on Kane's trail. His haul of weaponry includes atomic space bombs — apparently in the 25th century, nuclear weapons are available for the asking.

In the meantime, Buck and Wilma are attempting to track the exhaust trail of Barney's ship. Will they succeed? We'll never know, since the rest of the storyline no longer exists. Well, we do know heroes always win. In this case, we just don't know how.

The radio show seemed to succeed in just the same way the original prose did. It concentrated on throwing incredible gadgetry at us, took enough time to explain how it all worked, then constructed an adventure story around this. Buck and Wilma are welcome to fall in love if they want and Dr. Huer can deliver yet another lecture on his newest invention, but the main reason we hang out with them at all is because they have those nifty anti-gravity belts.

Buck Rogers on radio:
CBS: 7/7/32–5/22/36 (serial)
Mutual: 4/5/39–7/31/39 (serial)

Mutual: 5/18/40–7/27/40
Mutual: 9/30/46–3/28/47 (serial)
Buck: Curtis Arnall, Matt Crowley, Carl Frank, John Larkin
First prose appearance: *Armageddon 2419 A.D* (1928),
by Philip Francis Nowlan

Dimension X and *X Minus One*

Amazing Stories demonstrated that science fiction specialty magazines were commercially viable and it wasn't long before many of the other seemingly countless publishing companies that existed in the 1920s jumped into the pool as well. The Clayton magazine chain gave S-F a try with *Astounding Stories of Super Science* beginning in 1930.

A few years later, the Clayton chain went bankrupt and several of their titles, including *Astounding*, were bought by Street & Smith, one of the more successful publishers of the era. Now edited by F. Orlin Tremaine, the magazine began to take a new editorial direction that would heavily influence science fiction and become a driving force in the maturation of the genre.

Tremaine wanted stories he categorized as "thought variants" — stories that would explore new and challenging ideas. Though Buck Rogers–like space operas were still printed, so were stories that featured more human characterizations and more realistic science. Many concepts that are now old-hat to modern science fiction fans — such as genetic engineering or alternate realities — were found within the pages of *Astounding* while they were still new.

When writer John Campbell took over as *Astounding*'s editor in 1938, the quality of the magazine improved even more. Campbell is one of the most influential personalities in modern science fiction. During his thirty-four years as editor, he discovered or provided guidance to many of the most important writers in the genre, including Isaac Asimov, L. Sprague de Camp, Clifford Simak, Lester del Ray, and Robert Heinlein.

Campbell would often work one-on-one with writers to help develop their ideas. He and Isaac Asimov, for instance, worked together to come up with the basic concept for Asimov's Foundation stories. These involve a group of scholars who can use complex mathematical formulae to predict the future in large-scale terms and thus hope to save humanity from an impending era of barbarism. Asimov excelled at this type of concept-driven storytelling and the Foundation series is perhaps his best work. So when NBC began to air a science fiction anthology show in 1950, turning to *Astounding* magazine for story ideas was the single best move the network could have made.

Dimension X was a very low budget affair. Using staff already under contract to the network, it managed to eek out weekly episodes for about one-sixth the amount of money that the average half-hour series would spend. But such is radio that the tiny budget was sufficient to take us far into the future and across the galaxy, confronting aliens, robots and time travelers.

A few of the stories were original scripts, but most of them had first appeared in *Astounding* or (occasionally) another magazine. In fact, the show included a plug for *Astounding* during the opening narration. "We went the adaptation route," remembered producer Van Woodward, "simply because that's where the best stories are."* Staff writers George Lefferts and Ernest Kinoy were both intelligent storytellers able to adapt a prose story to a new medium without unnecessary changes.

Concentrating on short stories allowed them to remain very faithful to the source material — the tales would fit nicely within the thirty minute time slot with little if any of the plot trimmed away. But the August 18, 1950 broadcast of "The Martian Chronicles," based on Ray Bradbury's classic novel, is extraordinary in how well it manages to condense the story into a single episode.

Bradbury's book is itself episodic, being made up of stories that were originally published separately. It begins with the first tragic encounters with Martians by Earth explorers, then moves on to the settlement of Mars by colonists after the Martians die out. This is followed by the destruction of civilization on Earth via nuclear war. Bradbury's remarkable prose, which often manages to sound both conversational and poetic at the same time, perfectly complements his equally remarkable imagination. The novel drips with a real understanding of human nature, both good and bad, and ultimately ends on a note of cautious hope.

Ernest Kinoy's adaptation cherry-picks key moments out of the novel

---

*Widner, 28.

and streamlines them together into a beautiful half-hour of radio that manages to convey all the same feelings with almost the same intensity as the original. It is this model of clear, concise storytelling that allowed *Dimension X* to present great stories without dumbing them down in terms of either plot or theme.

The show ran for fifty episodes (most of which still survive today). Nine more Bradbury stories were used, along with tales by Robert Heinlein, Jack Vance, Isaac Asimov and other established leaders in the genre. The selection of stories covered a lot of territory. Vance's "The Potters of Firsk" is about humans dealing with an alien culture that they don't really understand. H. Beam Piper's "Time and Time Again" is an unusual time travel story. Asimov's "Nightfall" is about a planet with multiple suns where nightfall only comes once every 2500 years. Heinlein's "Universe," is about life on a spaceship during a multigenerational journey.

"Adventures in time and space," the opening narration promises us each week, "told in future tense." With just a little bit of money and a lot of imagination, the creative staff of *Dimension X* regularly kept this promise.

Many of the same creative people — most notably writers George Lefferts and Ernest Kinoy — brought high-class science fiction back to NBC radio for one more try in 1955. By this time, though, television was seriously cutting into network radio's advertising revenues. The new show, titled *X Minus One*, would have to make do with an even smaller budget than its predecessor. Live music was dropped in favor of recorded cues. Actors were paid minimum scale. The producers cut a deal with *Galaxy* science fiction magazine, plugging that periodical and one of its upcoming stories at the end of every episode. In return, they were able to buy the rights to stories from *Galaxy* for just $50.00 apiece.

Despite the production limitations, *X Minus One* was every bit as good as *Dimension X*. The first fourteen episodes, in fact, were remakes of *Dimension X* scripts, including Bradbury's "Mars is Heaven" and Heinlein's "The Green Hills of Earth." Another 111 episodes followed (including a few remakes of earlier episodes), with the last one airing in January 1958. Lefferts and Kinoy continued to turn out faithful and entertaining adaptations of the source materials. The stories chosen continued to cover a wide variety of themes.

Theodore Sturgeon's "A Saucer of Loneliness" is a heart-breaking story of loneliness and empathy. A number of yarns by Robert Sheckley, including "The Native Problem" and "The Lifeboat Mutiny," manage the difficult task of telling a humorous science fiction tale without turning it into parody. Isaac Asimov's "C-Chute" is about a timid man who must risk his life to escape from hostile aliens.

L. Sprague de Camp's "A Gun for Dinosaur" was first published in *Galaxy* magazine in 1956 and was dramatized on *X Minus One* that same year. Its main character is an Australian big game hunter named Reginald Rivers, who uses a time machine to take his customers on dinosaur hunts. The prose story is constructed around Rivers recounting the events of one particular safari to a drinking companion, explaining why he no longer takes anyone back in time who isn't muscular enough to fire a large-bore rifle — the only type of weapon capable of knocking down a dinosaur. The one time he did do this, the consequences were tragic.

The radio play retains this structure, providing a perfect way to introduce Rivers and have him act as narrator throughout the story. The result is an extremely faithful — sometimes word-for-word — adaptation of the original. Even a few details not essential to the plot are retained, such as Rivers telling his clients how a museum once sent a heavy machine gun crew back in time to kill and skin a brontosaurus. It wasn't a detail strictly needed to tell the main story, but it added verisimilitude to both the plot and the characterizations. Though the roars of the dinosaurs were a little on the wimpy side (probably a result of the tiny production budget), it was as engaging a story on radio as it was in print.

Perhaps the finest episode was based on Tom Godwin's "Cold Equations." Here the main character is the pilot of a small space ship designed to make emergency runs, such as his current mission to deliver badly needed serum to sick men on a remote planet. The tiny ship is equipped with just enough fuel to make the trip.

Not long after taking off, the pilot discovers a stowaway, a young girl who wants to visit her brother on the planet. But in hiding aboard, the girl has invited disaster. Her extra weight means the ship no longer has enough fuel to reach the planet and land safely. This obligates the pilot to consider throwing her out the airlock.

There is literally no other choice. The pilot can't sacrifice himself for her because she can't fly the ship. He can't go down with her because then the men who need the serum would then die. Desperate, the pilot radios his mother ship for help, but none can be given. It's all simple math — a cold equation that states too much weight means too little fuel.

The whole situation could have been nothing more than contrived melodrama, but in the hands of a skilled writer, it became a frank examination of both physical and moral courage. When George Lefferts turned it into a radio play, he kept all the virtues of the story intact. The only major difference (which was perhaps a concession to network censors) was turning the teenaged girl into a young adult — the wife, rather than sister, of one of the men on the planet. This did little to change the emotional intensity of the story, though.

At the beginning of each episode of *X Minus One*, announcer Fred Collins tells us "These are stories of the future, adventures in which you'll live a million could-be years on a thousand may-be worlds." All 125 episodes of *X Minus One* survive today to demonstrate the truth of this. Without any money to speak of, without CGI, without visuals of any sort, with only the imagination of each individual listener doing all the important work, both *Dimension X* and *X Minus One* provide us all with some of the best science fiction ever.

Dimension X:
NBC: 4/8/50–9/29/51

X Minus One:
NBC: 4/24/55–1/9/58

Exploring Tomorrow

There was one last attempt in the late 1950s to bring mature science fiction to the radio. *Exploring Tomorrow* debuted on the Mutual network in June 1957, airing thirty episodes before cancellation six months later.

The show was hosted by John Campbell, who also chose the stories. Campbell was still editing *Astounding* magazine at the time, but (unlike *Dimension X*) *Exploring Tomorrow* had no direct connection with that periodical. Nonetheless, since Campbell was picking stories he liked, most of them turned out to be among those he had originally printed in *Astounding*.

Campbell introduced each story, telling us "The program you are about to hear is fiction — science fiction. We make no guarantees, however, how long it will remain fiction." He then popped up between acts and again at the end, commenting on the specific story being told. His commentaries, he later wrote "were designed to act as bridges between parts of the show and save time otherwise needed for scene-setting action."*

Considering the show's twenty-five minute running time (five minutes having been shaved off to make room for a news update), this sounds good in theory. In reality, Campbell often ended up just restating the theme or moral of the episode, regardless of how obviously those points had been made in the story itself.

"The Trouble with Robots," based on a story by Randall Garret, is a good example of this. The plot involves the dictator of a small country who uses a robotic security device to guard himself. When the dictator is assassinated regardless, a U.N. diplomat is falsely accused of the crime. He goes on the run, pursued by both soldiers and a robot helicopter. He ends

---

**Widner*, 106.

up saving himself by making use of the robot's literal interpretation of its orders to capture him alive, forcing it to protect him from the soldiers.

The point of the story — that the inherent limitations of machines make it a bad idea to give them authority over people — is completely obvious. But Campbell reminds us of this in his introduction, then again at the act breaks, then again as an epilogue, pretty much beating us over the head with the idea in order to give himself something to say.

The episode itself is a fine one. Because of the low budget, narration was used to replace the need for sound effects in several instances, but the script and the acting were both good. The only real flaw was Campbell's completely unnecessary commentary. John Campbell's talent and his enormous contributions to science fiction are beyond question, but acting as a radio host was apparently outside his expertise.

A dozen or so episodes of *Exploring Tomorrow* survive and the same thing can be said of all of them. The stories chosen for the show were of high-quality and the adaptations were done well, but the commentary never added anything concrete to them. It just sort of sits there and takes up space.

Another minor flaw was the theme music. *Exploring Tomorrow* used "As Time Goes By" as its theme — a fine choice in of itself, but the canned version used on the show sounds very weak.

Still, both the commentary and the theme music are easy enough to tolerate as long as the individual episodes are good. One of the best surviving episodes is "Liar," based on an Isaac Asimov story.

"Liar" is one of Asimov's Robot tales. These are based on the Three Laws of Robotics, which Asimov and Campbell had originally worked out together. Asimov presents a world in which intelligent robots are a common part of the work force. All robots have the Three Laws programmed into them. First, they must never harm a human, or allow a human to come to harm. Second, the robot must always obey a human, as long as this did not violate the First Law. Third, the robot must protect itself, as long as it does not violate the first two Laws in doing so.

Asimov then used unforeseen consequences of the Three Laws to construct a series of enormously entertaining S-F stories. "Liar" is one of the best of these. It involves a telepathic robot named Herbie. Herbie can read minds, an ability that he was given be accident during the construction of his complex artificial brain.

When a group of scientists study him, Herbie responds to the First Law of Robotics by protecting them from mental harm. In other words, he begins lying to them in order to encourage romantic fantasies or salve damaged egos. All this leads to a lot of emotional messiness, of course, forcing Herbie into a state of mechanical catatonia when he finds he can't avoid hurting people's feelings no matter what he says.

"Liar" is a great match for radio. The story is dialogue-driven, allowing it to transfer faithfully to the new medium. The characterizations, sometimes a weak point in Asimov's fiction, are very good. The character of Dr. Susan Calvin, a frumpy and asocial academic who is convinced by Herbie that the man she loves is also in love with her, is particularly well-done. Unfortunately, the actress who plays Dr. Calvin in the radio play is unidentified — she did an excellent job and it would be nice to give her the credit she's due.

"Liar" also presented one of the few times Campbell's introductory commentary served a dramatic purpose. His succinct review of the Three Laws helped set up the conditions needed to understand the plot.

It's very possible that Campbell's choice of stories was modified by the need to work within a low budget. Most of the adaptations required only a few speaking parts and few complicated sound effects. But producer-director Sanford Marshall managed pretty well with the resources he had. *Exploring Tomorrow* is not as good as *X Minus One*, but it's still a worthwhile and entertaining production.

As long as the stories are well-told, science fiction and radio are natural partners. The writers and directors are tasked with the necessity of conveying sometimes complex plot points clearly to their listeners; but once they pull that off, the unlimited special effects budget that resides inside each of us takes over. As stated earlier, those of us listening play a vital and enormously satisfying role in bringing the story to life.

Exploring Tomorrow:
Mutual: 12/4/57–6/13/58
Host: John Campbell

Part V

General Anthologies

The Damon Runyon Theater

When Damon Runyon turned his skill with words and his eye for unusual characters to sports reporting, he eventually earned himself a spot in the writer's wing of the Baseball Hall of Fame. In the late 1920s, when he turned those same attributes to fiction, he produced some of the most purely entertaining yarns of the last century. His stories were set in a section of New York City that does not quite exist in real life. It's a place where the thugs and the riff-raff have personality and heart; where the bad guys rarely seem to actually hurt anyone and can be won over by the smile of a pretty girl.

Runyon was a master of the short story, exclusively using first person narration to quickly introduce and define his characters, then move the plot along rapidly. What makes his tales unique, though, is the slang-filled vernacular his unnamed narrator employed. Some critics refer to it as "Runyonese"—a style of prose that sounds the way we *think* Prohibition-era gangsters should talk. Whether anyone in reality actually spoke the way Runyon's characters do is beside the point. In a Runyon story, it sounds right.

In "Runyonese," women are exclusively referred to as dolls. A gun is a John Roscoe. Someone wondering how to get enough money to pay his rent is "thinking of very little except how I can get hold of a few potatoes to take care of the old overhead." It's a language where contractions are rarely used—"you are" and "I am" are preferred to "you're" and "I'm."

The stories practically demand to be read aloud, because the sentence structures and word choices are just so much fun: "Of all the scores made by dolls on Broadway the past twenty-five years, there is no doubt but what the very largest score is made by a doll who is called Silk, when she knocks off a banker by the name of Israel Ib, for the size of Silk's score is three million bobs and a few odd cents."

This prose is supported by memorable characterizations. Few of the people in these stories make an honest living. Sam the Gonoph is a ticket scalper. Sorrowful is a bookie. Big Butch is an ex-safecracker who bootlegs beer. Other denizens of Broadway — Dave the Dude, Handsome Jack, Harry the Horse, The Seldom Seen Kid — earn money in similarly shady manners.

But, despite this, we rarely meet anyone in these stories that we don't like. These are criminals with hearts of gold — present them with a spunky young lady in need of help or a baby who needs to be fed and the toughest of thugs suddenly finds he's something of a hero. The end result is a series of stories that have their own distinctive rhythm to them. Runyon was usually (and successfully) going for humor, but he would just as effectively produce an occasional tragedy. Whatever his intent, though, the reader will have a good time getting there.

Both the style of the prose and the first person narration make these tales natural fodder for radio, but it wasn't until 1948 (two years after the writer's death) that anyone seemed to realize this. Fifty-two episodes of *The Damon Runyon Theater* were produced for syndication in that year. Starring John Brown as the narrator, now named "Broadway," each episode was a wonderfully faithful dramatization of one of Runyon's stories.

Brown was easygoing and amiable as Broadway, while other roles were filled by some of radio's best character actors: Gerald Mohr, Sheldon Leonard, William Conrad, Alan Reed (later the voice of Fred Flintstone), Ed Begley and Parley Baer were just a few of those who appeared. All of them aptly handled the peculiar rhythms of Runyonese and helped retain the charm of the original stories. The jazzy theme and background music was also vital in providing the right atmosphere.

But writer Russell Hughes (who also worked on quality mystery shows like *Box 13* and *Nightbeat*) is probably most responsible for the show's artistic success. A lot of the original prose could be transferred to radio verbatim through the narrator, but in any dramatization, it is necessary to replace descriptive passages with dialogue. When this was required, Hughes was able to replicate Runyon's style with near-perfection.

In the story "Hold 'em, Yale," we meet Sam the Gonoph, who takes a half-dozen of his guys to New Haven to scalp tickets to the big Yale-Harvard game. The group meets a seventeen-year-old "little doll" outside the stadium, crying her eyes out. She's run away from Mrs. Peevy's School for Girls to marry her fiancé, but he hasn't shown up.

Sam and his men have decided to attend the game, curious to see "what makes suckers willing to pay so much for [tickets]." (Remember that this story takes place when football was a very minor part of American culture.) The doll, they discover, has a brother on Yale's team. Having assumed en masse a fatherly protectiveness towards the girl, they invite her along.

The rest of the story plays with the idea of Sam's thugs intimidating anyone who dares root for Harvard and later assisting the girl in stopping Harvard fans from stealing the goal posts. Along the way, they inadvertently help her discover that her fiancé is just after her father's money.

The radio adaptation follows the story without major changes. Sam the Gonoph is changed to Pete the Peddler. This is one of several examples throughout the series in which ethnically based nicknames from the original stories were dropped. (Gonoph, at least according to Runyon, is Yiddish for thief.) It's a minor and arguably unnecessary change, but it doesn't affect the quality of the story at all.

What makes the radio version so good is not just how much of the original prose it retains, but also how effectively dialogue written for the show compliments that prose. New jokes sounded perfectly natural when spoken by a Runyan character ("Kick off? They're going to rub someone out in here?") and were laugh-out-loud funny when heard in proper context during the broadcast.

"Butch Minds the Baby" is another example of this. In the original, three men use Broadway as a middleman to contact Big Butch. They want him to use his expertise to rob a safe of $20,000, but the job has to be pulled right away, before the money is transported elsewhere.

The trouble is that Butch is watching his baby while his wife attends a wake. The solution? Bring the baby along on the job. But babies cry at inopportune moments and Butch is determined to see the little guy is fed on time, even if that means pausing halfway through the job to heat up a bottle of milk.

The radio play dropped a character to keep the cast manageable, while broadcast standards of the day dictated other changes. In the original, Butch had retired from safe-cracking and now bootlegged beer. In the radio play, he had gone completely straight and now worked as a plumber. Also, the group was no longer stealing money, but has been hired to recover papers from the safe. Some gunplay between a couple of the characters and the police was dropped.

None of these changes hurt the story, since the source of humor (babysitting while safecracking) wasn't affected at all. Once again, a nice balance between keeping the original prose and inserting fresh dialogue was maintained.

One of Runyon's best known stories is "Little Miss Marker," in which a perpetually sad-faced bookie named Sorrowful is stuck caring for a three-year-old girl. The girl was left as a marker for a bet by her father, who then never came back.

Sorrowful is annoyed at first, but soon finds himself growing fond of the little doll. Always so stingy with money in the past, he rents a better apartment and hires a nanny. People are shocked to see him actually smile from time to time. He starts a sort-of fatherhood-by-committee system, meeting with other gamblers and bookies to discuss what is best for the girl. Among other things, the group decides keeping the girl out all night in speakeasies and nightclubs is probably a bad idea.

Then the girl gets very sick. Sorrowful spares no expense and one of his friends arranges for a medical specialist to be kidnapped and brought to the hospital. But it may already be too late....

The radio adaptation, with Gerald Mohr doing a great job as Sorrowful, is yet another example of balancing Runyon's prose with new dialogue. But in this case, the show chickened out by partially backing away from the original tragic ending. Still, taken on its own merits, the ending the radio play gives us fits the rest of the story nicely.

All fifty-two episodes of *The Damon Runyon Theater* still survive today. Like the original stories, the show dealt with a class of people who never quite existed in real life, but who seem very real and human to us nonetheless. Whether in prose or on radio, we really enjoy spending time with Runyon's characters. We just need to take care no one lifts our wallets while they're around.

The Damon Runyon Theater:
Syndication: 1948
Broadway: John Brown

Favorite Story

The premise of *Favorite Story* was a fun one — ask a prominent public figure (often, but not always, an actor) to name his or her favorite novel or short story. Then adapt that story into a half-hour radio play. It was an idea that originated at radio station KFL in Los Angeles in 1946, then soon jumped to national syndication and ran through 1949. Actor Ronald Colman often played the lead role each week and, in 1947, also became the host.

The stories chosen were nearly always established classics, covering a fairly wide variety of themes and genres. It was always a little interesting to hear who chose the particular story each week — Irving Berlin picked *Alice in Wonderland*; comedian Fred Allen, *Frankenstein*; Alfred Hitchcock, *Dr. Jekyll & Mr. Hyde*. Father Edward Flanagan, founder of Boy's Town, picked (not surprisingly) *Oliver Twist*. More important, though, was that the adaptations were skillfully done and nearly always entertaining.

Favorite Story was a half-hour show. For short stories, this was nearly always a perfect fit. Nathaniel Hawthorne's "Dr. Heidegger's Experiment," picked by actor Robert Walker, is a succinct tale about three old men and an old woman, all guilty of wasting their lives in various sinful ways. When they are given an opportunity to drink water drawn from the Fountain of Youth, all four of them claim that, given a second chance, they would learn from their past mistakes. But, upon regaining their respective youth, they immediately fall back into their old patterns of behavior, leading to the tale's ironic denouement.

Hawthorne's Gothic prose was well-suited to establish the creepy atmosphere needed to make the story work and included a detailed description of Dr. Heidegger's strange study, where the action of the story takes place. The radio adaptation replaced this prose with dialogue, concentrating a little less on establishing atmosphere in lieu of introducing us to the characters and providing us with their individual histories. The plot of the adaptation, though, follows the original very faithfully, giving us the same theme of moral fallibility and the same effective ending. The dialogue was well-written and flowed along naturally. It all made for a satisfying and well-spent thirty minutes.

For a novel, the half-hour format was problematic. The adaptation of *Oliver Twist* manages to recount the basic story, but the listener gets little sense of Dickens' extraordinary prose or characters. Most notably, Fagin and the Artful Dodger are largely stripped of their unique personalities and become one-dimensional villains.

But in many cases, *Favorite Story* managed the incredible feat of jamming a classic novel into half an hour and still giving us a rewarding experience. *Frankenstein* is a prime example of this — the novel was expertly shaved down to a self-contained short story.

In Mary Shelley's novel, the bulk of the story is told in the first person by Victor Frankenstein, as he recounts the events of his life to another character, a ship's captain named Walton. The radio play uses a similar bit of story construction. Victor, played by Hans Conried, is telling his story to his friend Henry Clerval, describing how "I devoted myself, day and night, to the most arduous — the most revolting work a scientist has every undertaken." In other words, he created a monster that would soon turn on him and destroy the people he loved.

The adaptation follows the bare bones of the novel's plot with reasonable faithfulness, but there is a key thematic difference. In the novel, immediately after bring the creature to life, Victor is horrified at what he's done and pretty much just runs away. He returns home, assuming the creature must have died of starvation or exposure. So when the creature turns up alive, this rejection by its creator is one of several plot elements that make him a sympathetic character despite his brutal actions.

But in the radio play, the creature is brought to life by a bolt of lightning during the night. Victor enters his laboratory the next morning to see "the dry papery lips move" as the creature mumbles inarticulately. The creature flees and Victor spends months searching for him before giving up. There's no outright rejection involved.

On top of this, when the creature returns to murder Victor's young brother, he does so pretty much because he just likes to kill. Victor realizes that his creation has no soul and thus is inherently evil. There is no attempt at all in the radio play to generate sympathy for the creature.

It's an important difference and it does render the adaptation much less dramatically effective than the novel. But it works quite well as a scary short story and it is this change in theme that allows it all to fit into its tiny time slot. In her novel, Mary Shelley is making important sociological and philosophical points about science, religion and human nature. The radio play is just trying to scare the pants off you.

And it does a pretty good job of this. The creature eventually kills Victor's wife. While Clerval is telling Victor he doesn't believe a word of the story, the creature shuffles up from behind and kills *him*. With his friends and family all dead, Victor has become "the most wretched, lonely man who ever walked the Earth." The play ends with Victor warning the audience that "The monster I created is still at liberty, roaming the dark places of the night. Beware of him — with one short stroke of his finger, he can crush out your life."

Jules Verne's *Around the World in 80 Days*, chosen by World War I flying ace Eddie Rickenbacker, was another successful adaptation. The key to getting the novel right is getting the character of Phileas Fogg right. Fogg was Verne's best ever character and any successful adaptation *must* capture his eccentricities and his unflappable determination to succeed in circumventing the globe in a set time. Do this and everything else will fall into place.

For the *Favorite Story* adaptation, host Ronald Colman took the role of Fogg, playing him with class and intelligence. The adaptation moves along quite leisurely at first, taking nearly eight of its thirty minutes to establish Fogg's personality and set up his wager to travel around the world in eighty days. Then the story takes off like a bullet. Many of the events of the novel are covered in a line (or even a word) of dialogue, but we are given a more detailed account of Fogg's rescue of the beautiful Aouda from Kali-worshipers in India. ("Mr. Fogg," she declares after her rescue, "you are a man of heart." "When I am twelve hours ahead of schedule," he casually replies.) Later, the story pauses again when he arrives in America and bribes a train engineer to risk running the train full speed across a rickety bridge. When he arrives back in England, there is just time enough to realize he had lost track of one day during the journey and win the bet in the nick of time. It's wonderfully entertaining, exactly recreating the key elements that make the novel so much fun to read.

A total of 118 episodes of *Favorite Story* were produced. A good number of them survive today and are worthy additions to the collection of any old-time radio aficionado. If the show could not help but take quite a few liberties with the novels and stories it adapted, it did so with wit and intelligence. Any show that can get Phileas Fogg around the world in thirty minutes must be doing something right.

Favorite Story:
Syndicated: 1946–49
Host: Robert Colman (from 1947)

The Mercury Theatre on the Air and The Campbell Playhouse

Richard Wilson, a member of the famed Mercury Theatre, once said of Orson Welles: "He thought of [radio] as a gathering of people in the town square just to hear a story."*

Orson Welles was, in fact, a magnificent storyteller. A brilliant actor, a skilled director, a talented writer and an enormous ham, Welles made his mark on Broadway as an actor in 1935, at the age of nineteen. Soon, he had formed a creative partnership with producer/director John Houseman and the two men scored both artistic and commercial successes with several plays.

In 1937, they staged *The Cradle Will Rock*, a play with anti–capitalist themes that made the WPA (which was funding the play) very nervous. When the theater was closed and the actors forbidden by their union to appear on stage in the play, Welles and Houseman managed to book another theater at the last moment. They then marched the audience twenty blocks to the new theater, where the actors performed while standing in the aisles. Soon after, the two men formed the Mercury Theatre company and debuted an acclaimed version of *Julius Caesar*, which kept the actors in modern dress to turn the play into an allegorical condemnation of fascism.

All this brought Orson Welles fame, but even successful theater during the Depression generated very little profit. For almost as long as he had been working along Broadway, Welles had also been working in radio.

*From *The Mercury Company Remembers* (audio documentary), 1988.

It was his main source of income, but it was also a medium he recognized as having tremendous dramatic potential.

Welles was, of course, the Shadow during that show's first season. He also appeared regularly in *The March of Time* and *Cavalcade of America*, along with a number of other shows. Able to perform a part reliably without prior rehearsal, he was soon in demand by all the networks. It wasn't unusual for him to hire an ambulance to race him, sirens blaring, from the theater after a rehearsal or matinee to NBC to do a broadcast, then to Mutual for another broadcast, then back to the theater once again for the evening performance. By 1937, before he even began his run on *The Shadow*, he was already a veteran of over two hundred broadcasts.

His first important creative leap into radio was in that year, when he and other actors from the Mercury adapted Victor Hugo's massive novel *Les Miserables* into a seven-hour radio play for the Mutual network. Broadcast in seven parts between June 23 and September 3, with Welles starring as Jean Valjean as well as directing, it demonstrated that the 22-year-old prodigy had already become an expert in radio drama.

Welles was determined to do a faithful adaptation of the book, lifting passages verbatim to use as narration for the show. Dialogue was also taken directly from the book. Throughout the adaptation, Welles used montages of dialogue to help condense the story without losing track of the plot. Michael Dawson, a filmmaker who is an expert on Welles, notes that "the use of rapid-fire dialogue with backdrop effects allows the elimination of large sections of detailed narrative."* In other words, thirty pages of descriptive prose in the novel could be effectively communicated to the radio audience by replacing it with thirty seconds of dialogue.

Welles also understood how to use music and sound effects properly, producing a synergy of elements that resulted in a coherent and emotional piece of melodrama. Both Hugo's plot and his themes of redemption and compassion are kept intact. *Les Miserables* is wonderful radio drama, as good today as it was seven decades ago.

In the summer of 1938, the Mercury Theatre was offered a regular time slot on CBS to produce adaptations of classic stories. Welles jumped at the chance and thus he and Houseman were tasked with producing an hour of radio every week without any lessening of their theatrical work. Howard Koch, who was brought on as a writer several months later, remarked that the partners "considered sleep a luxury which, for the most

---

*Dawson, 13.

part, they denied themselves as well as their staff."* In fact, Houseman often worked from his bed all day, writing radio scripts and administrating the theater, because he couldn't afford to take the time to get up and dress.

Welles picked *Treasure Island* for the premier broadcast, but changed his mind with only three days to spare, choosing to do *Dracula* instead. He and Houseman spent seventeen straight hours at an all-night restaurant, working on the script.

What they came up with is a hair-raising and entertaining abridgment of Bram Stoker's novel. The novel is written in the form of letters and diary entries, providing a convenient justification for using the various characters to provide narration. To fit the story into the one hour time slot, several of the major characters were dropped. Most notably, three of the vampire hunters from the novel were combined into a single character for the radio play. The plot was also streamlined, but the simple idea of shrinking the number of protagonists meant that many of the events of the actual story could be saved. For instance, the novel includes a gripping sequence in which Dracula one-by-one kills the crew of the ship bringing him to England. It was something that could have been dropped without affecting the overall plot, but it was left in and, in fact, is arguably the creepiest part of the broadcast.

Welles once again pulls the various elements (dialogue, sound effects and music) together to create the proper atmosphere. The basics of the original plot are all covered: Jonathan Harker's trip to Transylvania; Dracula's arrival in England; Lucy Westenra's death and resurrection as one of the undead; the gathering of the vampire hunters under the leadership of Professor Van Helsing; the detective work in tracking down Dracula; the chase that leads back to Transylvania. The absence of several characters required an altered ending, which had originally featured the heroic death of a character who had been cut from this version of the story. But the alternate ending Welles and Houseman came up with was just as satisfying.

Welles played both one of the vampire hunters and Dracula, managing to give each character a distinctive voice. Other members of the Mercury Theatre, including George Coulouris, Martin Gabel, Ray Collins and Agnes Moorehead, were all superb.

Dracula was broadcast on July 11, 1938. Welles got around to *Treasure Island* the next week, starring as both the adult Jim Hawkins (who

---

*Koch, 12.

provides narration) and Long John Silver. Thirteen-year-old actor Arthur Anderson played young Jim Hawkins. Once again, the adaptation is faithful, intelligent and entertaining. It is, in fact, pretty close to perfect, though listeners familiar with the book will be a little irked by one aspect. In Robert Louis Stevenson's novel, the sequence in which Jim sneaks back on board a ship now controlled by pirates, cuts the anchor cable and has his deadly encounter with Israel Hands is both exuberant high adventure *and* vital to Jim's growth as a character. In the radio play, these events are covered in just a few lines of dialogue. The upside of this was that it gave the play plenty of time for interaction between Jim and Long John, but it's still disappointing.

The Count of Monte Cristo suffers a similar problem. The first half of the radio play, involving Edmond Dantes' escape from prison, is beautifully done — a model of clear, concise storytelling. But his later elaborate plans to exact revenge on his enemies are too simplified and covered too quickly to be truly satisfying. Still, in both these cases, the good parts are more than good enough to carry the show through to the end.

The Mercury Theatre on the Air soldiered on through the summer and into the fall of 1938, never garnering high ratings but always maintaining high quality. Dickens, Dumas, Shakespeare, Verne and other giants of literature each got their turn. Almost as fun as the adaptations themselves were Welles's brief introductions to each week's story. For instance, he opened *Treasure Island* with:

> We calculate that no decent, law-abiding citizen is immune to pirates. There are cowboys and Indians. There are gangsters and G-men. But these delights are inconstant, like the short skirt. I don't care how young you are: nothing charms — nothing ingratiates — nothing wins like a one-legged, double-barreled buccaneer with earrings, a handkerchief on his head and a knife in his teeth.

And *The Count of Monte Cristo*:

> It's no secret and no shame either that the Chateau Monte Cristo is haunted by many ghost writers. And that its owner signed his name to more books than anyone could ever write. It's not expected of Pharaoh that he build with his own hands his own pyramid. And the mere blueprint of one Dumas plot is an airtight alibi for a whole career ... one Dumas plot persists as the most ingenious tall story ever perpetrated by the mind of man; God's vengeance on radio script writers and your indestructible delight in spite of us.

And "Sherlock Holmes":

> Well, tonight it's back to Baker Street — back to that unlikely London of the 19th century where high adventure awaits all who would seek it — in a hansom cab or under a gas lamp in an Inverness cape. For tonight we pay tribute to the most wonderful member of that most wonderful world. A gentleman who never lived and who will never die.

For the October 30 broadcast, Welles decided to do H.G. Wells' *War of the World's*. Howard Koch was given the job of turning out the script, but soon ran into problems. He felt the novel was dated and unbelievable. Koch and Houseman tried to convince Welles to do *Lorna Doone* instead. But Welles overruled them — they were going to go with *War of the Worlds*.

Welles also wanted the story modernized, constructed around a series of news broadcasts. This wasn't meant to fool anyone — who would believe that Martians were invading, anyway? — but would add a sense of urgency and verisimilitude to the story. That meant a truly faithful adaptation wasn't possible this time around. Only the basic idea of the invasion from Mars and the description and tactics of the Martians could be retained.

With Houseman's help, Koch gradually pulled a script together. He closed his eyes and stuck a pencil in a map, thus choosing Grovers Mill, New Jersey as the starting point of the invasion. From there, he had the Martians advance on New York City.

The script was ready for the Sunday night live broadcast. Welles, as director, did a beautiful job of pacing the show. It starts very slowly with a simulated dance music program, interrupted several times for "news bulletins" about strange eruptions seen on Mars, then by the news of a large meteor landing in Grovers Mill.

That was no meteor, of course, but rather the cylinder containing the horrific Martian fighting machines. They mow down the crowd of onlookers with a heat ray, then later emerge to destroy a regiment of infantry.

Here, the pace of the show speeded up dramatically. Events that would have realistically covered hours or days take place in the space of a few minutes, but nobody listening would notice simply because the story was so engrossing. The Martians swat the military aside, spraying poison gas as they approach New York. As the first half of the show ends, a lone ham radio operator is desperately asking "Isn't there anyone on the air? Isn't there anyone?"

The second half of the show employed first-person narration as Orson Welles's character wandered across the devastated countryside and city streets until the Martians die of exposure to Earth bacteria. Welles ended the broadcast with a scripted remark about how this had been the "radio version of dressing up in a sheet and jumping out of a bush and saying Boo!" Neither he nor any other member of the Mercury Theatre yet realized that they had panicked a nation.

The panic resulted in large part because so few people listened to the Mercury Theatre on a regular basis. The ratings powerhouse on Sunday nights was the Edgar Bergen and Charlie McCarthy comedy show, which often had ten times the listeners than were tuning into *The Mercury Theatre*.

On October 30, one of Bergen's guests was singer Nelson Eddy. Eddy was popular at that time, but all the same there were a fair number of listeners who didn't care for him. Several minutes into the show, he began to sing. Many people turned their radio dials to find something else, stumbling across a news report of a meteor landing in New Jersey. That caught their attention. The heat ray that spewed forth to slaughter scores of people caught their attention even more deeply.

It was definitely time to panic. Men tossed their families into automobiles and fled the cities. People frantically called friend and relatives or flooded police stations and government offices with pleas for help, jamming the phone lines.

It was later estimated that as many as 1,200,000 people heard the broadcast and believed it. Why? One reason was its high quality and the fine acting. Frank Readick (the original voice of the Shadow) played the reporter at the scene of the initial encounter with the Martians. To prepare for the role, he repeatedly listened to a recording of the live report from the *Hindenburg* disaster, then very successfully worked to reproduce that same desperate tone. Kenny Delmar played "The Secretary of the Interior," making an official announcement about the government's response to the invasion, but did it using a spot-on imitation of President Roosevelt's voice. Everything about these performances was convincing.

Another reason for the panic was the world political situation. By late 1938, it was seeming more and more likely that the world would soon be at war again. Many people assumed that the "Martians" were actually invading Germans, perhaps employing some sort of secret weapon.

For a few tense hours that night, it seemed to Welles and Houseman that their careers were over. But after everyone had calmed down, they began to realize that *The War of the Worlds* would be the ultimate career boost. No one had been hurt and some commentators saw the broadcast as a useful object lesson in just how unprepared the nation was for war. Ratings for *The Mercury Theatre on the Air* rose and the Campbell Soup company came aboard as a sponsor. Renamed *The Campbell Playhouse* in December, the show ran for nearly two more years. (The series was eventually broadcast from California after Welles signed a movie contract with RKO.) Input from the sponsor meant they would occasionally adapt modern best-sellers and even movies in addition to classics, but the overall quality remained high. Stories included *Beau Geste*, *Mutiny on the Bounty*, *A Christmas Carol* and *Lost Horizon*. The Mercury players revisited *Les Miserables* in April 1939, running microphones into the leaky studio bathroom to simulate the ambiance of the Paris sewers. They ended up accidentally broadcasting a flush after someone used one of the toilets during the live broadcast.

The best of the Campbell shows is perhaps *The Adventures of Huckleberry Finn*, from March 17, 1940. In Mark Twain's novel, the backbone of the story is the relationship between Huck and the escaped slave Jim. Twain took his time with this, very believably showing us Huck's gradual realization that Jim was a real human being deserving of his friendship and loyalty.

This would have been difficult to present with anything like the same depth and care in just one hour (though, as we will see in a later chapter, not impossible). Instead, the radio play is constructed to emphasize Twain's mastery of the English language. As in the book, the radio play is structured around Huck's narration. Former Little Rascal Jackie Cooper played Huck. Welles played one of a pair of con men who join up with Huck and Jim for a time. But Welles also played himself, engaged in a sort of friendly competition with Huck over who gets to read the really good descriptive passages taken verbatim from the novel.

The single best bit of prose in the English language is the beginning of Chapter 19 of the book, in which Huck describes a sunrise on the Mississippi river in such vivid, loving detail that it nearly breaks your heart. When this point is reached in the play, Huck begins to read it. But Welles interrupts him, politely yet firmly insisting that Huck is tired and he (Welles) should read the passage. Huck reluctantly yields the narration to Welles for a time.

The story remains intact and the friendship between Huck and Jim is still there. But the purpose of the play is to celebrate Mark Twain's beautiful and biting prose. There are few things in the world more worthwhile of celebration and this particular show is one of the high points of the Mercury Theatre.

Since the film that eventually drew Orson Welles away from full-time radio was *Citizen Kane*, one supposes we must be forgiving. Besides, Welles would return to radio from time to time throughout that medium's Golden Age, guest-starring on comedies or playing the lead in several episodes of the anthology show *Suspense*. In 1946, he and many of the Mercury players returned to radio for a few months for *The Mercury Summer Theater*, doing some high-quality original stories as well as adaptations.

In later years, Welles would occasionally speak with some bitterness about how much of his life had been wasted trying to find investors to fund his movie making. But, really, the guy once convinced over a million people that they were being invaded by Martians. There was no way he was ever going to top that. And there was no reason at all that he shouldn't have been satisfied with his creative accomplishments. Even if you look *only* at his work on radio, you see him standing taller than nearly everyone else.

Mercury Theatre on the Air:
CBS: 7/11/38–12/4/38
Host: Orson Welles

Campbell Playhouse:
CBS: 12/9/38–3/31/40
Host: Orson Welles

The World's Great Novels and *NBC University Theater*

It's all a matter of time — of simply giving a creator the time he needs to properly create. For the writers and directors of a radio show attempting to adapt a classic novel, the more time they had to work with, the better. Orson Welles had seven hours for *Les Miserables* and did a magnificent job. With *Mercury Theatre on the Air* and *The Campbell Playhouse*, he had a mere hour. It's a tribute to just how good the Mercury players were that the shorter adaptations are, for the most part, wonderful stories. But there's no denying that many episodes rush through the story a bit too frantically or leave out some of the really good parts.

The World's Great Novels, produced at WMAQ in Chicago and broadcast nationally on NBC, gave director Homer Heck and his writers more time in which to tell these stories. Each individual episode was only a half-hour long, but dramatizations of specific novels were spread over multi-episode story arcs. This was what was needed — time to do proper justice to the plot and the character; time to leave in the small moments and details that give depth to the story.

Judging from the few surviving episodes, *The World's Great Novels* made good use of this extra time. *Moby-Dick*, for instance, was spread out over four episodes. Of course, for a book as dense as Herman Melville's classic story of whaling and obsession, even a total of two hours demands doing some scene-crunching. The sermon Ishmael attends before shipping out on the *Peqoud*— vividly recounting the story of Jonah — is sadly absent. Most notably, poor Queequeg, the cannibal harpooner, seems to have been almost completely forgotten after the first episode. But most of the remaining good parts are there. Most importantly, Melville's rhythmic prose and dialogue is faithfully reproduced. There's no feeling of anarchism at all —

everyone sounds as if they are living in the early 19th century. Many of the best quotes are still there, such as Ahab's "I'll chase him round Good Hope and round the Horn and round Perdition's flames before I give him up."

The first part of the adaptation takes its time introducing us to Ishmael and recounting his unusual meeting with Queequeg. As in the novel, we hear ominous hints about Captain Ahab long before we meet him. Ishmael's encounter with the prophetic old sailor named Elijah is included, adding to the sense of doom that hangs over the whaling ship *Pequod*. Everett Clarke does a good job as Ishmael, while Jess Pugh brings across Ahab's hatred and anger very effectively without overdoing it.

The second episode included a sequence in which the crew of the *Pequod* hunts down a random whale. One can't help but wonder if the staff of the show wished whales did something more than occasionally sing — that they roared, moaned or growled when battling for their lives. Such sounds would have been very useful in generating excitement in a radio dramatization. But the whale hunting sequence is exciting nonetheless, with the character of Starbuck, played by Donald Gallagher, verbally urging the crew of his boat on as they approach and attack the whale. His intense dialogue, combined with the sound effects of rushing water and oars creaking, were more than enough to make the scene work.

The third episode slowed the action again in order to build up the suspense for the finale. Ahab's encounter with another captain who also lost a limb to Moby Dick is here, as is his refusal to help search for a young boy lost at sea so as not to give up a chance to catch the white whale.

The finale covers Ahab's successive attacks on Moby Dick, losing men and boats on every attempt. Ishmael's narration and Ahab's vengeful monologues carry the plot along quickly and effectively. It's a solid and sincere dramatization of an epic story.

The World's Great Novels ran from October 1944 until July 1948. A week after its last broadcast, its successor took to airwaves for a two-and-a-half year run. The *NBC University Theater* was produced in Hollywood with Andrew C. Love directing, with a different set of writers and actors, but the overall quality remained high.

Novels had already cut a deal with the University of Louisville to accredit the series as a part of a correspondence course. *University Theater* built on this, arranging with several other colleges to also provide the course. During the intermission halfway through each episode, an author, critic or teacher would give a short talk on the book being dramatized.

These mini-lectures weren't dry or overly academic, though, but rather another interesting part of an entertaining show.

NBC University Theater was a one-hour show through most of its run, so the dramatizations weren't as in-depth as they had been in *Novels*. But the writing staff at NBC, including Ernest Kinoy, George Lefferts, Claris A. Ross and Richard E. Davis, were among the best in the business. Like Orson Welles's efforts on CBS a decade earlier, the novels were expertly condensed and presented with excellent acting and sound effects.

John Steinbeck's *The Grapes of Wrath* was presented in a January 1949 episode, using a third person narrator to set the scenes and describe conditions of the Oklahoma dust bowl and the migration to the supposed promised land of California. As in the novel, the trials of the Joad family were then used to humanize these events. Jane Darwell, who won an Oscar playing Ma Joad in the 1940 film adaptation, reprised the role for radio, while Wally Maher was Tom Joad.

Richard E. Davis astutely picked incidents from the book to tell the story in the form of quick vignettes, linked by the narration. One aspect of the book captured vividly in the radio play is the contrast between the different people the Joads encounter during their odyssey. There were those who reacted out of bigotry or greed, but this was balanced by those who acted humanely. One of the strengths of Steinbeck's novel is that it recognizes both the good and the bad of human nature. An incident from the book where the hard-bitten lady owner of a road-side café gives the Joads a break on the cost of bread is particularly memorable and it makes for a brief but effective scene on radio.

The intermission lecture is given by J. Donald Adams, a critic who wrote for a column for the *New York Times Book Review*. He only had a minute or two to speak, but managed to intelligently cover the novel's importance as a work of social protest, its stunning sense of humanity, and the extraordinary characterizations.

Ernest Kinoy wrote the 1950 adaptation of *The Adventures of Huckleberry Finn*, with Jerry Farber sounding like he's having fun with the part of Huck. Jack Kruschen and Parley Baer are hilarious as the King and the Duke (the con men Huck and Jim meet up with during their escape along the river). Felix Nelson gives a subtle performance as Jim.

Mark Twain's novel is very episodic, so an adaptation has some leeway in what incidents to use and what to keep while still maintaining the overall integrity of the plot. The *NBC Theater* version starts with a laugh-out-loud scene between Huck and Tom Sawyer, in which Tom's vibrant imagination clashes with Huck's more pragmatic view of life. In fact, Kinoy managed to keep a lot of the funnier scenes intact, including the King's side-splitting mangling of Hamlet's soliloquy during a stage performance in a small town.

It's interesting to compare this adaptation to the *Campbell Playhouse* version done in 1940. Orson Welles and his troupe did a tribute to Twain's mastery of the English language, with the story being an almost secondary consideration. The later version didn't try to recreate Twain's prose verbatim, but covered the basics of the plot and nicely emphasized the growing friendship between Huck and Jim. Both versions pick up on different aspects of the novel, but both do it justice in their own ways.

Some shorter novels did fit in the one-hour time slot quite nicely. A May 1949 adaptation of *The Red Badge of Courage*, with John Agar as Henry Fleming, is nearly perfect. All the major incidents from the book are covered and Henry's journey from cowardice to courage makes for an exceptional hour of radio. Deserving special mention is Noreen Gammill as Henry's mother. During a flashback scene in which Henry remembers leaving home after joining the army, his ma tries to be matter-of-fact as she tells him about the extra socks she's packed for him. But the almost unnoticeable quiver in her voice is beautifully done and brings a very human poignancy to the scene.

Other authors covered during the series include Ernest Hemingway, James Hilton, George Orwell, Joseph Conrad and Miguel Cervantes. Late in 1949, the series name was shortened to *NBC Theater* and the intermission lectures were dropped, but the quality of the adaptations remained high. In the end, trying to fit a novel into one brief hour is rarely completely satisfying, but the *NBC University Theater* managed to come pretty close.

The World's Great Novels:
NBC: 10/14/44–7/23/48

NBC University Theater:
NBC: 7/30/48–2/14/51

Mystery in the Air

Mystery in the Air was more or less based on the premise that it would be entertaining to listen to Peter Lorre go insane once a week. Airing on NBC in 1947 as a summer replacement for *Abbott and Costello*, it ran from July through September of that year. It was an anthology series in which, as announcer Harry Morgan would inform us, "Peter Lorre brings us the excitement of the strange and unusual — the dark and compelling masterpieces culled from the four corners of world literature."

It was a format that was a perfect fit for that particular actor. Lorre, a native of what was then Austria-Hungary, had gained fame in Europe in 1931, portraying a child murderer in the Fritz Lang–directed film *M*. When the Nazis gained power in Germany, Lorre came to America, where he had demonstrated his versatility in many films. He was able to do character parts such as the effeminate Joel Cairo in *The Maltese Falcon* or the sleezy Ugarte in *Casablanca*; he played Rashkolnikov in a 1935 adaptation of *Crime and Punishment*; he showed a talent for comedy in *Arsenic and Old Lace*; and, as mentioned in an earlier chapter, he did a wonderful job portraying the Japanese detective Mr. Moto in eight films.

Despite this wide variety of roles, he'd been type-cast in the mind of the public as a horror movie icon. *Mystery in the Air* played off this image, taking some of the creepier tales from the classics and placing Lorre in the lead roles.

Radio historian John Dunning accurately describes Lorre's work on the show as "intense, supercharged performances of men tortured and driven by dark impulses."* He was backed up by a strong supporting cast (including Peggy Webber, Agnes Moorehead and Ben Wright) and literate scripts that remained faithful to the source material.

---

*Dunning, 477.

It's not surprising that the producers and writers turned to Edgar Allan Poe for at least two episodes. Sadly, the adaptation of "The Tell-Tale Heart" has not survived, but the September 18, 1947 broadcast of "The Black Cat" is still around and is worth close examination.

Poe's mastery of the English language is perhaps surpassed only by Dickens and Twain. When telling his dark tales of murder and insanity, he always picked exactly the right words and sentence structures to generate an atmosphere dripping with terror. Poe, like the otherwise completely different Damon Runyon, had a prose style that demands to be read aloud. This, in addition to his habitual use of a first person narrator, makes him ideal fodder for dramatic radio.

"The Black Cat" is structured as the final confession of man about to hang for murdering his wife. The radio play retains this conceit, allowing Lorre to narrate the action and thus keeping much of Poe's original prose intact. The play makes no major changes — its one cheat (probably a concession to the network censors) comes when the main character, acting in "fiendish malevolence," mutilates his pet cat. In the original, he deliberately cuts out one of the cat's eyes. In the radio play, he beats the cat and inadvertently tears off one of its ears. The radio play is less horrific and thus slightly less effective for building up the proper atmosphere, but it's a minor glitch in an otherwise excellent half-hour. In all other aspects — the narrator's descent into alcohol-fueled brutality, the killing of the cat, the house fire, the appearance of the second cat, the murder of the wife and the discovery of the body by the police in the famous and still shocking climax — the radio play does not significantly deviate from Poe. With Lorre's strong performance at the center, it is dramatic radio at its best.

In each of the seven other surviving episodes, Lorre is equally good. Apparently, he would perform alone at his own microphone (the supporting cast would gather around another mike), gesturing wildly as he worked up to the extreme level of emotion necessary to play the roles he was given. On one occasion, partway through the first half of the show, he got a little too carried away and threw his script into the air, scattering it about the studio. Some judicious improvisation got him to the commercial break and allowed time to gather the script up and get the pages back in order.

The August 14 broadcast was "The Horla," by French author Guy de Maupassant. This is the story of a man who becomes convinced that he's being stalked by an invisible and malevolent being called a Horla. Whether the man is simply insane or the Horla is genuine is never really made clear.

Once again, Lorre's strong performance and a good script made for a magnificently eerie thirty minutes. In fact, the radio play improves upon the original short story in one respect. A particularly ghastly moment comes late in the story, when the protagonist sets fire to his home in hopes of destroying the Horla. In the original, he realizes with horror that the servants are still inside and that it's now too late to save them. It's an effective scene, but less so than it might have been since the servants were faceless characters, never given any personalities of their own.

In the radio version, we get to meet one of the servants — Marie the maid, played by Peggy Webber. Despite having relatively few lines of dialogue, Webber infuses Marie with enough individuality to make her likeable. When she and the other servants are trapped in the burning building, Lorre's character is too far gone into his obsession to even notice. It's a touch that adds an additional level of drama to the story.

It also adds a nifty little bit to the ending, where Lorre breaks character and brings his panic over the Horla into "real life," ranting at the cast and crew that he knows he's still on the air, but the invisible monster will get them all nonetheless.

The September 11, 1947 episode took the audience on a figurative trip to Russia for an adaptation of Alexander Pushkin's *The Queen of Spades*. Here we listen to Lorre become obsessed with the idea that an elderly Countess can tell him exactly what three cards to bet on in a game of faro. Peggy Webber once again provides Lorre with excellent support, playing the young lady Lorre seduces in hopes of getting access to the Countess. And, once again, he's commits a murder and ends up in an asylum by the time the episode ends.

Of the surviving episodes, the only one that fails to completely satisfy is the adaptation of *Crime and Punishment*. Lorre returns to the role of Rashkolnikov, the poverty-striken student who commits murder and is overcome by guilt and paranoia. It's fine for what it is, but you really need a bit longer than a half-hour to do proper justice to Dostoevsky.

But that's just one small stumble amidst some otherwise great radio. It's a pity *Mystery in the Air* didn't have a longer life or that more episodes didn't survive. Because, yes, it *really is* entertaining to hear Peter Lorre go insane once a week.

Mystery in the Air:
7/3/47–9/25/47
Host: Peter Lorre

The Weird Circle

If the producers and writers of *Mystery in the Air* liked Poe, then the creative staff behind *The Weird Circle* absolutely loved him. This syndicated show was produced in 1946–47 and premiered with an adaptation of "The Fall of the House of Usher." During its brief run, it returned to Poe on at least seven other occasions.

Who exactly was responsible for the show is today a mystery worthy of Poe's detective character Auguste Dupin. *The Weird Circle* never bothered to credit any of its staff or actors on the air. In fact, it usually didn't bother to mention the authors of the stories they were adapting each week. But whoever they were, they were good at what they did. Drawing primarily from tales of gothic horror, they were responsible for some very entertaining and atmospheric radio.

The show did a good job of establishing its atmosphere right up front. With the sound of the surf pounding on the sand in the background, an announcer, speaking in a low, sinister voice, would tell us "In this cave by the restless sea, we are meant to call out of the past stories strange and weird. Bellkeeper, toll the bell so that we all may know we are gathered again in the weird circle."

Sometimes, the ensuing radio play would use the story it was adapting as a jumping off point for something largely original. The premier show is an example of this. Poe's "The Fall of the House of Usher" is a tale of despair and premature burial that broadly hints that Roderick Usher, his twin sister Madeline and their ancient family home all share a single soul. When the two Ushers die, the decaying ancestral mansion finally collapses.

The radio play took that concept in a different direction by making Roderick much more selfish and forceful than the weak, despairing man Poe created. Here, Roderick openly acknowledges that he shares a soul with

Madeline and callously wants her dead in order to break this connection. This converts him into a straightforward villain and the story thus loses much of the subtlety that made the ending of Poe's tale so horrific.

Another change was made by dropping the original narrator and adding two new supporting characters. Because of this, the story was told through dialogue rather than first-person narration. This left little opportunity to keep any of Poe's wonderful prose in the script.

But despite all this, the story is still very effective. Taken on its own terms, it's well-constructed, with good acting and production values. Straying from the original plots and themes when adapting the classics is dangerous; the classics *are* classics, after all, because they got everything right the first time. But if it's done well, it can still be worthwhile. *The Weird Circle*'s version of "The Fall of the House of Usher" still raises its share of goose bumps as it leads up to a climax largely identical to Poe's, marred only slightly by an awkward romantic epilogue involving the supporting characters.

"The Cask of Amontillado" is also quite different by the time it entered that weird circle in the seaside cave. In the original, the narrator, driven by the need to avenge some perceived insult, lures the unfortunate Fortunato into a wine cellar, chains him to a wall in a niche, then bricks up the niche.

The radio play provides a detailed back story. The narrator, now named Angelo, is about to be married when he is kidnapped and sold into slavery. Years pass before he escapes and returns home, only to discover that his best friend Fortunato has married his old love. He soon learns that Fortunato is responsible for his kidnapping and subsequent slavery. When the girl, mistreated by Fortunato, dies, Angelo determines to seek revenge. In the short story, we get the feeling that the narrator is just plain nuts. In the radio play, his actions are logical and arguably justified.

It's so thematically different from Poe's tale that had the names Fortunato and Amontillado been changed, a listener might not have connected it with Poe at all. But, once again, it's a very good story. The uncredited actor playing Angelo is particularly excellent when he succinctly recounts his years of slavery, while the themes of unrequited love, revenge and justice are all smoothly mixed together.

In other episodes, the show remains very faithful to the source material. The adaptation of Edward Everett Hale's short novel "The Man Without a Country" kept the plot and much of the dialogue from the original prose intact as it told the tale of a young army officer named Philip Nolan.

Early in the 19th century, Nolan fell in with Aaron Burr. When Burr's plots against the young United States are exposed, Nolan is caught up in the scandal and court-martialed. Losing his temper during the proceedings, he rants "Damn the United States! I wish I would never hear of the United States again!"

He gets his wish. He is sentenced to serve aboard Navy vessels and to be transferred from ship to ship so that he never sets foot in the United States again. Though he is otherwise treated with dignity, officers and crew are all forbidden to speak to him about their native land. Books and newspapers are censored so that all news of the U.S. is kept from him. For forty years, he is denied any knowledge of the country he now realizes he loves.

Hale's straightforward narrative style transfers to radio very smoothly and the sad but ultimately uplifting story of Philip Nolan works nearly as well in that medium as it did in prose.

Samuel Taylor Coleridge's *The Rime of the Ancient Mariner* is also adapted faithfully and makes for an absolutely wonderful half-hour of radio. Coleridge's poetry is converted into conversational dialogue, but the primary events of the poem are all still there — including the Mariner's ship getting trapped in ice; the encounter with Death's ship after the Mariner kills the albatross; the reanimation of the dead crew; the sinking of the ship as it nears the Mariner's homeland once more; and his penance that drives him to tell his tale to others. The poem's original moral — that we must respect all God's creatures "both great and small" is also still there. With eerie sound effects and a strong script, it's a perfect story for radio, allowing each listener to build his own mental image of the bizarre sea voyage.

The Weird Circle also paid tribute to, among others, Mary Shelley, Robert Louis Stevenson, Nathaniel Hawthorne, Washington Irving, Charlotte Brontë, and Emily Brontë. Sometimes the scripts remained faithful to these authors, other times they would wander astray. But in nearly every case, the ghostly and forgotten people lurking inside *The Weird Circle* demonstrated that they understood good storytelling.

The Weird Circle:
Syndicated: 1946–47

NBC Presents: Short Story

Perhaps the best anthology show to look to the short story for inspiration was *NBC Presents: Short Story*. Directed by Andrew C. Love, who had also directed *NBC University Theater*, it had an all-to-brief run from February 1951 until May 1952. Using the same staff of skilled writers as did *University Theater*, it did fantastic adaptations of tales by some of the best writers from the 19th and 20th centuries. Charles Dickens, Ernest Hemingway, John Steinbeck, Conrad Aiken, and Ring Lardner were among those represented on the show.

As we've already seen with shows such as *Favorite Story* and *The Weird Circle*, the short story and the half-hour radio drama were a perfect match. The creative staff of *Short Story* made good use of this match, picking stories that could be brought faithfully to radio without losing their emotional impact.

Shirley Jackson's classic tale "The Lottery" certainly has emotional impact. It involves a small rural community, where the villagers gather together for an annual lottery. We're not told what the lottery is for, but we soon learn that it's an old tradition, going back many generations. The villagers have a minor debate over the exact method — should they all pick scraps of paper out of the old wooden box or go back to picking chips of wood like their grandfathers did — that helps establish just how deep a tradition it is.

Thus, we are presented with the image of a quiet small town with a strong sense of community. It's obvious that the lottery — whatever its purpose — is an important part of that community. But there are subtle — very, very subtle — hints that something is not quite right almost from the beginning. There's the way the children collect stones, for instance, filling their pockets or making "a great pile of stones in one corner of the square and guarding it against raids of the other boys."

It's all very understated and when we learn the fate of the lottery "winner" in the last few brutal paragraphs, it is one of the most emotionally jarring moments in American literature. Shirley Jackson's horror stories are all the more horrific because of her ability to set them against a normal, everyday background. "The Lottery" is her finest example of this.

The radio play, using a friendly fiddle to provide background music, does an outstanding job of establishing the same sense of friendly community, with one of the characters providing narration that leaves much of Jackson's original prose intact.

The radio play adds some new dialogue involving one of the local farmers that hints a little more broadly that all is not as serene as it seems. This might have been a mistake; Jackson had a perfect sense of just how much foreshadowing was needed to give the ending its full impact. But the radio play preserves many of the small details that make the story as a whole so effective: the casual discussion over who (wife or older son) should pick a paper out of the box for someone with a broken leg; the old man who brags that this is his 77th successive lottery; the contemptuous references to other villages who have given up the lottery in recent years and thus violated tradition.

By the time the lottery nears its end, with one family singled out and the individual members of that family picking papers out of the box to decide the final "winner," the tension has been built up to a remarkable level. Unfortunately, the radio play gives in to the temptation to allow the narrator to do a little anticlimatic moralizing after the tale's proper conclusion—it would have been much better to simply allow the story to speak for itself. But this, like the added foreshadowing, is a minor mistake at best and the overall adaptation is still exceptional.

F. Scott Fitzgerald's "Crazy Sunday" is about a young screenwriter named Joel Coles who "was twenty-eight and not yet broken by Hollywood." Over the course of several Sundays, he attends different parties and becomes involved in the lives of a famous director named Miles Calman and Calman's wife Stella.

It's the sort of thing that Fitzgerald did so well—a study of complex relationships set against a Jazz Age background, involving people who superficially have everything they could ever want but inevitably manage to destroy themselves. If the story were summarized in any detail at all, it would sound like a soap opera, but Fitzgerald's ability to create characters that immediately seem real lifts it far above that level.

The radio play changed the third-person narration to first-person provided by Joel, but otherwise kept the plot intact. As with "The Lottery" and many other *Short Story* adaptations, much of the original prose is retained within the narration. The NBC writers were themselves enormously talented men and women, quite able to intelligently insert new dialogue or narration when necessary. But they also knew when to leave well enough alone and let the original author speak for him or herself.

In fact, picking stories like "Crazy Sunday" is an indication of how justifiably confident the *Short Story* staff was in their ability to do great radio. Fitzgerald's story is dialogue-driven, making it ideal for radio in that sense. But the flip side of this is that there's no action in the traditional sense — no murders, death traps, or shoot-outs. Everything revolves around character relationships. An even slightly awkward adaptation would have been boring or stilted, but a skillful script by Claris A. Rose and a great job by Lawrence Dobkin playing Joel made it a spellbinding half-hour.

Short Story didn't hesitate to jump from one genre to another — any story of high quality was fair game for them. They jumped from the Jazz Age to the Space Age when they turned to Ray Bradbury's "The Rocket." The story involves a poor family man named Fiorello Bodoni, who every night watches rockets taking off for Venus or Mars. He wants desperately to take a ride on one of those rockets, but he knows that space travel is only for the rich. When he scraps together enough money to send his wife or one of his children on the Mars rocket, they all realize that it wouldn't be right for just one of them to go and leave the others behind.

Despite needing his money for his small business, he impetuously spends it on a full-scale mock-up of a rocket. Then, with the useless make-believe space craft sitting outside his home, he suddenly realizes that there is indeed a way to take his children to Mars. It's a tale that lets us visit with a family full of love and meet a father who finds a way to give his children a very remarkable gift.

When "The Rocket" came to radio, a third-person narrator was used to once again preserve as much of the original prose as possible and the story flowed along flawlessly. Ernest Kinoy, who would later help bring a lot more Bradbury tales to radio on *Dimension X* and *X Minus One*, wrote the script. The sound effects are particularly good in this time around and Don Diamond is pitch-perfect as Bodoni. Bradbury's very human story about the power of love and imagination fit just fine in a medium that depended on the imagination of its audience to be truly effective.

Short Story looked to Poe as well, as all radio anthology shows inevitably did. An adaptation of "The Tell-Tale Heart" is an interesting effort, though it fails to capture the same level of intensity as the original story. Conversational dialogue between the narrator, his uncle and a neighbor is added to help emphasize that the uncle is a pleasant, inoffensive fellow. This, and the voices the narrator keeps hearing in his head ("If thine eye offends thee, pluck it out!"), is used to set him up as an obsessive paranoid. Besides, the story is *so* short that a completely faithful adaptation wouldn't fill up a half-hour of airtime.

It's still good storytelling and the heartbeat sound effect used in both the murder scene and the finale is effectively creepy, but the departures from the original do weaken the episode somewhat. We simply don't need all that extra stuff to tell us the main character is nuts. The fact that he wants to hack his uncle to death because he doesn't like the man's deformed eye is really more than enough to make that point. Also, those paranoid voices echoing in his head get a little annoying after awhile. *Short Story* was its best when it was able to stay as faithful to the source material as possible.

Despite being titled *Short Story*, the show did try to cram a novel into its time slot on a couple of occasions. *Dr. Jekyll and Mr. Hyde*, a short novel to start with, made for a relatively faithful if somewhat rushed half-hour. *Frankenstein* was turned into a short story by bringing it to an end right after the Monster had killed Victor's wife, leaving the wretched scientist alone "to suffer my full share of misery, as [the Monster] as suffered his."

NBC Presents: Short Story is one of the best examples of the power of radio drama. By jumping to different genres and themes each week, it showed us just how versatile the medium is. Many anthology shows stuck to a general theme for most of their story choices — *Escape* was adventure–oriented, while *The Weird Circle* emphasized gothic horror. But *Short Story*, along with *Favorite Story,* showed us that radio can truly take us anywhere — whether it be inside the head of a madman or into the heart of a father who loves his children.

NBC Presents: Short Story
NBC: 2/21/51–5/30/52

Miscellaneous Adaptations

Anthology shows were popular on radio during the 1930s and 1940s. Most of these primarily used original materials, but would from time to time turn to the printed word for inspiration.

Suspense was one of the most popular shows during radio's Golden Age, running on CBS from 1942 to 1962. It specialized in stories of, well, suspense. During the height of its popularity, the conceit it used to draw in a large audience was to feature a different movie star playing the lead role each week. Cary Grant, Gregory Peck, Jimmy Stewart, Bette Davis, Humphrey Bogart and many other movies stars took their turn behind the *Suspense* microphone. Many comedians, such as Jack Benny and Bob Hope, were given a chance to play cheats and killers.

But this wasn't just a publicity stunt — Lucille Fletcher, John Dickson Carr and other talented writers provided scripts that were more than worthy of the actors. *Suspense* is a wonderful show and old-time radio fans are fortunate that over nine hundred episodes survive today.

When *Suspense* turned to short stories and novels for source material, the scripts maintained this same quality. When "Leiningen vs. the Ants" and "Three Skeleton Key" made a splash on *Escape*, those same scripts were later used on the higher-rated *Suspense*.

Richard Connell's "The Most Dangerous Game," was produced on *Suspense* in 1943, with Keenan Wynn as the protagonist and Orson Welles giving a melodramatic but entertaining performance as the insane hunter General Zaroff. To provide justification for Wynn's first-person narration, the plot was very slightly reorganized. The story opens with Wynn's character already running through the jungle with the sound of Zaroff's dogs closing in on him. Most of the adventure is then presented as a flashback, as Wynn explains how he ended up in this situation.

In 1944, Orson Welles was back for a two-part adaptation of Curt

Siodmak's science fiction novel *Donovan's Brain*. This is a wild story about a scientist who manages to preserve the disembodied brain of a dying man named Donovan. Soon, though, the scientist realizes that the brain is telepathically taking control over his body.

The script gave Welles a chance to effectively play two characters, both the scientist as himself and the scientist possessed by Donovan. Doubling up on parts in a single broadcast was something Welles had done from time to time on the *Mercury Theatre* and he does a typically fine job with it here. The novel is short, so a total of one hour was sufficient to do it justice. One minor but interesting change was made for radio: a physical mannerism the scientist takes on when he is possessed is changed to habitually muttering the phrase "Sure, sure, sure." It's a small thing, but demonstrates just how well the creative staff of *Suspense* understood the medium.

Not surprisingly, *Suspense* turned to Edgar Allan Poe. John Dickson Carr wrote an interesting adaptation of "The Pit and the Pendulum" that ran a total of four times between 1943 and 1959. Henry Hull, Jose Ferrer, Vincent Price and Raymond Burr all took a turn as the protagonist.

The original story, like most of Poe's stories, was narrated in the first person by the protagonist. Carr's script added characters, including a very effective sequence recounting the hero's trial in front of the judges of the Inquisition. Later, when the hero is tossed into the pitch-dark dungeon, he is visited by the spirit of his wife, who provides him with encouragement and advice. This was a little contrived, especially when she admits right off the bat that she is just a feverish hallucination. But the actors manage to pull it off (especially in the Vincent Price version, with Ellen Morgan playing the wife) and the conceit gives the hero with an excuse to provide a fervent verbal description of his actions as the story progresses.

Inner Sanctum, famous for the creaking door heard at the beginning of the show (and the bizarre verbal interplay between the morbid host and the always-cheery Lipton Tea lady who plugged the sponsor's product), also turned to Poe. An odd adaptation of "The Tell-Tale Heart" aired in 1941. Boris Karloff played the killer, but the premise was altered drastically.

Karloff was a man with an incredibly acute sense of hearing, capable of hearing "every sound on Earth." His traveling companion has supereyesight that allows him to see a lost cow hidden on the other side of a forest. When Karloff's companion decides to use his ability for dishonest profit, Karloff realizes he must kill him. The story ends with a new twist meant to change our perspective on the whole story.

It's one of those cases where the radio play ends up bearing little resemblance to the original story. It's good for what it is, though, primarily due to Karloff's typically excellent performance. He appeared often on *Inner Sanctum*, showing a talent for radio acting that few of his colleagues from the motion picture industry could match.

One of the oddest places to find a Poe story was *Family Theater*. Running from 1947 to 1956 on the Mutual network, *Family Theater* was created by a Catholic priest to promote prayer and the importance of family. It might have been corny, but the stories were well written and skillfully produced. This and the legitimacy of its moral objective made it a vigorous and entertaining show. Most of its scripts were original, but in 1949 it celebrated the one hundredth anniversary of Poe's death with an adaptation of "The Gold-bug."

Host Maureen O'Hara introduced the episode with an explanation of story's importance to the mystery genre. The episode itself is great, with Howard McNear doing a wonderful job as the treasure hunter William Legrand. The story was intelligently condensed; in the original prose, Legrand first finds a buried pirate treasure, explaining afterwards how he located it by using deductive reasoning to follow up obscure clues he found on an old parchment. The radio play has him explaining the clues to a companion *as* they conduct the search. It was a change that allowed the story to fit into its thirty minute time slot and still emphasize Legrand's methodical intelligence.

Family Theater did a few other adaptations during its run. In 1950, there was a largely successful attempt to fit Jules Verne's *20,000 Leagues Under the Sea* into its half-hour format. Professor Aronnax is played by Gene Lockhart, who provides enthusiastic descriptions of undersea wonders. Most importantly, his interaction with Captain Nemo, played by Bill Woodson, is done very well, successfully presenting the mysterious submariner as a tragic, sympathetic figure.

The Columbia Workshop, an experimental program that ran on CBS in the 1930s and 1940s, gave us Lewis Carroll, Jonathan Swift, Herman Melville, and others. *The CBS Radio Workshop*, a revival of *The Columbia Workshop* that aired in 1956–57, premiered with a two-part adaptation of Aldus Huxley's *Brave New World*, narrated by Huxley himself. Perhaps the best episode of *Workshop* was "1489 Words," which featured William Conrad reading several poems, including Alfred Noyes' long narrative poem "The Highwayman." Intended to demonstrate the power of the spoken word on its own (though it cheated a little by including background music written by Alexander Courage), "The Highwayman" section succeeds in telling a story just as powerfully as a straightforward dramatization could have done.

Adaptations of prose fiction are just one part — albeit an important one — of the rich cultural history of old-time radio. The medium provided us with a vibrant and engaging form of storytelling that even the best of motion pictures and television can never quite equal. Sadly, it is something that has largely disappeared from our popular culture. It's still out there for those who look for it, though. Several satellite stations specialize in old-time radio broadcasts. Many of the shows have fallen into the public domain, making them easily available to those who seek them out. Through radio drama, we can journey to Treasure Island; help solve a murder; face down a gunman on the streets of Dodge City; fight a dinosaur while armed with nothing but a hunting knife; visit alien worlds and lost cities — all without even having to open our eyes. We each provide our own set designs, casting and fight choreography. We each see the story in our own individual way. It just doesn't get any better than that.

Bibliography

Barer, Burl. *The Saint: A Complete History in Print, Radio, Film and Television*. Jefferson, NC: McFarland, 1993.
Bruce, Scott, and Dan Soper. *Lunch Box: The Fifties and Sixties*. San Francisco: Chronicle Books, 1988.
Dawson, Michael. *Les Misérables*. Introduction to compact disc recordings. Smithsonian Historical Performances. Schiller Park, IL: Radio Spirits, 1995.
DeAndrea, William L. *Encyclopedia Mysteriosa: A Comprehensive Guide to the Art of Detection in Print, Film, Radio, and Television*. New York: Prentice Hall, 1994.
DeForest, Tim. *Storytelling in the Pulps, Comics and Radio: How Technology Changed Popular Fiction in America*. Jefferson, NC: McFarland, 2004.
Dunning, John. *On the Air: The Encyclopedia of Old-Time Radio*. New York: Oxford University Press, 1998.
Fitzgerald, Stephanie, and Brian Fitzgerald. *Edgar Allen Poe*. Introduction to compact disc recordings. Schiller Park, IL: Radio Spirits, 2004.
Gibson, Walter B., and Anthony Tollin. *The Shadow Scrapbook*. New York: Harcourt Brace Jovanovich, 1979.
Grams, Martin, Jr. "In the Shadow of Fu Manchu." *Scarlet Street* no. 39, 2000.
_____. *The Radio Adventures of Sam Spade*. Churchville, MD: OTR Publishing, 2007.
_____. *Radio Drama: A Comprehensive Chronicle of American Network Programs, 1932–1962*. McFarland, 2000
Harmon, Jim. *The Great Radio Heroes*. Jefferson, NC: McFarland, 2001.
_____. *Radio Mystery and Adventure and Its Appearances in Film, Television and other Media*. Jefferson, NC: McFarland, 1992.
Hutchison, Don. *The Great Pulp Heroes*. Buffalo, NY; Mosaic Press, 1995.
Koch, Howard. *The Panic Broadcast*. New York: Avon Books, 1970.
Lackmann, Ronald W. *Comic Strips and Comic Books of Radio's Golden Age, 1920s–1950s*. Boalsburg, PA: BearManor Media, 2004.
The Mercury Company Remembers. Audio documentary. Produced by Frank Beacham, 1988.
Nachman, Gerald. *Raised on Radio*. Berkeley: University of California Press, 1998.
Nevins, Francis M., Jr., and Ray Stanich. *The Sound of Detection: Ellery Queen's Adventures on Radio*. Madison, IN: Brownstone Books, 1983.
Penzler, Otto. *The Private Lives of Private Eyes, Spies, Crime Fighters, and Other Good Guys*. New York: Grosset & Dunlap, 1977.
Sampson, Robert. *Yesterday's Faces, volume 1—The Glory Figures*. Bowling Green, OH: Bowling Green University Popular Press, 1984.

Terrace, Vincent. *Radio Programs, 1924–1984.* Jefferson, NC: McFarland, 1999.
Tollin, Anthony. *The Shadow: The Making of a Legend.* N.p.: Advance Magazine Publishers, 1996.
_____, and William Nadel. *The Ultimate Sherlock Holmes Collection.* Introduction to compact disc recording. Schiller Park, IL: Radio Spirits, 2003.
Widner, James F., and Meade Frierson III. *Science Fiction on Radio: A Revised Look at 1950–1975.* Birmingham, AL: A.F.A.B., 1996.

Index

Abbot and Costello 215
Adams, J. Donald 213
"The Adventure of the Circus Train" 73
"The Adventure of the Empty House" 87
"The Adventure of the Devil's Foot" 89
"The Adventure of the Speckled Band" 88
The Adventures of Ellery Queen 71–73, 88
The Adventures of Frank Merriwell 34–35
The Adventures of Huckleberry Finn 209, 213–214
The Adventures of Philip Marlowe 13, 115–118, 139, 159
The Adventures of Sam Spade 13, 108–112
The Adventures of Superman 173, 183
The Adventures of the Thin Man 99–100
After the Thin Man 98
Agar, John 214
Aherne, Brian 9, 12
Aiken, Conrad 221
The Airlords of Han 179–181
Aladdin Industries 170
Alexander, Joan 55, 67
Alice in Wonderland 199
All-Story 153, 154
Allen, Fred 199
Allen, Gracie 66–67, 94
Amazing Stories 179–180, 185
The American 23
American Broadcasting Company (ABC) 45, 67, 68, 72, 73, 88, 89, 90, 103, 104, 112, 123
Anderson, Arthur 206
Anderson, Marjorie 130
"The Angel's Eye" 7
Archer, John 130, 131
"The Arena of Death" 158

Armageddon, 2419 A.D. 179–181, 184
Arnall, Curtis 182, 184
Around the World in 80 Days 201
Arsenic and Old Lace 215
"Arson Plus" 104
Arthur, Louise 122
"As Time Goes By" 191
Asimov, Isaac 185–186, 187, 188, 191–192
Astounding Stories 185–186, 190
Autry, Gene 169
The Avenger 132–135
The Avenger 132–135

Backus, Jim 16, 18
Baer, Parley 160, 196, 213
Bagli, Gwen 160
Bagli, John 160
Bar 20 168, 173
Barrier, Edgar 9, 12
Bartell, Harry 83
Beadle and Adams 58
Beau Geste 163, 209
Beck, Jackson 67, 68, 173, 175
Beeton's Christmas Annual 85
Begley, Ed 44, 45, 196
Bellah, James Warner 159
Benny, Jack 225
Benson, Richard *see* The Avenger
The Benson Murder Case 63, 64–66
Bergen, Edgar 208
Berlin, Irving 199
Bierstadt, Edward Hale 128
The Big Sleep 113–115, 117, 118
Biggers, Earl Derr 41–42, 45, 146
Black Camel 42
"The Black Cat" 216
Black Hush 127

231

Index

Black Mask 13, 14, 15, 17, 101, 108, 113
Blackie, Boston 23–27, 28, 30, 42, 84
"Blackmailers Don't Shoot" 113
Blackwell, Frank 125
Blanc, Mel 72, 173
Bloch, Robert 148
Blore, Eric 30
"Blood Bath" 160
Blue Coal 128
Bogart, Humphrey 108, 225
Boston Blackie 25–27, 99
"Boston Blackie's Mary" 24
"The Bottle Imp" 146–147
Boucher, Anthony 72, 88
Bourke-White, Margaret 72
Box 13 196
Boyd, William 169–171
Boyle, Jack 23–24, 25, 27
Bradbury, Ray 186–187, 223
Brand, Max 167, 168
Brandon, Jim *see* The Avenger
Brant, Mel 34
Brave New World 227
Briggs, Donald 35, 55, 57
Brett, Jeremy 88–89
Britton, Barbara 95–96
Brontë, Charlotte 220
Brontë, Emily 220
Brook, Clive 90
Brown, Himan 99
Brown, John 196, 198
Bruce, Nigel 88–89, 90
Buck Rogers in the 25th Century 182–184
Bulldog Drummond 36–40
Burns, George 3, 67
Burr, Raymond 52, 56, 226
Burroughs, Edgar Rice 153–158, 179
Burroughs, Joan 156
Bushman, Francis X. 82, 84
"Butch Minds the Baby" 197–198
Butterfield, Herb 72

"C-Chute" 188
"The Caballero's Way" 172–173, 175
Cain, James M. 24
Calamity Town 70–71
Calkins, Dick 181
Campbell, John 185–186, 190–192
The Campbell Playhouse 76, 209–210, 211, 214
Campbell Soup 209
Carpenter, Laura Mae 130
Carr, John Dickson 225, 226

Carroll, Lewis 227
Carson, Kit 167
Carter, Nick 58–62, 91, 101
Casablanca 215
"The Case of the Calculated Risk" 83–84
"The Case of the Careless Victim" 76
"The Case of the Curious Cop" 20
"The Case of the Dirty Dollar" 21
"Case of the Giant Rat of Sumatra" 88
"The Case of the Party of Death" 83
The Case of the Sun Bather's Diary 54–55
"The Case of the Vanishing Visa" 21
The Case of the Velvet Claws 52, 53, 57
Casey, Crime Photographer 16–18
Casey, Flashgun 13–18, 82
"The Cask of Amontillado" 219
Cassidy, Hopalong 167–171, 173
Cat with Many Tails 71–72
Cavalcade of America 204
The CBS Radio Workshop 227–228
Cervantes, Miguel 214
Chan, Charlie 41–45, 46, 56, 95, 146
Chandler, Jeff 122–123
Chandler, Raymond 63, 66, 79, 113–116, 118, 146, 148
Charles, Nick 97–100
Charles, Nora 97–100
Charlie Chan 44–45, 99
Charlie Chan in Shanghai 43
Charteris, Leslie 7–9, 12, 19, 31, 87–88
Chick Carter, Boy Detective 61
Choate, Helen 61
Christie, Agatha 63, 74–78, 147
A Christmas Carol 209
The Cisco Kid 172–175
The Cisco Kid 173–175
Citizen Kane 210
Clark, Lon 61, 62
Clarke, Everett 212
Clayton Publishing 185
Clues Detective 132
Clyde, Andy 170
Cody, Buffalo Bill 167
"Cold Equations" 188–189
Coleridge, Samuel Taylor 220
"Collector's Item" 95
Collier 142
The Collier Hour 143
Collins, Ray 205
Colman, Ronald 199, 201, 202
Columbia Broadcasting System (CBS) 10, 12, 16, 18, 30, 31, 55, 57, 71, 73, 77, 78, 94, 96, 100, 112, 116, 118, 139, 140, 143,

145, 157, 159, 170, 171, 182, 183, 204, 210, 213, 225, 227
Columbia Pictures 25, 30
The Columbia Workshop 159, 227
"Command" 160
Conan Doyle, Arthur 13, 79, 85–90
Connell, Richard 161, 225
Connolly, Walter 42, 45
Conrad, Joseph 159, 214
Conrad, William 139, 160, 163, 196, 227
Conried, Hans 161, 200
The Continental Op 79, 101–103, 104, 107, 115
Conway, Tom 10, 12, 19, 89, 90
Cooper, Jackie 209
Corwin, Norman 72
Cotsworth, Staats 16, 18
Coulouris, George 39, 40, 205
The Count of Monte Cristo 206
Courage, Alexander 228
Courtleigh, Steve 131
Coxe, George Harmon 14–15, 17, 18
Coy, Walter 31–32
The Cradle Will Rock 203
Crane, Stephen 159
Cranston, Lamont see *The Shadow*
"Crazy Sunday" 222–223
Crime and Punishment 215, 217
"The Crooked Horse" 103
Crossen, Kendell Foster 136, 140
Crowley, Matt 16, 18, 182, 184
Crutchfield, Les 160
"Cry Foul" 95
Culver, Howard 72, 73
"The Curious Ride of the Sea Witch" 44
Curtin, Joseph 94–96, 99, 100
Curtis, Donald 123

Dahl, Roald 159
Daly, Carrol John 13
Daly, John C. 143, 145
Damon, Les 20, 22, 99, 100
The Damon Runyon Theater 196–198
Dannay, Frederic 64–73
Darwell, Jane 213
Davis, Betty 225
Davis, Richard E. 213
Dawson, Michael 204
DeAndrea, William 2, 36, 66
"Death from the Deep" 129
"The Death House Rescue" 129
de Camp, L. Sprague 185, 188
de Corsica, Ted 72–73

Dehner, John 160
Delmar, Kenny 208
del Ray, Lester 185
de Maupassant, Guy 216
Denning, Richard 95–96
Dent, Lester 132
Detective Story Hour 124–125
Detective Story Magazine 59, 124, 125
Diamond, Don 223
Dickens, Charles 200, 206, 216, 221
Dille, John 181
Dimension X 185–187, 189, 190, 223
The Dishonest Murderer 92, 93–94
Dividend on Death 119, 123
Dobkin, Lawrence 10–11, 72, 73, 83, 139, 223
"Dr. Heidegger's Experiment" 199–200
Dr. Jekyll and Mr. Hyde 199, 224
Donovan's Brain 226
Double Detective 136, 138
"Double Disguise" 61
Doud, Gil 108, 109, 160
Dracula 205
Dragnet 123, 160
Dresser, Davis 119–121
Drummond, Bulldog 36–40, 53
Duff, Howard 118–112
Dumont, Jethro see *The Green Lama*
Duncan, Henry W. 51
Dunne, Steve 111, 112
Dunning, John 1, 2, 108, 215

"Eager Witness" 116
Earth Abides 163
Eddy, Nelson 208
The Edge of Night 56
Eisinger, Jo 108, 109
Elliot, Bruce 127
Ellis, Georgia 139
Ellis, Herb 83
Emperor Fu Manchu 143
Ernst, Paul Frederick 132, 135
Escape 139, 159–163, 224, 225
Exploring Tomorrow 190–192

Fairlie, Gerald 37
The Falcon 19–22, 23, 25, 37, 39, 84, 89
The Falcon 19–22
Falcon, Gay see *The Falcon*
"The Fall of the House of Usher" 1, 218–219
The False Faces 30
Family Theater 227

Index

Farber, Jerry 213
The Fat Man 103–104
Favorite Story 199–202, 221, 224
Fer-de-Lance 79, 84
Ferrer, Jose 67, 68, 226
"Fifty Candles" 146
"The Final Problem" (short story) 86, 88, 89
"Firebug" 129
Fitzgerald, F. Scott 222–223
Flanagan, Father Edward 199
Fletcher, Louise 225
Ford, John 3
Foster, Hal 155
Foster, Richard *see* Crossen, Kendell Foster
"1489 Words" 227–228
Frank, Carl 182, 184
Frank A. Munsey Publishing 136
"Frank Merriwell" 33, 35
"Frank Merriwell's Nobility" 34
Frankenstein 3, 199, 200–201, 224
Frees, Paul 139, 140, 160, 161, 163
Frost, Alice 94–96

Gabel, Martin 205
Galaxy Magazine 187–188
Gallagher, Donald 212
Gammill, Noreen 214
Gangland's Doom 127
The Garden *Murder Case* 66
Gardner, Erle Stanley 52–54, 55, 56, 57
Garret, Randall 190
"The Gay Falcon" 19, 22
George Washington Coffee 88
Gernsback, Hugo 179–189
Gibson, Walter 125–127, 128, 131
Gielgud, John 89, 90
"The Gift of the Magi" 172
Gillette, William 88, 90
Godwin, Tom 188
"The Gold Bug" 227
The Golden Spiders 80
Gordon, Gale 143–144
Gordon, Richard 88, 90
Gothard, David 99, 100
The Gracie Allen Murder Case 66–67
Grams, Martin, Jr. 143
Grant, Cary 225
Grant, Maxwell *see* Gibson, Walter
The Grapes of Wrath 213
"The Greek Interpreter" 86
"The Green Hills of Earth" 187

The Green Lama 136–140
The Green Lama 139–140
Greenstreet, Sydney 82–84
Grey, Zane 167, 168
"A Gun for Dinosaur" 188
Gunsmoke 139, 159

Hale, Barbara 56
Hale, Edward Everett 219–220
Halliday, Brett *see* Dresser, Davis
Hammett, Dashiell 13, 79, 97–98, 100, 101–104, 105, 107, 108, 111, 112, 115, 146
Hands in the Dark 127
Hardwicke, Cedric 39, 40
Harmon, Jim 1, 2, 88
Hawthorne, Nathaniel 199, 220
Heck, Homer 211
Hector, Louis 90
Heflin, Van 115–116, 118
Heinlein, Robert 185, 187
Hemingway, Ernest 214, 221
Henry, O. 172–173, 175
Hercule Poirot 76–78
"High Tide Murders" 134–135
"The Highwayman" 227
Hindenburg 208
Hitchcock, Alfred 199
Hite, Kathleen 116, 160
"Hold 'Em, Yale" 196–197
Holmes, Sherlock 16, 20, 26, 64, 74, 75, 77, 79, 84, 85–90, 142, 153
Hopalong Cassidy 170–171
Hopalong Cassidy Enters 169
Hope, Bob 225
"The Horla" 216–217
The Hound of the Baskervilles 87
The House Without a Key 41, 45
Houseman, John 203, 204–205, 207, 208
Huber, Harold 76–78, 143, 145
Hughes, Arthur 143, 145
Hughes, Russell 196
Hugo, Victor 204
Hull, Henry 226
Huxley, Aldous 148, 227

Ibbett, G. Fred 143
Inner Sanctum 226–227
The Insidious Dr. Fu Manchu 142
Irving, Washington 220

Jackson, Shirley 221–222
Jamey, Leon 44
Johnson, Lamont 158

Index

Johnstone, Bill 130, 131
Johnstone, Jack 182–183
Julius Caesar 203

KaDell, Carlton 157, 158
"The Karaloff Papers" 51
Karloff, Boris 226–227
KFL 199
"Killers Are Camera Shy" *see Silent Are the Dead*
Kinoy, Ernest 186–187, 213–214, 223
Kipling, Rudyard 153, 159, 160
Koch, Howard 204–205, 207
Kollmar, Richard 26, 27
Kroeger, Barry 20, 22
Kruschen, Jack 213

La Curto, James 124
Lane, Richard 26
Lang, Fritz 215
Lang, Harry 174, 175
Lanyard, Michael *see The Lone Wolf*
Lardner, Ring 221
Larkin, John 55, 56, 57, 182, 184
The Late George Apley 46
"The Lazarus Caper" 110–111
Lee, Gypsy Rose 72
Lee, Manfred B. 69–73
Lefferts, George 186, 187, 188–189, 213
"Leinengen vs. the Ants" 162–163, 225
Lemay, Alan 3
Lenrow, Bernard 146, 148–149
Leonard, Sheldon 196
Lewis, Cathy 122
"Liar" 191–192
"The Lifeboat Mutiny" 187–188
Lipton Tea 226
"The Little Man Who Wasn't There" 131
"Little Miss Marker" 198
The Living Shadow 125, 131
Lockheart, Gene 227
Lockridge, Francis 91, 96
Lockridge, Richard 91, 96
Lombardo, Guy 72
The Lone Ranger 3, 35, 169, 174
The Lone Ranger 1
The Lone Wolf 28–32
The Lone Wolf 31–32
The Long Goodbye 113, 117
Lorna Doone 207
Lorre, Peter 49, 51, 215–217
Lost Horizon 209
"The Lottery" 221–222

Love, Andrew C. 212, 221
Love Story 127
Love Story Hour 127
Lovel, Leigh 88, 90
Loy, Myrna 98–99
Luke, Keye 43, 45

M 215
Macdonnell, Norman 116, 139, 159
Mahar, Wally 122, 123, 213
"The Make-Believe Murder" 62
The Maltese Falcon 13, 105–108, 112, 215
The Man Behind the Gun 159
"The Man Who Never Existed" 139–140
"The Man Who Would be King" 160
"The Man Without a Country" 219–220
Manson, Charlotte 61
The March of Time 204
Marlowe, Hugh 71, 73
Marlowe, Philip 17, 77, 113–118, 119, 123
Marple, Jane 74, 78
Marquand, John P. 46–49, 51
"Mars Is Heaven" 187
Marshall, Sanford 192
"The Martian Chronicles" 186–187
Mason, Perry 52–57
Mather, Jack 174, 175
Matthews, Grace 130
Maugham, Somerset 148
McCarthy, Joe 112
McNear, Howard 227
McNeile, H.C. 36–38, 40
Meet the Tiger 12
Meighan, James 20, 22
Meiser, Edith 87–88, 89
Melville, Herman 211, 227
Mercury Summer Theater 210
The Mercury Theatre on the Air 89, 129–130, 204–210, 211, 226
Merriwell, Frank 33–35
MGM 9
Michael Shayne 122–123
Mike Shayne Mystery Magazine 119
Miner, Jan 55
Les Miserables 204, 209, 211
Mr. and Mrs. North 94–96
Mr. Moto 50–51
Moby Dick 211–212
Mohr, Gerald 31, 32, 83, 116–117, 118, 196, 198
Molle Mystery Theater 146–149
Molle Shave Cream 146
Monks, James 50, 51, 134, 135

Moorehead, Agnes 129, 130, 205, 215
Morgan, Claudia 99, 100
Morgan, Ellen 226
Morgan, Harry 215
Morris, Chester 25, 27
Morrison, Bret 130, 131
"The Most Dangerous Game" 161, 225
Moto, I.A. 46–51, 215
Mowgli 153
Mulford, Clarence 167–169, 171
"Murder in City Hall" 146
Murder in Mesopotamia 74, 75–76
The Murder of Roger Ackroyd 74, 76
The Murder on the Orient Express 76
The Murderous Affair at Styles 74, 78
"Murders in the Rue Morgue" 79
Mutual Network 12, 19, 22, 31, 32, 38, 40, 44, 45, 61, 62, 76, 78, 82, 84, 88, 90, 122, 123, 129, 131, 170, 171, 174, 175, 182, 183–184, 190, 192, 204, 227
Mystery in the Air 215–217, 218

Nanovich, John 128
Nash, Ogden 66
National Broadcasting Company (NBC) 10, 12, 19, 22, 25, 27, 34, 35, 44, 45, 50, 51, 67, 68, 73, 82, 84, 87, 88, 89, 90, 99, 100, 112, 115, 117, 146, 149, 186, 187, 189, 204, 211, 213, 214, 215, 223, 224
"The Native Problem" 187–188
NBC Blue 19, 22, 45, 90, 96, 145
NBC Presents: Short Story 221–224
NBC University Theater 211–214, 221
Nelson, Felix 213
Nero Wolfe 82–84, 104
New York Times Book Review 213
New York Weekly 58
The New Yorker 91
"The Next Witness" 81–82
"Nick Carter, Detective" 60
Nick Carter, Master Detective 60–62
Night on Bald Mountain 160
Nightbeat 196
"Nightfall" 187
"Nightwalk" 95–96
No Hero 47–48, 51
Nolan, Lloyd 121
North, Jerry 91–96, 97
North, Pam 91–96, 97
The Norths Meet Murder 91–92, 96
Novak, Pat 17
Novello, Jay 32

Nowlan, Philip Francis 179–181, 184
Noyes, Alfred 227

O'Brien, Edmund 144
O'Hara, Maureen 227
Oland, Warner 42–43, 45
"The Old Detective's Pupil" 58, 62
Old Sleuth 59
Oliver Twist 199, 200
"Once Around the Clock" 14–15
"The Opera Murder" 94
"Operation Fleur-de-Lis" 160
Ortega, Santos 39, 40, 44, 45, 55, 57, 71, 82, 84
Osborne, Ted 143–144, 145

Parker, Robert B. 113
Pat Novak for Hire 13
Patton, William Gilbert 33–34
Peck, Gregory 225
Penzler, Otto 2
Perrin, Vic 160
Perry Mason 55–57
Petrie, George 20, 22, 67
Philo Vance 67–68
Pierce, Jack 156, 158
Piper, H. Beam 187
"The Pirates of Cape Bendeira" 158
"The Pit and the Pendulum" 226
"Plunder of the Sun" 160
Poe, Edgar Allan 79, 148, 159, 216, 218–219, 223–224, 226–227
Poe, James 161
Poirot, Hercule 74–78, 84
Poodle Springs 113
"The Potters of Firsk" 187
Powell, Dick 10
Powell, William 98–99
Price, Vincent 10–12, 31, 162, 226
"The Price of Principle" 27
Prisoner's Base 80, 81
"Project 77" 50–51
Pugh, Jess 212
Pushkin, Alexander 217
Queen, Ellery 69–73
The Queen of Spades 217

"The Ransom of Red Chief" 172
Rathbone, Basil 88–89, 90
Ravetch, Irving 161
Readick, Frank 124–125, 127, 131, 208
The Red Badge of Courage 214
"The Red-Haired League" 87

Red Harvest 102
"The Red Raincoat" 17
"Red Wind" 115, 116
Redbook 97
Reed, Alan 196
Renaldo, Duncan 173
Rensselaer Dey, Frederick Van 59, 62
"Return Engagement" 14, 18
"Return of Carnation Charlie" 130–131
The Return of Nick Carter see *Nick Carter, Master Detective*
The Return of Tarzan 155, 156–157
Richardson, Ralph 89, 90
Rickenbacker, Eddie 201
The Rime of the Ancient Mariner 220
"River of Ice" 133
RKO 209
Robeson, Kenneth *see* Ernst, Paul Frederick
Robinson, Bartlett 55
Robson, William N. 159
"The Rocket" 223
Rogers, Buck 179–184
Rogers, Roy 169
The Roman Hat Mystery 69, 73
The Romanoff Jewells 127
Romero, Cesar 173
Ronson, Adele 182
Rooten, Luis van 82, 84
Rose, Claris A. 213, 223
Rosenberg, Ed 103
Runyon, Brad 103–104
Runyon, Damon 195–198, 216

The Saint 7–12, 19, 25, 30, 31, 37, 84, 88, 89
The Saint 9–12, 31
The Saint in New York 8–9
Sanders, George 19
Saturday Evening Post 41, 46, 54
"A Saucer of Loneliness" 187
Savage, Doc 132
"A Scandal in Bohemia" 86–87
Scribners 63
"Scylla, the Sea Robber" 60
The Searchers 3
The Shadow 1, 10, 60, 124–131, 132, 134, 136, 137, 140, 204, 208
The Shadow 1, 124–131, 134–135, 204
"The Shadow Challenged" 131
The Shadow Laughs 125
The Shadow Unmasked 125–126
Sharkely, Marion 130

Shayne, Michael 119–123
Sheckley, Robert 187–188
Shelley, Mary 3, 200–201
Sherlock Holmes 87–90, 207
Sherman, Harry 169
"A Shipment of Mute Fate" 160
Shirley Alfred 90
The Sign of Four 85, 87
Silent Are the Dead 15–16
Simak, Clifford 185
"The Simple Art of Murder" 63, 113
Siodmak, Curt 225–226
"The Sky Walker" 133
Smart, J. Scott 103, 104
Smith, Bill 72
Smith, Sydney 72, 73
"Smoke Screen" 50
Snowden, Eric 90
Sorin, Louis 173, 175
Spade, Sam 17, 105–112, 119, 123
"Spanish Blood" 146
Spier, William 108, 110
Stafford, Hanley 143–144
Standish, Bert L *see* Patton, William Gilbert
Stanley, John 89, 90
Stehli, Edgar 182
Steinbeck, John 213, 221
Stephenson, George 162
Sterling Drugs 148
Stevenson, Robert Louis 146, 206, 220
Stewart, George 163
Stewart, Jimmy 225
Stoker, Bram 205
Stopover Tokyo 49
The Story-Teller 142
Stout, Rex 24, 79–81, 82, 84
The Strand 86
Street and Smith Publications 125–128, 132, 185
A Study in Scarlet 85, 90
Sturgeon, Theodore 187
Suchet, David 76
Sullivan, Barry 10, 12
The Sun 91
Superman 3, 153
Suspense 30, 210, 225–226
Swift, Jonathan 227

Tallman, Bob 108, 109
Tarplin, Maurice 26
Tarzan 38, 153–158
Tarzan and the City of Gold 158

Tarzan and the Diamonds of Ashur 157
Tarzan and the Fires of Tohr 157
Tarzan and the Forbidden City 157
Tarzan and the Lost Empire 155
"Tarzan and the Lypagor" 158
Tarzan, Lord of the Jungle 155
Tarzan of the Apes 154–155, 158
"The Tell-Tale Heart" 216, 224, 226–227
Templer, Simon *see The Saint*
Ten Days' Wonder 71
Thank You, Mr. Moto 47, 48–49
The Thin Man 97–98, 100
Thorness, Cliff 162
"Three Skeleton Key" 161–162, 225
"The Tick Tock Murder Case" 67
"Time and Time Again" 187
Tinsley, Theodore 126
Tip Top Weekly 33
Toler, Sidney 43
"A Tooth for Paul Revere" 160
Toudouze, George G. 161
Town and Country Magazine 19
Tracy, Dick 35
Treasure Island 4, 205–206
Tremaine, F. Orlin 185
Tremayne, Les 20, 22, 99, 100
"The Trouble with Robots" 190
True Detective 129
Tuttle, Lurene 109, 111
Twain, Mark 209, 213–214, 216
Twentieth-Century–Fox 42, 49, 121
20,000 Leagues Under the Sea 227

The Uncomplaining Corpse 120–121
Under the Moons of Mars 153
Universal Pictures 88
"Universe" 187
University of Louisville 212

The Valley of Fear 86
Vance, Jack 187
Vance, Louis Joseph 28, 30, 32
Vance, Philo 2, 63–68, 69, 75, 173
Van Dine, S.S. 63–64, 66–67, 68
"The Vanishing Lady" 160
Vass, Victoria 182
Vendig, Irving 55–56
Verne, Jules 179, 201, 206, 227
Vittes, Louis 10, 31
The Voyage of the Scarlet Queen 13

Walker, Robert 199
"Wandering Fingerprints" 122–123

War of the Worlds 207–209
Warburton, Charles 143
Waring, Michael *see The Falcon*
Warner, Gertrude 55, 130
Warner Brothers 13
Washburn, L.J. 119
"The Wave of Death" 138
Wayne, John 3, 72
Webb, Jack 123, 160
Webber, Peggy 215, 217
Weird Circle 218–220, 221, 224
Weird Tales 148
Welles, Orson 76, 89, 129, 13, 203–210, 211, 213, 214, 225–226
Wells, H.G. 159, 179, 207
West, Harry 90
Wever, Ned 39, 40
WHN 134
"The Whosis Kid" 102
"Wild Jack Rhett" 160
Wildroot Cream Oil 111
Williams, Warren 30, 66
Wilson, Richard 203
Winslow, Paula 144
The Winter Murder Case 67
Winters, Roland 43
Wister, Owen 167
"Witness for the Prosecution" 147
WMAQ 211
Wolfe, Nero 20, 26, 64, 75, 79–84, 91
Woods, Lesley 26, 130
Woodson, Bill 227
Woodward, Van 186
Woolrich, Cornell 148
World's Greatest Novels 211–212
WPA 203
Wright, Ben 89, 90, 139, 215
Wright, Robert 162
Wright, Shirley 170
Wright, Walter 170
Wright, Willard Huntington *see* Van Dine, S.S.
Wynn, Keenan

X Minus One 187–189, 192, 223

Young, Carleton 72, 73
"Yours Truly, Jack the Ripper" 148
Yours Truly, Johnny Dollar 183

Zemba 127
Zerbe, Lawson 34–35
Zorro 60

www.ingramcontent.com/pod-product-compliance
Lightning Source LLC
Chambersburg PA
CBHW051219300426
44116CB00006B/640